Women's Letters as Life Writing 1840–1885

I0592962

Examining letter collections published in the second half of the nineteenth century, Catherine Delafield rereads the life writing of Frances Burney, Charlotte Brontë, Mary Delany, Catherine Winkworth, Jane Austen and George Eliot, situating these women in their epistolary culture and in relation to one another as exemplary women of the period. She traces the role of their editors in the publishing process and considers how a model of representation in letters emerged from the publication of Burney's *Diary and Letters* and Elizabeth Gaskell's *Life* of Brontë. Delafield contends that new correspondences emerge between editors/biographers and their biographical subjects, and that the original epistolary pact was remade in collaboration with family memorials in private and with reviewers in public. *Women's Letters as Life Writing 1840–1885* addresses issues of survival and choice when an archive passes into family hands, tracing the means by which women's lives came to be written and rewritten in letters in the nineteenth century.

Catherine Delafield is an independent scholar based in Devon. She is the author of *Women's Diaries as Narrative in the Nineteenth-Century Novel* (2009) and *Serialization and the Novel in Mid-Victorian Magazines* (2015). She has also published articles on life writing and serialisation.

The Nineteenth Century Series
Series editors: Joanne Shattock and Julian North

The series focuses primarily upon major authors and subjects within Romantic and Victorian literature. It also includes studies of other nineteenth-century British writers and issues, where these are matters of current debate: for example, biography and autobiography; journalism; periodical literature; travel writing; book production; gender; non-canonical writing.

Recent in this series:

Wordsworth and Evolution in Victorian Literature
Entangled Influence
Trenton B. Olsen

Edward Lloyd and His World
Popular Fiction, Politics and the Press in Victorian Britain
Edited by Sarah Louise Lill and Rohan McWilliam

Science, Language, and Reform in Victorian Poetry
Political Dialects
Barbara Barrow

Victorian Culture and the Origin of Disciplines
Edited by Bernard Lightman and Bennett Zon

Literary Experiments in Magazine Publishing
Beyond Serialization
Thomas Vranken

Women's Letters as Life Writing 1840–1885
Catherine Delafield

For more information about this series, please visit: https://www.routledge.com

Women's Letters as Life Writing 1840–1885

Catherine Delafield

Routledge
Taylor & Francis Group

NEW YORK AND LONDON

First published 2020
by Routledge
605 Third Avenue, New York, NY 10017

and by Routledge
2 Park Square, Milton Park, Abingdon, Oxon, OX14 4RN

First issued in paperback 2021

*Routledge is an imprint of the Taylor & Francis Group, an
informa business*

Copyright   © 2020 Taylor & Francis

Publisher's Note
The publisher has gone to great lengths to ensure the quality of this
reprint but points out that some imperfections in the original copies
may be apparent.

Library of Congress Cataloging-in-Publication Data
A catalog record for this title has been requested

ISBN 13: 978-1-03-223907-1 (pbk)
ISBN 13: 978-0-367-85911-4 (hbk)

Typeset in Sabon
by codeMantra

Contents

Acknowledgements

I would like to express my gratitude to the organisers of conferences significant to the production of this book: Life and Works (Anna Barton and David Amigoni), Lives in Relation (Amy Culley and Rebecca Styler), Victorian and Edwardian Lives and Letters (Janice Norwood and Andrew Maunder), Writing Lives Together (Felicity James and Julian North) and Silence in the Archives (Lyndsey Jenkins and Alexis Wolf). These and other gatherings have provided stimulating environments for the development of ideas. This research has also been made possible by the efforts of the unseen compilers of online material.

I am grateful to Amy Culley and Valerie Sanders for their generous feedback, and to the anonymous Routledge reader for direction and suggestions. I would like to thank Joanne Shattock for her continued encouragement and to acknowledge the long-term friendship of the late Heather Kerr. George, as always, has been my mainstay throughout the writing process.

Introduction
Re-reading Letters as Life Writing

In her published *Diary and Letters*, the novelist Frances Burney set out her own view of the published letter collection when she analysed the letters of Samuel Johnson produced by their friend Hester Thrale Piozzi (1788). For Burney, the letters should have been selected and amended to make them readable, and edited to maintain an exalted view of the 'ever-revered' doctor (Barrett 1842d, p. 15). Burney herself was at Court in 1778 and trying to work on the memoirs of her friend Mary Delany by helping Delany to re-read and destroy the letters of a lifetime. Burney read Piozzi's edition in an unpublished form and used this to renovate the character of Johnson in a conversation with Queen Charlotte (pp. 16–7). She then wrote in a journal letter jointly addressed to her sister Susan and her friend Frederica Locke: 'The few she [Piozzi] has selected of her own do her, indeed, much credit: she has discarded all that were trivial and merely local and given only such as contain something instructive, amusing or ingenious' (p. 15). Preservation, selection and the concept of the writer's own words in print are concerns for any editor of a letter collection. The means of migrating letters into life writing were part of the publishing dilemma Burney left with her extensive collection of family papers when she died in 1840.

Using 1840 as its starting point, this book investigates the role of letters within women's life writing of the later nineteenth century and explores how life writing emerged from the nineteenth-century letter collections of six women: Frances Burney, Charlotte Brontë, Mary Delany, Catherine Winkworth, Jane Austen and George Eliot. The influential women discussed in this book were presented as exemplary of womanhood despite their public roles. Women's letters were authorised as domestic duty but for women who had professional writing careers or a public profile there would be speculation about role-playing and fictionalisation. For the purposes of life writing, a letter sent out as a performance of the self was hoarded and objectified and then collected, curated and recuperated as a life in a new context. The narrative was unconsciously created by the original letter writer and would be reconstituted by the reader of the collected form. The letter recovers an historical relational narrative but this is in opposition to the original 'theatre of usage' (Stanley 2004, p. 217). Even the discovery of an apparently reliable source through concerted research into the process of preservation might also show that the letter has been influenced by contingencies or emergencies, and by other forms of writing.

The Letter as a Vehicle for Life Writing

A personal letter is a document of self writing and may seem to fulfil the criteria associated with autobiography, but the role of writing intent within the letter, of absence made present, of correspondent, collection and future collation, changes the boundaries drawn around the writing moment. A letter brings with it the freight and weight of expectation, social mores, codes of behaviour and the impact of the original burden of correspondence. The 'life and letters' style of life writing makes assumptions that a life can be found within letters that themselves have a performative function (Summerfield 2013). Letters use the evolving technology of communication throughout their cycle of transmission and they become a suspect means of life writing in relation to their companion function as a fictional device used to authorise reading in the lives of the newly literate during the eighteenth century. As an emerging genre, the novel adopted the dailiness of letter writing in order to be legitimised as a narrative form, and this fictionalisation, in turn, raises questions about the life to be found in a letter. The life of the letter, and the impact of time, preservation and survival, has additionally prioritised one piece of life writing in epistolary form over another, and the family who inherit have a vital role in writing, receiving, preserving, relinquishing and publishing letters re-valued over time.

The letter as life writing occupies a place on the auto/biographical continuum that should be interrogated using an understanding of the letter-writing choreography and geography within the lives being lived. Women's letters of the eighteenth and nineteenth centuries were weighted in a number of ways. Letters were a form of family communication and a site for gossip that may or may not otherwise be shared. The letters bore the logistical marks of their composition and transmission, and some editions are more assiduous than others in explaining or unravelling the survival path of the text. Women's letters were predicated on travel or separation, and on events that had a value within the sociability of the communication process. The circumstance or place for writing was part of that account. It was from the original writing, response and negotiation for existence that a literary process of self-expression developed. The transition into print involved a further complexity enhanced by the already fraught role of the women exemplar and her public existence constructed by reviewers and in obituaries.

The distinctive style of Hester Thrale Piozzi noted by Burney impacted on another letter writer, and the letter-as-life-writing community is presented in miniature by this single piece of correspondence.

On 11 June 1799, at the turn of the page in a letter written from Bath, Jane Austen exclaimed to her sister Cassandra: 'So much for Mrs Piozzi. I had some thoughts of writing the whole of my letter in her stile, but I beleive I shall not' (Le Faye 1995, p. 44). In surviving, this letter informs its new readers that Jane Austen has traded a muslin veil for a black lace one as a present for Mary Austen, an outlay of 16 shillings that she hopes will not be too expensive for Cassandra to share 'on the altar of Sister-in-law affection' (p. 46). This letter's onward transmission after Cassandra received it at her Steventon home was by a bequest to their niece Fanny Knight and thence to her son Lord Brabourne, editor of Austen's letters. The text of the letter was published by Brabourne (1884) and then by twentieth-century editor R. W. Chapman (1932). The physical manuscript was sold to a private collector in 1886 and presented to the National Library of Australia in 1911 (Le Faye 1995, p. 369); a facsimile has also appeared (Modert 1990). The letter displays interest in letterness and refers to available models before it follows a trajectory into curation and life writing. From daily record to collected works, *Women's Letters as Life Writing* explores this narrative arc.

The Case Study Texts

The book follows the paths of letters as 'multifocal', 'reciprocal' and 'marked by the context of reading' (Stanley, Salter and Dampier 2012, p. 281; p. 269). It explores the wider community of life writing for the case study women as well as the afterlives created by lives in relation (Culley and Styler 2011). Chapter 1 considers five introductory areas that contextualise the discussion in Chapters 2 and 3 of two foundational texts: Burney's *Diary and Letters* (Barrett 1842–46) and Elizabeth Gaskell's *Life of Charlotte Brontë* (1857). The model emerging from this discussion is then explored in Chapters 4–7, using four further examples of women's letters as life writing. Chapter 8 considers both the afterlives of the letters and the hidden lives within.

Chapter 1 introduces the letter as life evidence by providing an overview of life-writing theory relating to the letter before moving on to discuss unseen collaborations in the creation and survival of the letter: correspondence, collection and editing. The chapter then considers how letters become life writing before briefly introducing women's letters of the nineteenth century.

Chapter 2 identifies a model for the letter as life writing through the work of Frances Burney as editor, diarist and family correspondent. Burney entrusted the publishing of her *Diary and Letters* (1842–46) to her niece Charlotte Barrett who enlisted her nieces and the publisher Henry Colburn as participants in the final project. The journal letters were also edited by their own *dramatis personae* since Barrett and Colburn were petitioned by the families of those mentioned in it to exclude some of the material. The reception – or ongoing community – of the diary and letters was also constructed through the responses first of John Wilson Croker (1842) and then of Thomas Macaulay (1843), writing in the quarterly reviews about the *Diary and Letters* and also about Burney's *Memoirs* (1832) of her father. The example of Burney highlights five elements that inform the model of letters as life writing. Letters are openly traded and circulated but also withheld. Letters are used as places for self-narration but may also be fictionalised. Finally, the published letter must contest any suggestion that it was originally written for publication.

Chapter 3 reinforces and supplements the model by examining the use of letters in Elizabeth Gaskell's *Life of Charlotte Brontë* (1857). The *Life* mines letters for material but also negates them as a genre by transforming extracts into self writing in order to use Brontë's own words. Gaskell was responding to reviews and to her own conflicted view of Brontë. She consciously and openly deployed her own letters to provide a commentary written to the moment and also used authorship to define an epistolary pact with Brontë over *Cranford* and *North and South*. Gaskell's *Life* adds a further four elements to the model: the importance of the letter writer's own words, the role of identity, the place of the biographer's life/letters and the overarching narrative of recovery and duty. According to the Barrett-Gaskell model, exemplary women bequeath letters that write their lives but must be re-domesticated within the context of their own fame.

Chapter 4 discusses *The Autobiography and Correspondence of Mary Granville, Mrs Delany* (Llanover 1861–62) that was in part a riposte to Burney. The descendants of Delany were among those who had excluded themselves from (or been anonymised in) the *Diary and Letters*. At the same time, the texts occupied the same space because they were recognised as court memoirs and were promoted for publication on the basis of royal anecdote. Delany's image and reputation were already in circulation before the edition produced by her great-great-niece, but Lady Llanover tried to answer the reviewers of letters as life writing and to remove the taint of association with Burney and her family by invoking contemporary sources and the hereditary might of the Granvilles.

Chapter 5 traces the biographical links between Gaskell's *Life* and Susanna Winkworth's *Letters and Memorials of Catherine Winkworth* (1883, 1886). The latter text was compiled by an editor sister who was herself a professional editor and translator of letters. Winkworth uses withholding and trading very consciously and preserves self-narration as a form of duty to future generations. The chapter draws out comparisons between Gaskell and the Winkworths as life writers, exploring the role of translation and family memorials in the privately printed, but publicly circulated, *Letters and Memorials*.

Chapter 6 examines Lord Brabourne's edition of Jane Austen's *Letters* (1884) as a family record split across letter survivals superintended by

Cassandra whose task was probably impacted by the early volumes of Burney's *Diary and Letters*. Brabourne's *Letters* was a memorial to his own mother Fanny Knight but also a riposte to James Edward Austen-Leigh's *Memoir* (1870, 1871), to biographical records such as that of Sarah Tytler (1880) and to the example of Burney. The chapter considers how the voices of Jane and Cassandra Austen emerge despite the suffocating weight of Brabourne's accompanying commentary.

Chapter 7 demonstrates how *George Eliot's Life* (1885) was arranged from her letters by her husband John Cross in part as a response to the 'Eminent Women' biography by Mathilde Blind (1883) but also within the context of a range of reviews and obituaries circulating after Eliot's death. The chapter traces Cross's interventions and his narrative of recovery that recuperated Eliot's domestic character and re-presented her as member of the Cross family.

In conclusion, Chapter 8 uses the lives of Christina Rossetti to look beyond the parameters already established and to retrace the letter-as-life-writing continuum. The chapter also provides an overview of the afterlives of the case study texts using an accompanying Appendix. Rossetti's life was hidden by her role as Pre-Raphaelite model and lyric religious poet, and the chapter concludes with a brief analysis of hidden lives that emerge from within the case studies, focussing on Charlotte Barrett and Elizabeth Gaskell, the 'authors' of the model.

Letters are circumstantial and circumscribed life writing because they focus on a life lived at the moment of composition that was later subsumed by other family and biographical agendas. The level of transparency in letters as self writing was affected by the situation and writing intent of the letter writer and by the models of writing and duty being fulfilled through the text. For women, it should be argued that the opportunity and authorisation to write affected their level of empowerment which has been re-drawn by the onward circulation and preservation of those texts. It is in the passage to retrospective memoir that the letters are mired in new ways of thinking and in the new tradition of life writing. The very validity of the letter comes to be undermined by the writer's daring to have found a place for self-expression or a consciousness of writing for future publication.

Letters are, however, a chancy medium for preserving a life in print. Survival, choice and other women writers' lives have shaped the letter-written life. In their different ways, the authors and editors of the case study texts demonstrate their knowledge of the range, permeability and narrative potential of the letter. In the case of women with exemplary lives that were attractive to publishers, life writing also had to take its cue from the response of reviewers. This book revisits the material conditions for letter writing and addresses some of the issues of editing when an archive passes into family hands, examining how women's lives came to be written and rewritten in letters in the nineteenth century.

Bibliography

Austen-Leigh, James Edward (1870, 1871) *A Memoir of Jane Austen, by Her Nephew*. London: Bentley.

Barrett, Charlotte (ed.) (1842, 1843, 1846) *The Diary and Letters of Madame D'Arblay* (7 vols). London: Henry Colburn.

Barrett, Charlotte (ed.) (1842d) *The Diary and Letters of Madame D'Arblay. Volume 4: 1788–1789*. London: Henry Colburn.

Blind, Mathilde (1883) *George Eliot*. London: W. H. Allen.

Brabourne, Lord (Edward Knatchbull-Hugesson) (ed.) (1884) *Letters of Jane Austen* (2 vols). London: Bentley.

Chapman, Robert W. (ed.) (1932) *Jane Austen's Letters to Her Sister Cassandra and Others*. Oxford: Oxford University Press.

Croker, John Wilson (1842) 'Diary and Letters of Madame D'Arblay, Vols I, II, III', *Quarterly Review*, 70, pp. 243–87.

Cross, John Walter (ed.) (1885) *George Eliot's Life as Related in Her Letters and Journals* (3 vols). Edinburgh: Blackwood.

Culley, Amy and Styler, Rebecca (2011) 'Editorial: Lives in Relation', *Life Writing*, 8(3), pp. 237–40.

Gaskell, Elizabeth (1857) *The Life of Charlotte Brontë* (2 vols). London: Smith Elder.

Le Faye, Deirdre (ed.) (1995) *Jane Austen's Letters*. Oxford: Oxford University Press.

Llanover, Lady (Augusta Hall) (1861–62) *The Autobiography and Correspondence of Mary Granville, Mrs Delany* (6 Vols). London: Bentley.

Macaulay, Thomas Babington (1843) 'Diary and Letters of Madame D'Arblay', *The Edinburgh Review*, 76, pp. 523–70.

Modert, Jo (ed.) (1990) *Jane Austen's Letters in Facsimile*. Carbondale: Southern Illinois University Press.

Piozzi, Hester Lynch (1788) *Letters to and from the Late Samuel Johnson, LLD* (2 vols). London: Strahan and Cadell.

Stanley, Liz (2004) 'The Epistolarium: On Theorizing Letters and Correspondences', *Auto/biography*, 12, pp. 201–35.

Stanley, Liz, Salter, Andrea and Dampier, Helen (2012) 'The Epistolary Pact: Letterness and the Schreiner Epistolarium', *a/b Auto/Biography Studies*, 27(2), pp. 262–93.

Summerfield, Penny (2013) 'Concluding Thoughts: Performance, the Self, and Women's History', *Women's History Review*, 22(2), pp. 345–52.

Tytler, Sarah (1880) *Jane Austen and Her Works*. London: Cassell, Petter & Galpin.

Winkworth, Susanna (1883, 1886) *Letters and Memorials of Catherine Winkworth* (2 vols). Clifton: Austin.

1 Women's Letters Becoming Life Writing

There is a generic instability within the letter as life writing. It is a vehicle for recollection and for writing events and collating news, but it has been preserved through the agency of third parties who make choices or collations/curations of letters. The life-writing moment has been recalibrated by an editor and un/authorised reader who provides linking passages to re-genericise the original letter in a new context. The letter migrates through autobiography into biography and into auto/biography (Stanley 1992; Marcus 1994). At a level of interpretation within this new narrative, the letters may, in turn, write the editing biographer's own life. This chapter introduces the factual and fictional letter in life-writing theory and discusses the collaborative nature of life writing in letters through correspondence, collection and editing. The chapter then explores the letter as life writing and women's letters of the nineteenth century.

As documents, letters provide both narrative evidence and circumstantial denials of their own veracity. For instance, Arthur Bell Nicholls demanded of his new wife Charlotte Brontë that all her correspondents should consent to the destruction of her letters once received. Brontë, in turn, explained in a letter to her friend Ellen Nussey on 31 October 1854 that Nicholls thought women 'most rash in letter-writing' and that he mistrusted 'the accidental passing of letters into hands and under eyes for which they were never written' (Barker 1997, p. 394). This letter nonetheless survives, of course, along with approximately 370 other letters to Nussey of the 500 she has claimed were written to her. Three volumes of Brontë's letters have been edited for a modern audience (Smith 1995, 2000, 2004). The text of 1854 survives but appears to deny its own existence, and history has shown, as Charlotte described it to Ellen on 7 November, that 'a letter may fall into any hand' (Barker 1997, p. 395).

The letter as a text comes into existence through acts of writing and sending. Each stage in the progression from written immediacy to collected edition involves a collaborative act, ranging from the application of models established by letter manuals to the conservation of the accumulated texts of a lifetime. The letter is affected by the occasion of writing and the mode of transmission. Its receipt and circulation by a recipient or addressee dictates its survival and onward transmission into a collection. A further process of collation occurs during the selection of letters to be preserved and ordered for publication. It is from this process that a written life emerges across a wide spectrum of potential re-readings. The collator may claim that the letters contain the life and allow the writer to speak for herself in her own words, whereas selective and targeted quotation from letters serves the purposes of the biographer. The letter thus follows a process of composition, transmission and reception followed by a first reading, shared reading or re-reading and then a re-transmission, all of which take place within a revised context. Any retention or collection decision that is made re-values the letter as an object or as a memorial, and the new holder of the document assumes a position of power over it. Within a publishing or editing context, this power redefines the 'epistolary pact' (Altman 1982, p. 89; Stanley, Salter and Dampier 2012) originally established between first writer and first correspondent. Where life writing takes the form of a letter, the revised audience acts as a 'fourth wall' in the onward reception and classification of the letter.

For women of the nineteenth century, the letter at the time of its composition represented a negotiated and authorised space for reflective discussion and communication, for writing a self. The incorporation of such life writing into domestic responsibilities and thence family memorialisation acted as a palliative, allowing women to write but without addressing the causes of their exclusion from life writing. The manuscript letter might be written as part of a family duty or as an exercise in literacy or politeness. Crucially there was already a planned instability within the written text because it could circulate further to both intended and unintended audiences. The printed form might re-stabilise the text within a written or biographical sequence but the letter was now addressing an unplanned audience. When letters are invoked as evidence of life writing and written immediacy becomes retrospective testimony, the life-writing moment is questioned.

Life-Writing Theory and the Letter

The letter at that moment of immediacy is autobiographical writing (Stanley, Salter and Dampier 2012, p. 264) and it has been suggested that autobiography is a retrospective transformation of the self into a text (Fleishmann 1983, p. 33). The letter as life writing is, however, an unstable source for autobiographical moments since the narrative transformation of the self ostensibly occurs further along the continuum towards biography, at a point where the original text is restructured, published and packaged for the consumption of family and future public.

Laura Marcus observes that for the Victorians, autobiography was a sub-category of biography, and that, until the 1980s, there was an andocentric tradition of 'Great Men' that excluded the forms of life writing

adopted by women (1994, pp. 1, 273). It has been more recently suggested that it is the 'great' who are represented and that most 'minor'
lives were also hidden until the advent of the *Dictionary of National
Biography* (Atkinson 2010, pp. 4, 11). Despite their exclusion from some
of the seminal discussions of auto/biography (Altick 1966; Renza 1977),
women's texts have been brought into the canon. Sidonie Smith suggests
that the use of the letter as life writing by 'culturally silenced' women
threatens the established order (1987, pp. 43–4). Mary Jane Corbett
sees a motivation for women who become exemplars and whose written
lives have to be shaped by domestic ideology, to represent the private
sphere in public (1992, pp. 12, 15). Trev Lynn Broughton approaches
the 'contested terrain' of life writing by suggesting a need to manage
difference and to find 'alternative myths of selfhood' (1999, pp. 9, 11).
Letter writing in the eighteenth and nineteenth centuries was a role for
a woman in the private sphere despite the fact that she might be operating in public in the roles of author, charity worker, hymn writer or
lady-in-waiting. Marcus broaches the subject of letters as texts in their
own right and of gender as a genre that changes the operation and reception of a text (1994, p. 231), and the very term 'life writing' more readily accommodates women's and 'minor' forms of self-narration (Kadar
1992; Lang-Peralta 1997, pp. 24, 40). The letter can become life writing
beyond its fulfilment of domestic roles because it authorises the writer to
assert herself as 'I' and to identify herself with the logistical viewpoint
of correspondent.

The variety within the letter as a genre causes theorising to cross
other boundaries of language and discipline. In the narrative theory
of the novel, the 'narrative of transmission' (Duyfhuizen 1992) maps
a process of accounting for the existence or 'transmission' of letters,
giving the letter a life as well as helping to derive the life of the participants from the text of that letter. The seminal *Yale French Studies*
issue of 1986 offered a number of perspectives for the letter as life
writing. English Showalter charted the migration of a correspondence
into a self-conscious literary production (1986, p. 126), Mireille Bossis
opened the debate on collaboration (1986, p. 68) and Janet Altman
considered publication as a 'reinscription' (1986, p. 19). From the
perspective of social science theory, Liz Stanley defines the letter as
dialogical, perspectival and emergent (2004, p. 202–3). In working
on the letters of Olive Schreiner, Stanley has reached an understanding of letter collections by coining the term 'Epistolarium' and four
classifications within it. Letters comprise the extant material of the
writer but must also account for all her potential epistolary activity,
including what has not been preserved. The 'epistolarium' should also
include the writer's correspondents and may finally be compacted into
an edited published collection derived or divorced from the manuscript
(Stanley 2004; Stanley, Salter and Dampier 2012).

The different schools of thought on epistolary theory maintain their own correspondence. In considering letters as life writing, Stanley's assumption of 'reciprocity and exchange at the core of correspondence' (2012, p. 262) tends towards an absolute definition of letters as sociological evidence rather than as philosophically tuned documents contributing to the adjacent genres of auto/biography. Stanley and Margaretta Jolly (Jolly and Stanley 2005) have made a feature of their divergent approaches within the academic study of the letter through a correspondence conducted in public in the journal *Lifewriting*. In their shared article, Jolly contends that 'editing letters can be more straightforwardly autobiographical than their original writing' whereas Stanley maintains her stance that there is an ethical dimension to transcription and selection (pp. 107, 111). The reader has to be able to trust the editor to print representative material. Stanley describes edited collections, as well as the unrecoverable (and unreadable) epistolarium, as 'unnatural' (p. 108).

Any theory of completeness or evidence-based reading should be able to accommodate the parallel fact that nineteenth-century correspondence was governed and affected by the use made of an evolving postal service, by the absence of such a service and by the basic need to signal being alive (Thomas 2012). The context of the life writing published between 1840 and 1885 must also include letters in the lives of women at much earlier periods. Mary Delany was born in 1700 at a crossroads between Early Modern and eighteenth-century sensibility. Delany used the letter form as part of her sociability within the Bluestocking circle and as a reinforcement of her family identity. Her letters published in the 1860s were then refracted through a new celebrity culture that undid the earlier pattern of communication and redefined the author of the letters as a safely antiquarian relic.

Furthermore, the letters of the eighteenth and nineteenth centuries were also in correspondence with their fictional counterparts. Samuel Richardson's *Pamela* emerged from the market for letter-writing manuals, reinforcing the recognition that factual and fictional letters shared the same models of composition. Frances Burney's published letters opened with the announcement of her authorship of an epistolary novel, *Evelina*. Jane Austen, who abandoned the epistolary form of *Lady Susan* 'to the great detriment of the Post Office revenue' and revised *Pride and Prejudice*, was presented as an admirer of the work of Richardson, especially *Sir Charles Grandison* (Austen 1818, p. xv; Austen-Leigh 1871, p. 84). A symbiotic relationship develops. The factual letter collection receives back a suspicious veracity to be redefined and reinterpreted by the actions of the letter writer in her real life. In the novel, fiction has been designed to appear real and to recommend itself as a truth-telling medium using the everyday form of the letter, and this conversely brings the truth of the letter collection into question.

Theorising about the letter as fiction (Altman 1982; MacArthur 1990; Favret 1993; Cook 1996; Gilroy and Verhoeven 2000) thus redounds on critiques of the letter as life writing providing parallel and interacting models of the letter as evidence and as narrative. In the case of the fictional letter, the story is mapped out and every letter is significant in the unfolding of the plot. The plot of an actual life told in letters is compiled from materials composed in an uncharted sequence that will be reordered and re-contextualised by the memorialist, editor or biographer. Altman additionally argues that '*published* correspondences' become literature and that there are 'literary values... implicit in the reinscription of letters as books' (1986, pp. 18, 19). Rosemary Bodenheimer's 'writerly fictionality of letters' (1994, p. 19) assumes that the new reader is capable of recognising the exploitation of letters and of understanding that the letter was not always written with life writing in mind. Life writing can be achieved through a form that has been popularised as fiction but the level of trust that the letters are about the life is in a constant state of flux. Elizabeth MacArthur observes that letter writers interpret in the midst of events; that 'a series of present moments of letter-writing predominates, and the future is yet to be decided' (1990, pp. 3, 9). The unknown outcome is part of the fiction of the novel, reflecting real-life letter writing. Conversely, the letter written in life and published as life writing becomes part of a known, completed future to which the editor of a collection is directing readers through revision or selection within the editing process. There is a suspicion that correspondences in real life might have been conducted as fiction and preserved as fact – that they were maybe destined for publication all along. The very bookness of the letter in published form suggests its potential 'fictionality'. There is no reason why the letter writers themselves should not be writing in imitation of their fictional counterparts but the fact that *Pamela*, *Clarissa* and *Evelina* were composed through the letters of women will not be forgotten when lives come to be written in the mid-nineteenth century.

Collaboration: Correspondent, Collector, Editor

Life writing has been explored recently as 'communal' (James and North 2017, p. 133) and as 'a relational literary form' (Culley and Styler 2011, p. 238). Linda Peterson (2003) has discussed the family practice of autobiography and Linda Hughes (2016) traces 'shared life writing' through correspondence. Cynthia Huff's work on the 'imagined communities' of women's life writing describes women's letters in the nineteenth century as sleepers waiting to challenge the 'narrative possibilities' for telling a life (2005, p. 15). Huff considers the role of non-textual and digital media in the contemporary recovery of lives (pp. 15–6). In the mid-nineteenth century, a wider range of women had access to the new technology of the post as well as new means of telling stories through literacy and logistics denied them in previous centuries. Amy Culley too has pointed out that sociability enhances the 'relational and communal aspects of self-representation' where the woman writer is not the 'solitary genius' of autobiography but presented as part of a family or community (2014, p. 2).

Correspondent

At the initial stage of this collaboration, at the autobiographical moment of life writing, a letter is dependent for its existence on an absent correspondent. In its created moment where the separation between correspondents is overcome by a letter, there is, as Esther Milne has suggested, a sense of simultaneity and 'a shared present' (2010, p. 59). Through her absence, the correspondent manipulates the letter medium to encourage role-playing and create a letter-reading and letter-writing circle. In receiving letters, the correspondent has also played her part in the creation and deployment of talisman or hostage letters that may influence and distort the reception of the life written later.

Letter writing was influenced by the identity and location of a correspondent. Within letter collections, there are saved sequences of letters devised for specific 'journalising' purposes that provide a developed type of auto/biographical evidence. Some were written once there had been a chance for reflection as exemplified in the letters written by Elizabeth Gaskell to her American friend, Charles Eliot Norton. These letters have themselves been collected (Whitehill 1932) and have a retrospective character that distinguishes itself from Gaskell's day-to-day correspondence on family and business matters. This segmentation of letters by correspondent is a sub-category of collected letters that highlights the identities adopted by the letter writer. Mary Delany in particular has been subject to these segmentations. Nine letters from Delany to Samuel Richardson appeared in his letters published in 1804 (Kerhervé 2004, p. 30; pp. 139–40) and there have been collections of her letters to Frances Hamilton (*Letters* 1820) and to Lord North (Kerhervé 2009). Gaskell's letters to Norton adopted her recognisable tone but offered alternative perspectives on evolving circumstances such as her daughters' engagements: Meta's that was broken off and Marianne's to her cousin Thurstan Holland (Chapple and Pollard 1966, pp. 487–93; pp. 502–7; pp. 743–6). Gaskell memorialised and valued her long-distance correspondence and marvelled that the materials of its creation would be received by the Nortons across the Atlantic. On 5 February 1865, she wrote to congratulate them on the birth of a daughter, 'To think you will really touch this bit of paper!' and, on 28 September 1857, 'I feel as if one ought to have great events to write about before beginning a letter into another continent' (Chapple and Pollard 1966, pp. 474, 743). In the modern edition of Gaskell's letters, the re-reader can apprehend that her style was tailored to her correspondents but also had a characteristic vitality and spontaneity occasionally found to be ill-judged and regretted in the new context of the retrospective collection. It also becomes apparent that Gaskell's letters were supplemented, and sometimes even written, by her daughters who will later copy Brontë's letters for the Brontë biography.

In being published, letters have destroyed their corresponding selves because one half of a relationship is not available. As Bossis observes, 'A correspondence is a joint endeavour in which meaning is the product of collaboration' (1986, p. 68). The letter, according to Huff, is a form determined by 'readers, intended or unintended' (Huff 2001, p. 954). Thus, Frances Burney's style and tone has lost the response in kind and encouragement from her sisters and from Samuel 'Daddy' Crisp and her friends such as Frederica Locke. John Abbott explains in his introduction to Burney's journals and letters for 1784–86 that her prose 'is consistently shaped by the sister's relationship [and] by the eye she knew was reading' (2015, p. xvi). The letters were originally read at the time of transmission and have been redelivered into an uncertain future without their corresponding links and responses. Correspondents were collaborators whose collusion in future life-writing projects, intended or otherwise, is part of the life writing itself.

Collector

Life writing at the moment of composition was taking place in a form different from that which will be transmitted and mediated into the forms of edited collection and biography. At the stage of composition, the time for writing and the timing of writing contributed to the content of the correspondence. This temporal dimension caused some events to be prioritised over others within the account of the life. The selective preservation process also denies the reciprocity of that correspondence – with its literal meaning of 'answering together' – because a letter has been dispatched and has survived without its answer. Emergent dialogues of friendship, sisterhood and authorship are themselves hedged or couched within a further round of inheritance and survival that dictates the letters' operational place within a life-writing project. In the preservation process, letters come to be redefined by their valorisation as objects, and letter collections also have lives and contingency. The intervention of the collector has dictated the type of life writing produced from the letters published within the six texts discussed in later chapters. In the introduction to her annotated bibliography, Cheryl Cline observes that '[b]etween a woman's impulse to write down something of herself and ours to read it stands a host of intermediaries: editors, publishers and executors' (1989, p. xxvi). Letters might be valued at the time of receipt for their content or length or the occasion of their composition, and they have then been subject to both family and public valuation. They have been segmented by family holdings and by the retention practices of significant correspondents. Collections appear to be fixed but are later updated by rediscoveries and new identifications within 'lost' archives. Stanley points out that 'letter-writing is characterised by fragmentation and dispersal' (2004, p. 204) but we must also consider disposal and disposition in any reconstruction of life writing through letters.

The letter collection is thus both a collated and a withheld sequence. It has been pointed out that such archives are not neutral and that their organisation and context are affected by 'contingencies of value' (Gerson 2001, p. 7). For women's archives, Carole Gerson expresses concern about a lack of cataloguing and unevenness in preservation (p. 12). Social scientists of the 1960s conclude that 'the episodic and private record' provided by an archive involves a 'selective filter' since '[a]lthough the investigator may not himself contaminate the material, he may learn that the producer or repository already has' (Webb, Campbell, Schwartz and Sechrest 1966, p. 111). On top of such suspicions comes the adaptation of the text itself. Frances Burney was both archivist and editor, and for her, Cline's 'impulse' was guided by decorum and social pressures. When Annie Raine Ellis edited Burney's early diary and letters in the later nineteenth century, she, in turn, endorsed and respected Burney's prepared text. For the new reader in 1889, Ellis noted the diarist's editorial intervention on the blue wrapper or cover of the 'Juvenile Journal, No. 1': 'Curtailed and erased of what might be mischievous from friendly or Family Considerations' (Ellis 1889, p. 1). In their preservation and contamination, collections are markedly affected by 'family considerations'.

Looking more closely at the example of the extensive Burney collection, much of it was sold in 1924 to a bookseller in London whence it was acquired by Owen D. Young, President of General Electric. In 1941, Young was persuaded to accept half the value of his 'hoard' in order to donate it to the Berg Collection in the New York Public Library where it now resides (Hemlow, Burgess and Douglas 1971, pp. xiii–xiv). There are over 10,000 Burney family letters from the years 1749 to 1878 in collections including Berg in New York, the Barrett Collection in the British Library and the Osborn Collection at Yale (Hemlow, Burgess and Douglas 1971, p. xviii). For Burney at the time, it began to feel as if letter collections were burdens to be carried. Her son Alexander urged his mother to destroy her hoard in the 1830s but she deemed it right that, once 'family considerations' were dealt with, the letters and journals might be educational to future generations. This process has been fraught for Burney descendants who have published the letters or used them as life writing. Burney has been accused of self-aggrandisement, unwomanly self-promotion and downright lies by family members of letter recipients and by reviewers in the prestigious magazines of the nineteenth century including John Wilson Croker in the *Quarterly* and

Thomas Macaulay in the *Edinburgh Review*. As discussed in Chapters 4 and 6, descendants of Mary Delany, Burney's friend at Court, and of Jane Austen have accused Burney of exploiting family connections and of using an ostensibly domestic and private communication to write for posterity and publication. These were not just 'family considerations' but issues of reputation and the revaluation of the collection within a new era.

It is notable for family preservation purposes that Burney was linked with Jane Austen in reviews of Burney's *Diary* since Cassandra Austen's reported destruction of many of her sister's letters occurred around the same time in 1842. One Austen letter that survived this cull serves to illustrate the intricacies of transmission and inheritance. The letter resurfaced in 2014 when its present owners proposed to sell it on once more in response to funding cuts and at a time convenient for the Austen bicentenaries. In 1799, this letter to Cassandra written on 8 January from Steventon to Godmersham in Kent mentioned '*first impressions*' which is the first known reference to *Pride and Prejudice* in its original form. In the next sentence, Austen thanked Cassandra for restoring to her 'an old petticoat' (Le Faye 1995, p. 35). On Cassandra's death, the letter passed to their niece Fanny Knight, who had lived at Godmersham, and it was published in the 1884 Brabourne edition of Austen's letters. The letter was probably sold by the family in 1893 before becoming part of a collection of 4,000 documents owned by Hester Pengelly (later Forbes-Julian), daughter of the founder of the Torquay Museum in Devon. After her death in 1934, the collection was gifted to the museum and remained un-investigated until 1989 when the manuscript of this letter first came to light (Le Faye 1995, p. 366). Its content has been transmitted to twentieth-century editions through the Brabourne *Letters* (1884a, p. 191) but dispersal from the original collection occurred through the valuation of the letter as an object to be collected in a new context.

Before its publication and editing for a new audience, the letter collection has already made a hazardous journey beginning with the postal system and followed a route through many collectors ranging from family historians like Cassandra Austen to autograph hunters like Hester Pengelly and custodial controllers such as the librarians of the Berg Collection. Letters structure the life while it is being lived and help to document the life-writing project. The path of transmission betrays dispersal through sale and valuation as 'Brontëana' or any number of other 'anas'. The Delany (Llanover 1861–62) and Winkworth (1883) papers were preserved as family projects that are now mined for localised information and biographical contextualisation that sets the lives of the letter writers to one side. The movements around salerooms and within libraries make explicit the value that has accrued to the lives contained, and apparently accounted for, in documents in New York, London and, in the case of that one Austen letter – together with another from Charlotte Brontë – Torquay. The lives of these women were shaped by those who collect, with hidden texturing from what Gladstone called 'the tapestry in reverse' (1889, p. 603) woven by people like Charlotte Barrett, Ellen Nussey and even Hester Pengelly and a Mrs H.G. Frankel who has un-accountably donated two Burney letters to the Berg Collection. Modern collections must recover provenance and signal this other trajectory of a letter which, to paraphrase Arthur Nicholls, has passed into hands and under eyes never envisaged by the writer.

Editor

The original letter archive or hoard was a monument, mausoleum or re-pository of the memorialised and objectified family member. The editing of the resulting collection entails re-articulation in a new context within which the editor must decide how much the reader can be expected to form a judgement and, in turn, what degree of guidance and interpreta-tion should be given. Editors were responsible for reframing, curtailing and collation. The further need for a narrative thread, however, creates a requirement for longer interpretative passages to guide the reader, and this leads to another hybrid form of life writing that incorporates the letter. The editor becomes a biographer but a biographer who can still engage with his subject by allowing her own words to appear in the text. This new epistolary narrative has been created through linking passages and interpretative notes and the re-evaluation of the narrating subject as a biographical construct. William Merrill Decker identifies in this process the privileging of 'narrative possibilities' and the expectation of editorial guidance for the 'posterior readership' of letters (1998, p. 5). Although the letters stand in for the life, the editor adapts evidence to support a contemporary thesis or 'family consideration'.

The Austen family collaboration, for instance, became divorced from original memory so that even the physical image of the author was re-fixed in the time period of her inheritors (Kirkham 1983). Within this process, there are clearly talisman letters which act as touchstones for the representation of a life, and hostage letters which circumscribe a chosen interpretation. James Edward Austen-Leigh's *Memoir* re-read and misunderstood Austen's injunction about writing with a fine brush on a 'little bit of ivory' (1871, p. 155). Austen-Leigh described the letter of 16 December 1816 written to himself (Le Faye 1995, pp. 323–4) as 'her description of her own style of composition' (Austen-Leigh 1871, p. 153) without appreciating the context and his role as nephew within the correspondence. This picked up Henry Austen's equally wilful use of an extract in his 1818 'Biographical Notice' (p. xvii). Other editors of the case study texts also follow specific agendas. Lady Llanover ignores evidence of Mary Delany's fondness and concern for Burney. Elizabeth

Gaskell values the Nussey letters and tries to gloss over Ellen's exclusion from the knowledge of Brontë's authorship of *Jane Eyre*. Families were remembering together in public and yet apart, as can be seen in the split holdings of the Brontë and Austen circles and the hoarding of Burney's, although Burney was given a second chance at life writing in letters because she also inherited. The letter publications discussed in this study were also reacting to texts already in circulation including obituaries, reviews and earlier biographies. The life shared passes from correspondent to commemorator to commentator within the family and then out into public gaze.

Once the correspondents and inheritors have played their part in the reframing process, there are also self-professed but invisible collators who become biographers without necessarily announcing themselves. John Cross paradoxically laid claim to self-effacement in his *Life of George Eliot* (1885a, p. vi). The resultant life writing then reflects in parallel or in relief the life of the editor-collator. Such collators range from Susanna Winkworth, who lived her life contemporaneously with her sister Catherine, to Lord Brabourne who devoted a hundred pages of his *Letters of Jane Austen* to himself even though he was not born until 12 years after the death of his great-aunt. Even within the reality of words direct from the letter writer, there is room to question whose life is being presented to the nineteenth-century audience of book purchasers. Within the archive, a reading afterlife for a letter written at a moment of necessary communication is cultivated by such acts of editing. The 'power relationship' of the editor or biographer comes into question (Stanley 1992, p. 251), and Bernard Duyfhuizen observes that the actions of an editor create a further 'double narrative', one of the narratives of transmission (1992, p. 64). For the purposes of this study, it is essential to debate the reliability of the textual evidence offered by the editor-collator at the point of publication. There are a range of narratives that uncover the means by which letters become life writing and thus where the compiler exists in relation to the narrating subject.

The original nineteenth-century 'Life and Letters' emerging from the archive with its 'sagging circumstantiality' has been largely condemned, and Richard Altick describes 'biography-told-in-documents' as 'chaos in three volumes' (1966, pp. 193, 199). A.O.J. Cockshutt observes rather testily that 'a batch of letters and dates is not a biography' (1974, p. 12). Altick acknowledges the need for a subject to speak in his own words but criticises 'mere compilers' who assumed 'it was axiomatic that the letters of a man *contained* his life' (1966, pp. 193, 194, 196). More recently, David Amigoni has suggested that the discourse of Victorian biography emerged from the more complex textual process of representing not just the 'life' but the 'times' (1993, p. 1). The reader of the life was expected to recognise this narrative, and Paul de Man posits the 'specular nature of autobiography', a mirroring effect through which the author and reader share their interiorisation within a text (1979, p. 921). Mireille Bossis points out that celebrated lives cause a correspondence to gain a different 'weight' with 'a fixed and univocal referential value' presented from the viewpoint of the author's ultimate fame (1986, p. 65). Additionally, however, the collaborating editors and correspondents appear in a complex reflection or refraction of their subjects that might be termed 'umbral'. This study would contend that 'univocal' content and de Man's mirroring impact on the reproduction or re-inscription of a correspondence. The hidden lives both of other correspondents and of the editorial or biographical overseer reappear in the umbral space between.

The collation of letters refracts the collator as well as creating what could be termed a false narrative. An editor must account for references to other letters that no longer exist. The loss of contextualisation in the edited collection might add significance that is not a true representation of the life. Letters may have been written as an excuse for a correspondence flagging and no longer valued. Letters may have been lost in sharing or merely through carelessness, or never written at all. The interpretation of such absences from a sequence affects the further interpretation of a life. The editor might speculate on whether the letters have been destroyed deliberately by the writer or recipient and why. Brabourne cannot account for the loss of Jane Austen's correspondence during time spent in Bath and in Southampton (1884a, p. 300). There is a gap between 27 May 1801 and 14 September 1804 even in the modern edition (Le Faye 1995, p. 92). John Cross tried to avoid accounting for a change in George Eliot's relationship with her friend Sara Hennell but latterly the two women appeared to communicate only on their birthdays. In the early twentieth century, William Michael Rossetti (1908, p. viii) will later struggle with letter sequencing because he has himself given power over Christina Rossetti's letters to her biographer Mackenzie Bell.

In shaping this archive of autobiographical letter writing, a biographer will choose a path through a life to make a life-writing construct, and the imposed narrative is significant to the received understanding and readability of the life being written. As Hermione Lee points out, 'Biography has to omit and to choose' (2005, p. 27). The biographer along with the editor effectively becomes a new correspondent or collaborator in the life-writing project and subsequent chapters of this book explore the roles of these collaborators. Gaskell and Susanna Winkworth are correspondents and biographers; Mathilde Blind (1883) and Mackenzie Bell (1898) ambush the process to create a narrative before the collected letters of Eliot and Rossetti can appear. In the process, the immediacy of the original letter becomes past time and 'I' becomes 'she'. Reading letters is part of an exchange for lack of autobiography and indeed a resistance to it.

The collaborations between letter writer and editor-collator produce a patchwork, mosaic or audit of the life writing within letters. The letter might ask for editorial intervention as an antidote or anti-model for those 'life and letters' tomes but the process of composing a connecting narrative also effaces the original writer of the letter and tends to undermine the value of that letter as the document of a life. The mosaic obscures factors of composition and transmission that are significant for the life as presented by the letters in real time. This results in a debate about whether letter collections fix or free up the content of that life.

Letters as Life Writing

The letter is fixed by its original written form and its placement within a letter-writing sequence but it is also pliable, or perhaps pliant, in the sense of being available for narrative purposes. The identity of the self and the prevailing relationship with a correspondent dictates the appearance of self writing in the communicated text. Having been a part of life-writing immediacy, the letter is then repurposed as material for a life 'written' by someone else. The letter stands within a sequence unpicked and reinstated by publication to become autobiography or is alternatively reinterpreted from a biographical point of view within the planned narrative structure of the biographer. This section considers first the physical production, appearance and composition of the letter at the lived moment and secondly the letter as evidence, including its narrative of transmission and the retrospective valuation of celebrity within the archive.

Letters negotiate their existence within a framework of epistolary exchange and have ongoing textuality as documents that can be verified through marks of exchange such as greeting, closure and postscript. Many of these elements were dictated in the eighteenth and nineteenth centuries by handbooks or the taught experience of letter writing. These marks were also dependent on the nature of an epistolary relationship and its openness to other recipients through the practice of reading aloud. Retaining these marks legitimises the original writing intent but reinstates also the triviality of the form. As against the self-conscious and potentially transgressive effort of self writing indicated by a diary, anyone could write a letter, and for women of the time, the vehicle of the letter offered the motivation and opportunity for self-record. Many of the letters composed within the case study texts were for a family circle and would have stood in for the presence of the letter writer in her absence. The letters set scenes that indicated a planned time for composition or alternatively a time snatched from other duties. The letters' reference models were classical, domestic and fictional (*The British Letter-Writer* 1760; Kerhervé 1763; *The Complete Letter-Writer* 1776; Johnson 1779), and Eve Bannet has described the influence on 'letteracy' of the much-reprinted letter-writing manuals including their reproduction of direct speech (2005, p. xvii). She suggests that the manuals were themselves collaborating in the letter writing (p. 314). At a further level of correspondence, the physical texts of letter-writing manuals were themselves inscribed by the women who had owned them. Imaginary women write the letters being presented as models but the actual edition of *The British Letter-Writer* published by J. Cooke at 1s 6d held in the British Library is inscribed 'Jane Wells her Book 1771' and then 'Miss Smith July 14th 1815'.

This should raise questions about the extent to which letters can be autobiographical since their structure, narrative and timing were dictated by the life's original contingencies. The sending process ostensibly gave no opportunity for reflection or recall of the life-writing moment, and the writer herself did not have power over the presences, absences and functions of duty within that life. The letters themselves record a process of acknowledgement and management with references to composition, receipt, planned future composition and the opportunity to write. The letters comment on, and worry about, progress towards finishing a letter and about its consequent transmission. Susan Whyman, discussing the eighteenth-century use of the letter as a newly 'accessible technology', suggests that letter writing offered opportunities to practise constructing narratives, to record life stories and to communicate over distances (2009, pp. 227, 330). Letters controlled chaos and offered dating, location and 'a system of serial ordering' (p. 227). This is a viewpoint, however, that glosses over the fictionality of the letter-writing opportunity and assumes a level of survival and preservation unhoped-for even within the households of exemplar women.

For the texts that survive, dated or dateable letters appear to construct a dateable life but hoarded letters are divorced both from a sequence and from the life context. At its basic level, the edited form of a published collection may deny letters their generic epistolary characteristics such as greeting style or closing address. The materiality of the original letter is often lost although it may be described in modern editions. Letters before 1840 were constrained by the cross-post system but were then freed up by the uniform penny post (Hall 1999; Smith 2012, pp. 115–6) and in real time, the writer may have had to prioritise communication for a given correspondence to ensure family needs or economic criteria were met. The letter was originally constructed to meet the demands of the postal system. It could be curtailed in length for reasons of cost, dictated by the departure of the mail coach or retained to allow for communication in person. On 26 June 1808, for instance, Jane Austen resolved to send her regular letter despite the fact that her sister Cassandra would read a letter already sent by their niece Fanny: 'The two letters will not interfere, I dare say; on the contrary they may throw light on each other' (Le Faye 1995, p. 134). On 26 October 1813, however, she told her sister: 'It is throwing a letter away to send it by a visitor [who] can tell most things as well' (Le Faye 1995, p. 245).

The modern reader has also lost the appearance of being hurried or measured in composition. In her more recently published letters, Elizabeth Gaskell refers to pens and paper, and to the timescale of her letters' composition. '(This is such very bad paper... and yet I have no other)', she explains on 12 December 1850 to Lady Kay-Shuttleworth who will be instrumental in her meeting Charlotte Brontë (Chapple and Pollard 1966, p. 137). To George Smith, publisher of *The Life of Charlotte Brontë*, she excuses her 'very bad pen' on 25 July 1864 because she really needs a better one to ask for an advance on her serial *Wives and Daughters* (p. 736). Gaskell tells her daughters who are away in Bradford, 'I was so glad to hear from you, though my pen does not look very like it' (p. 652) and opens a much earlier letter to Marianne, 'My dearest Polly — (Oh —— the pen & my want of a penknife)' (p. 271). She apologises to John Forster on 3 May 1853 in a letter about Brontë's visit to Manchester: 'I have written amid the distraction of children' (p. 231). The new reader cannot see the background material circumstances of her composition. Notes to published editions might give back a sense of the letter's appearance but we are no longer educated in the art of reading the crossed paragraph or squeezed postscript that strikes home when seeing originals or facsimiles of once ephemeral texts. The new reader cannot now understand how difficult it was to write without blotting, or how crossing a paragraph to save money may have impacted on a letter's content and length. The original writing and reading experience was governed by conditions that cannot be recreated such as variance in script size, the positioning of a postscript or address, delay in receipt, hiding from prying eyes or the sequencing of other letters now lost.

In reading the letters out of context, it is also important to consider the journal letter, a form highly relevant to the letter-writing practices of the eighteenth and nineteenth centuries. In its shorter form, it was a letter written over the course of a week to meet the day of the post so that the day or days of composition and posting have an important part to play in the creation of the original text. Communication was achieved through a longer compilation of news over a number of days, enforced by distance or lack of postal opportunity. In this way, a form of authorship and textual manipulation becomes readily apparent. Thus, for instance, Austen wrote from Godmersham over three days of her stay in June 1808 to include an account of a visit to Canterbury 'as Mrs J.A.'s letter to Anna cannot have given you every particular of it' (Le Faye 1995, p. 128). Susanna Winkworth's representation of the letters of her sisters was controlled by her conflicting family and professional agendas, and many letters have internal dates because of news retained or overflowing. A letter from Emily Winkworth to their sister Catherine on 7 May 1849 opened with an ellipsis '... Interrupted yesterday' and was further interrupted by a visit from Gaskell that prompted a new date for news internal to the text (Winkworth 1883, pp. 178, 179). The discussion about Frances Burney's more deliberate processes is ongoing (Hemlow, Cecil and Douglas 1972, pp. xxxi–v; Clark 2012), and her 'extended journal letters' are regarded as life writing (Sabor 2012, p. 72). Such a form of writing offered greater opportunity for self writing because of the longer time period and authorisation to use a reflective narrative form. It could be that shorter and extended journal letters have greater claims to autobiographical status because they explicitly acknowledge this narrating self. The generic boundaries are tested and redrawn, but at the same time those boundaries may be re-fixed by editorial labelling that conceals the serial-writing process within the single date selected for the text.

Social science has been most active in classifying letters as evidence but with a *caveat* based on context. In his broad definition for the *Encyclopedia of Life Writing*, Bernard Bray suggests that letters may be practical instruments of communication, sociological documents or fragments of literature. Their forms are contradictory because they use known ingredients but are composed to appear natural and spontaneous (2001, pp. 552–3). In the collation of letters as documents or as evidence of life writing, the texts under discussion within this book are arguably engaged in all three activities. Earlier social scientists are wary, however, of letters as a source of research data. Only a complete sequence of letters, to include correspondents and a balance of other factors with 'a more textured series of comparisons', can be evidence of a life (Webb, Campbell, Schwartz and Sechrest 1966, pp. 89, 105). This suspicion of letters was challenged by Ken Plummer's *Documents of Life* in 1983, itself revised in 2001. Plummer puts the case for letters as a narrative form from within a life while still seeing letters as 'interactive products' that should not be divorced from their context (2001, pp. 51–5). His suggestion that there is a bridge between science and humanities (p. 9) itself represents the spectrum and variation found between the apparently raw data of collected letters and their editing to form a narrative. If letters are life documents, any action to present the life through letters is, Plummer contends, 'a form of hidden censorship and selective screening' (p. 55). Liz Stanley has since revisited this seminal text in her quest for the 'narrative and biographical frame', specifically explored in her studies of the letters of Olive Shreiner (2013, p. 3).

Even before the collection of letters, a recoverable life has also been edited by the process of letter writing since absence/presence contributes to letter sequencing and unevenness of material and thus affects the timing, volume and content of surviving correspondence. At the post-composition stage, this emergent pattern may overvalue or overweight certain parts of the life because correspondence has been preserved to account for the active and celebrated period of life rather than for its origins. Importantly for the non-fictional letter sequence, a narrative emerges at a later stage in the collaboration when a life is re-valued by celebrity or by the desire for retrospective memorialisation. Cockshutt points out (1974, pp. 16–7), as does Bossis (1986, p. 65), that the reliance of nineteenth-century biography on documents meant that any life was top-heavily based on evidence from the period of the subject's fame. If the life and its explanatory origins are missing for a pre-celebrity period, it could also be argued, of course, that life writing cannot be authorised until exemplary status has been achieved, until the letters reach the stage of being re-found and re-circulated to represent the life already lived. Altman observes that the original letters are ephemera and based on a relationship with the original reader negotiated at the time (1986, p. 19). The re-publication in a recovered form is not so much reading letters but asking the (re) reader to compose a life from the mass. Relative celebrity has distorted the pattern of letters and their preservation, and this has also contributed to the unevenness of style which both editor and biographer try to smooth or excuse in the path to a coherent narrative.

The ensuing publication of the letter collection occurs for complex reasons through the vested interests of the original writer herself, the surviving family and the publisher. There are divided family factions and new social codes and fashions to take into account in the transmission of the letter to a new audience. The transition to life writing is blurred and the letters operate on that boundary described as auto/biography. Elizabeth Heckendorn Cook sees letters at a crossroads where 'the letter-narrative exposes the private body to publication' (1996, p. 8). In its function as evidence, the letter has behind it many narratives to be traced across the private/public, auto/biographical boundaries. Letters stand in for the life writing that did not take place in life since the phase of publication re-values the letters along with the life that can now apparently be derived from a correspondence worthy of both preservation and publication. At this point in the transmission, the editor or biographer will argue that the voice of the writer emerges from her letters but at the same time may seek to silence that writer for her own good. Susanna Winkworth uses many ellipses within the family letters she presents albeit in a largely private publication (Winkworth 1883). William Michael Rossetti must provide intrusive commentary to maintain the image of a woman without an autobiography at all (Rossetti 1908). At one level, a biographer re-collects letters out of sequence and out of context and interprets them but, as Malcolm Bradbury observes in his essay on 'The Telling Life', 'Biography is inclined... toward structure and assertion... Biographies are plots of life, not the life itself' (1987, p. 314). Other experts in the field acknowledge selectivity and contingency. Jenny Uglow, biographer of Gaskell and Eliot (1993, 1987), observes that 'chance has played a part in dictating what we write' (2004, p. 182). The letter as a life-writing tool is subject to vagaries of preservation, rearrangement and interpretation, and Charles Porter in *Yale French Studies* suggests that we should seek rather 'the plot of a correspondence' (1986, p. 14).

The cultural and social practice of letter writing included the rhetoric of friendship and duty but also an inherited code of debt, lack of writing materials – of pens, paper and information – and concerns about the means of sending. There was also a pattern of recirculation and destruction observable within letters that are latterly portrayed with a single trajectory and that have survived strict instructions to 'burn'. This creates a letter community and print afterlife that must be explored as they radiate from the central point supplied by models for letter writing into the specific conditions of writing for nineteenth-century women.

Women's Letters as Life Writing

Felicity Nussbaum has suggested that diary and journal recording in the eighteenth century were 'sites of resistance' based on an empowered 'written interiority' (1989, p. xii; p. xiii). Letters, however, have their authorisation from female roles that were not dependent on resistance but on family duties of news gathering and dispersal. More recently, Anne Collett and Louise D'Arcenis have described 'the unsociable sociability of women's life writing' that places women 'at odds with the social and institutional expectations placed on them' (2010, p. 6). The letter formed a part of the household accounting function, interacting with the diary/journal. The journal betrayed life recording and shaded into life-writing intent. Where the diary emerged from a sense of keeping literal household accounts (Delafield 2009, pp. 9–10), the letter or epistolary exchange functioned as a balance in a relationship, another type of accounting mechanism where a letter (or a life) was owed. The shading generic definitions within personal writing across the diary, commonplace book, journal and autobiography were made privately available to women. The organisation of correspondence for a subsequent life was a more complex negotiation particularly for women writers whose exemplary lives had to be without incident and to accommodate the writer's sociable role as wife or daughter. Michelle Levy has suggested that 'the discourse of authorship was systematically dismantled' (2008, p. 19) when domestic life was pitted against genius. The lives and letters of women writers came to present them as both 'eminent and obscure' (Atkinson 2010, p. 150).

Within the terms of the letter as life writing for women in the nineteenth century, a complex interplay of factors emerges. Letters were an authorised medium of communication but life writing was not. Valerie Sanders suggests that Victorian women could not write about themselves as women because of 'a web of prohibition against self-advertisement' and because they were untypical if they had a life to write about (1996, p. 169). Where a woman was a published author in the nineteenth century, letters provided audiences with material additional to her extant work that was then viewed within a new generic framework as autobiographical writing. It might also be misinterpreted as fiction. The suspicion that self writing had already taken place was deplored and this led to further misinterpretation of the auto/biographical practices of women and their editors. In addition, wholesale survival could paradoxically trivialise or mis-focus a life such as Delany's or Burney's, both of whose writing is undermined by repetition in the material of letters extant from their time at Court.

It has been assumed that letters arise from an autobiographical impulse and that the eighteenth- and nineteenth-century classification of the personal letter as a site for women's writing generated a self-reflective or self-fashioning opportunity (Milne 2010, p. 199; Caine 2015, p. 483). Kathy Mezei (2005) sees domestic space with its interruptions, surveillance and duties as a metonymical representation of women's writing, and this concept can be extrapolated into life writing through the medium of letters. Melanie Bigold observes that letters were, for women in the eighteenth century, 'a version of literary manuscript performance' and 'a way of... both creating and viewing a textual representation of oneself' (2013, pp. 7, 14). James Daybell's work has uncovered a mediated and layered form in writing across generations (2016, p. 232; Daybell and Gordon 2016, p. 7). The original authorisation for writing was bound up in the domestic duty to write according to a pre-planned communication pattern: a pattern dictated by travel, the postal system or the availability of other family members to convey news. Rebecca Earle describes the letter as an unstable artefact in a context, operating at an 'imprecise frontier' between private and public. The letter represents both a commodity and an obligation, and Earle points out that the letter cannot be 'unmediated' because of these factors in its existence (1999, pp. 1–8). Divorced from their original trajectory, letters become life writing without that being the ostensible intent at the time of composition when correspondent, context and the material conditions of writing were significant factors of production.

The process of recollection was not thought appropriate or possible for Victorian women. Sanders points out that autobiography 'implies selection, order, shaping; a complex interplay between the present self and the self as recalled at various stages of the recorded life-story' (1989, p. 4), and she cautioned in her early work against the one-sided narrative of the letter with its short-term retrospect (pp. 13, 19). Linda Peterson has defined Victorian women's autobiography as hybrid in that it was likely to combine first-person narrative with commentary; Peterson identifies the three categories of spiritual autobiography, 'chroniques scandaleuses' and family domestic memoir (1999, p. x, p. 4). The definition of autobiography as a 'retrospective prose narrative' (Eakin 1999, p. 2, quoting Phillippe Lejeune) appears to sideline the letter because correspondence lacks a retrospective dimension; it operates on an unfolding serial basis whose texts cannot be recalled. The letter has, however, been brought into the theorisation of women's writing about the self with its 'devalued position at the margins of the canon' (Smith 1987, p. 16). If women were being denied the opportunity for an autobiographical impulse or viewpoint, the letter provided a site for what Sidonie Smith terms 'self-narrating' and thus 'narrative coherence' (1995, p. 108). Mertxell Simon-Martin has sought to revalue the letter as 'a site of struggle and empowerment where the writer negotiates different subject positions' (2013, p. 226). In the process, letters have become more complicated and also questionable as acts of recording the self (Summerfield 2013).

Letters could be invoked within all three categories of Peterson's first person/commentary model, and the case study texts demonstrate how letters are called up as evidence of domestic duty that will pass the test of respectability within a nineteenth-century interpretation of womanhood. Paul John Eakin suggests that there is no such thing as the 'unstoried self' (1999, p. 140). Stories, of course, can be told through other media and may still be interiorised despite difficulties in communication or narrative. Editors were able to use letters to revise the 'master narrative' of autobiographical patterns based on men's achievements and to address somehow the politics of life writing using achievements from lives written back into domesticity (Gagnier 1991, pp. 6, 41; Broughton 1997, p. xv). Alexis Easley describes the masculinisation of literary authority that defined female texts as ephemeral and forced early nineteenth-century professional women to present themselves as amateurs in their writing (2004, pp. 18, 20). Rebecca Styler (2017) has more recently pointed out the potential for writing a self through a progression of biographies. All these approaches to life writing suggest collaboration through the interaction of the chosen text with women's roles and identities. The hybridity is part of the negotiation for a text. Women of the nineteenth century were disabled by gender but could still 'story' themselves in their letters and other allegedly or ostensibly domestic forms of self-expression. The case study women are novelists, editors, translators and a paper mosaic artist.

David Amigoni has described how Victorian biography was written as part of a 'cult of exemplarity' to make 'a monolithic contribution to master-narratives with much broader ambitions' (1993, pp. 1, 2). This might suggest the necessary exclusion of women from such narratives in the third person but Alison Booth's work on collective biography has demonstrated how women's lives provided celebrity prototypes within a didactic rhetorical frame (2004, pp. 10, 28). Of the case study women, Charlotte Brontë appears most frequently in the collections researched by Booth. In the years after Gaskell's *Life*, Brontë was 'The Worthy Daughter' (Dickes 1859), 'The Moorland Romanticist' ([Hope] 1886) and a 'Modern Sibyl' along with Eliot and Gaskell herself (Ritchie 1913). Austen was one of the original 'sibyls' (Ritchie 1883) along with Maria Edgeworth, Anna Laetitia Barbauld and Amelia Opie. Brontë's girlhood as a 'chapter in female biography' was deplored along with that of Burney in the same publication that lauded Delany's early life (Adams 1883). Eliot was a 'Queen of Literature' ([Hope] 1886), a 'Beacon Light of History' (Lord 1886) and one of 'Twelve English Authoresses' along with Austen, Brontë, Burney and Gaskell (Walford 1892). Rossetti was a 'Maid of Honour' among 'Twelve Descriptive Sketches of Single Women who have distinguished themselves in Philanthropy, Nursing, Poetry, Travel, Science, Prose' (Green-Armytage 1906). As Amber Regis observes, however, the collective biography becomes less coherent under stress (2019, p. 68). Although resident in Clifton, the author of *Maids of Honour* did not include in her collection the Winkworths, who had lived in the Bristol suburb since 1862, despite their contributions to philanthropy, translation, hymn writing and, of course, singleness.

As subjects of biography and 'self-help history' in the nineteenth century (Booth 2004, p. 50), women's lives nonetheless reflected the domesticity of those times: not their authorship or commercial negotiation. Their lives were to be exemplary of womanhood as 'girls', 'queens' and missionaries. Jane Austen herself described letters to Cassandra as 'important nothings' on 15 June 1808 (Le Faye 1995, p. 125), and the family later used her letters to represent Austen's ordinariness. Her nephew James Edward Austen-Leigh wrote of Austen's letters in his *Memoir* of her:

> [T]he materials may be thought inferior to the execution, for they treat only of the details of domestic life. ... They may be said to resemble the nest which some little bird builds of the materials nearest at hand, of the twigs and mosses supplied by the tree in which it is placed; curiously constructed out of the simplest matters.
>
> (1871, p. 57)

When Frances Burney's letters were edited by her niece Charlotte Barrett in seven volumes between 1842 and 1846, Barrett explained Burney's exemplary ordinariness in her 'Introductory Memoir':

> We would also hope there may be a moral use in presenting the example of one who, being early exalted to fame and literary distinction, yet found her chief happiness in the discharge of domestic duties, and in the friendships and attachments of private life.
>
> (1842a, pp. iv–v)

Burney, of course, was castigated by reviewers for including herself in history. Part of the negative response to her autobiographical works was owing to the publisher's pursuit of celebrity stories including Burney's accounts of time spent at the Court of George III and of her life on the continent during the Napoleonic Wars.

For the exemplary woman who must be re-domesticated, the early editor or biographer works within a coded representational form to show an exemplary life with its family responsibilities and its memorialisation potential. This is a woman who happens to have written preserved letters ostensibly offering an autobiographical viewpoint. Austen's biography was controlled by the family's ownership of her letters, initially held by Cassandra and then distributed across the branches of the family. Burney's much larger hoard has proved more problematical in its volume and provenance. There are some 2,000 extant letters, as opposed to 163 by Austen and 950 by Brontë. In the cases of all three women, the tension between the life, the letters and life writing has impacted on subsequent biographical interpretation and output. John Mullan describes Burney's letter-life as a 'copious gap-filled record' compared with the 'compacted obscurity' of Austen's (Mullan 2001, pp. 21, 23). By contrast, Burney has generated fewer biographical column inches than Brontë, and Austen has been written and rewritten starting with the family's *Life and Letters* (Austen-Leigh and Austen-Leigh 1913) through to the mischievous speculations of David Nokes (1997) and the 'fictionalised memoir or biographical novel' (Butler 1998, p. 3) of Claire Tomalin (1997) via Park Honan's meticulously researched *Jane Austen: Her Life* (1987).

The letter has come to represent hybrid authorship and a category at the border between private and public writing. The private texts of women with an alternative public voice were made public in the case study texts to be discussed in the succeeding chapters. The letter has had an exaggerated effect when redefined as life writing by giving letters emphasis over other non-surviving evidence. This should raise warning signals about the extent to which any life can be narrated within a letter. Charlotte Brontë's life is imbalanced because of Ellen Nussey's hoard and because of Gaskell's concealment of her infatuation with Constantin Heger. Frances Burney removed a whole year from her life because of family embarrassment over her brother's expulsion from Cambridge. The letters of Jane Austen and the Winkworth sisters have systematically concealed the existence of family members, their elder brothers.

Letters gave women access to life writing before the term was coined and allowed the creation of a 'storied' self. The life writing of the letters has its own plot or narrative of transmission to account for the letters' dating, chronology and narrative arcs. Letters were inherited or gifted as objects out of their context, and ownership of these letters implies ownership of the biographical subject. It is also implied that the letters are mine to destroy, and modern interpretations must account for the vandalism enacted by the family memorial on the letters of a woman whose life is both exemplary and transgressive. The letter as a preserved document of women's life writing has linked and concentric circles radiating beyond correspondents to the family and the external critical reception of the reshaped life built from letters. This book also suggests that the shaping performed on two particular letter-written lives – on Frances Burney's letters edited by Barrett and Charlotte Brontë's life written by Gaskell – gave a very specific direction to the writing of women's lives in the nineteenth century.

Bibliography

Abbott, John (2015) 'Introduction', in Cooke, Stewart (ed.) *The Additional Journals and Letters of Fanny Burney. Volume 1: 1784–86*. Oxford: Oxford University Press, pp. xv–xx.

Adams, William Henry Davenport (1883) *Childhood and Girlhood of Remarkable Women*. London: Swan Sonnenschein.

Altman, Janet Gurkin (1982) *Epistolarity: Approaches to a Form*. Columbus: Ohio State University Press.

Altman, Janet Gurkin (1986) 'The Letter Book as a Literary Institution 1539–1789: Towards a Cultural History of Published Correspondences in France', *Yale French Studies*, 71, pp. 17–62.

Altick, Richard D. (1966) *Lives and Letters: A History of Literary Biography in England and America*. New York: Knopf.

Amigoni, David (1993) *Victorian Biography: Intellectuals and the Ordering of Discourse*. Hemel Hempstead: Harvester Wheatsheaf.

Atkinson, Juliette (2010) *Victorian Biography Reconsidered: A Study of Nineteenth-Century 'Hidden Lives'*. Oxford: Oxford University Press. doi:10.1093/acprof:oso/9780199572137.001.0001

Austen, Henry (1818) 'Biographical Notice of the Author' and 'Postscript', in *"Northanger Abbey" and "Persuasion" by the Author of "Pride and Prejudice", "Mansfield Park" & c. Volume 1*. London: Murray, pp. v–xix.

Austen-Leigh, James Edward (1871) *A Memoir of Jane Austen, by Her Nephew*. 2nd edn. London: Bentley.

Austen-Leigh, William and Austen-Leigh, Richard Arthur (1913) *Jane Austen, Her Life and Letters: A Family Record*. London: Smith Elder.

Bannet, Eve Tavor (2005) *Empire of Letters: Letter Manuals and Transatlantic Correspondence, 1688–1820*. Cambridge: Cambridge University Press.

Barker, Juliet (1997) *The Brontës: A Life in Letters*. London: Viking.

Barrett, Charlotte (ed.) (1842a) *The Diary and Letters of Madame D'Arblay. Volume 1: 1778–1780*. London: Henry Colburn.

Bell, Mackenzie (1898) *Christina Rossetti: A Biographical and Critical Study*. London: Burleigh.

Bigold, Melanie (2013) *Women of Letters, Manuscript Circulation and Print Afterlives in the Eighteenth Century*. Basingstoke: Palgrave Macmillan. doi:10.1057/9781137033574

Blind, Mathilde (1883) *George Eliot*. London: W. H. Allen.

Bodenheimer, Rosemarie (1994) *The Real Life of Mary Ann Evans: George Eliot, Her Letters and Fiction*. Ithaca: Cornell University Press.

Booth, Alison (2004) *How to Make It as a Woman: Collective Biographical History from Victoria to Present*. Chicago: Chicago University Press.

Bossis, Mireille (1986) 'Methodological Journeys through Correspondences', *Yale French Studies*, 71, pp. 63–75.

Brabourne, Lord (Edward Knatchbull-Hugesson) (ed.) (1884a) *Letters of Jane Austen. Volume 1*. London: Bentley.

Bradbury, Malcolm (1987) *No, Not Bloomsbury*. London: Andre Deutsch.

Bray, Bernard (2001) 'Letters', in Jolly, Margaretta (ed.) *Encyclopedia of Life Writing: Autobiographical and Biographical Forms. Volume 2*. Chicago: Fitzroy Dearborn, pp. 551–3.

Broughton, Trev Lynn (1997) 'Preface', in Broughton, Trev Lynn and Anderson, Linda (eds) *Women's Lives/Women's Times: New Essays on Autobiography*. Albany: State University of New York Press, pp. xi–xvii.

Broughton, Trev Lynn (1999) *Men of Letters Writing Lives: Masculinity and Literary Auto/biography in the Late-Victorian Period*. London: Routledge.

Butler, Marilyn (1998) 'Simplicity', *London Review of Books*, 20(5), pp. 3–6.

Caine, Barbara (2015) 'Letters between Mothers and Daughters', *Women's History Review*, 24(4), pp. 483–9. doi:10.1080/09612025.2015.1015326

Chapple, John A.V. and Pollard, Arthur (eds) (1966) *The Letters of Mrs Gaskell*. Reprint, London: Mandolin, 1997.

Clark, Lorna J. (2012) 'Dating the Undated: Layers of Narrative in Frances Burney's *Court Journals*', *Lifewriting Annual*, 3, pp. 119–39.

Cline, Cheryl (1989) *Women's Diaries, Journals and Letters: An Annotated Bibliography*. New York: Garland.

Cockshutt, Anthony O. J. (1974) *Truth to Life: The Art of Biography in the Nineteenth Century*. London: Collins.

Collett, Anne and D'Arcens, Louise (2010) '"Femmes a Part": Unsociable Sociability, Women, Lifewriting', in Collett, Anne and D'Arcens, Louise (eds) *The Unsociable Sociability of Women's Lifewriting*. Basingstoke: Palgrave Macmillan, pp. 1–17. doi:10.1057/9780230294868

Cook, Elizabeth Heckendorn (1996) *Epistolary Bodies: Gender and Genre in the Eighteenth Century Republic of Letters*. Stanford: Stanford University Press.

Corbett, Mary Jean (1992) *Representing Femininity: Middle Class Subjectivity in Victorian and Edwardian Women's Autobiographies*. Oxford: Oxford University Press.

Cross, John Walter (ed.) (1885a) *George Eliot's Life as Related in her Letters and Journals. Volume 1*. Edinburgh: Blackwood.

Culley, Amy (2014) *British Women's Life Writing, 1760–1840: Friendship, Community and Collaboration*. Basingstoke: Palgrave Macmillan. doi:10.1057/9781137274229

Culley, Amy and Styler, Rebecca (2011) 'Editorial: Lives in Relation', *Life Writing*, 8(3), pp. 237–40. doi:10.1080/14484528.2011.579047

Daybell, James (2016) 'Gendered Archival Practices and the Future Lives of Letters', in Daybell, James and Gordon, Andrew (eds) *Cultures of Correspondence in Early Modern Britain*. Philadelphia: University of Pennsylvania Press, pp. 210–36.

Daybell, James and Gordon, Andrew (2016) 'Introduction: The Early Modern Letter Opener', in Daybell, James and Gordon, Andrew (eds) *Cultures of Correspondence in Early Modern Britain*. Philadelphia: University of Pennsylvania Press, pp. 1–28.

Decker, William Merrill (1998) *Epistolary Practices: Letter Writing in America before Telecommunications*. Chapel Hill: University of North Carolina Press.

Delafield, Catherine (2009) *Women's Diaries as Narrative in the Nineteenth Century Novel*. Reprint, London: Routledge, 2016. doi:10.4324/9781315233536

Dickes, William (1859) *Women of Worth: A Book for Girls*. London: Cassell, Petter and Galpin.

Duyfhuizen, Bernard (1992) *Narratives of Transmission*. London: Associated University Presses.

Eakin, Paul John (1999) *How Our Lives Become Stories: Making Selves*. Ithaca: Cornhill University Press.

Earle, Rebecca (1999) 'Introduction', in Earle, Rebecca (ed.) *Epistolary Selves: Letters and Letter-Writers, 1600–1945*. Aldershot: Ashgate, pp. 1–12.

Easley, Alexis (2004) *First-Person Anonymous: Women Writers and Victorian Print Media, 1830–70*. Aldershot: Ashgate.

Ellis, Annie Raine (ed.) (1889) *The Early Diary of Frances Burney (1768–1778). Volume 1*. London: Bell.

Favret, Mary A. (1993) *Romantic Correspondence: Women, Politics and the Fiction of Letters*. Cambridge: Cambridge University Press.

Fleishmann, Avrom (1983) *Figures of Autobiography: The Language of Self-Writing in Victorian and Modern England*. London: University of California Press.

Gagnier, Regenia (1991) *Subjectivities: A History of Self-Representation in Britain, 1832–1920*. Oxford: Oxford University Press.

Gerson, Carole (2001) 'Locating Female Subjects in the Archives', in Buss, Helen M. and Kadar, Marlene (eds) *Working in Women's Archives: Researching Women's Private Literature and Archival Documents*. Waterloo: Wilfred Laurier University Press, pp. 7–22.

Gladstone, William E. (1889) '*Journal de Marie Bashkirtseff*', *The Nineteenth Century*, 126 (October), pp. 602–7.

Gilroy, Amanda and Verhoeven, W.M. (eds) (2000) *Epistolary Histories: Letters, Fiction, Culture*. Charlottesville: University Press of Virginia.

Green-Armytage, Amy Julia (1906) *Maids of Honour*. Edinburgh: Blackwood.

Hemlow, Joyce, Burgess, Jeanne M. and Douglas, Althea (eds) (1971) *A Catalogue of the Burney Family Correspondence, 1749–1878*. New York: New York Public Library.

Hemlow, Joyce, Cecil, Curtis D. and Douglas, Althea (eds) (1972) *The Journals and Letters of Fanny Burney. Volume 1: 1791–92*. Oxford: Clarendon Press.

Hall, Nigel Hall (1999) 'The Materiality of Letter-Writing: A Nineteenth-Century Perspective', in Barton, David and Hall, Nigel (eds) *Letter Writing as Social Practice*. Amsterdam: John Benjamins, pp. 88–107.

Hope, Eve (1886) *Queens of Literature of the Victorian Era*. London: Walter Scott.

Honan, Park (1987) *Jane Austen: Her Life*. Reprint, London: Phoenix, 1997.

Huff, Cynthia (2001) 'Women's Letters', in Jolly, Margaretta (ed.) *Encyclopedia of Life Writing: Autobiographical and Biographical Forms. Volume 2*. Chicago: Fitzroy Dearborn, pp. 952–4.

Huff, Cynthia (2005) 'Towards a Geography of Women's Life Writing and Imaginary Communities: An Introductory Essay', in Huff, Cynthia (ed.) *Women's Life Writing and Imagined Communities*. Abingdon: Routledge, pp. 1–16.

Hughes, Linda (2016) 'The Shared Life Writing of Anna Jameson and Ottilie von Goethe', *Forum for Modern Language Studies*, 52(2), pp. 160–71. doi:10.1093/fmls/cqw003

James, Felicity and North, Julian (2017) 'Writing Lives Together: Romantic and Victorian Autobiography', *Life Writing*, 14(2), pp. 133–8. doi:10.1080/1448 4528.2017.1291063

Johnson, Charles (1779) *The Complete Art of Writing Letters*. 6th edn. London: Lowndes and Evans.

Jolly, Margaretta and Stanley, Liz (2005) 'Letters as/not a Genre', *Life Writing*, 2(2), pp. 91–118. doi:10.1080/10408340308518291

Kadar, Marlene (ed.) (1992) *Essays on Life Writing from Genre to Critical Practice*. Ontario: University of Toronto Press.

Kerhervé, Alain (2004) *Mary Delany (1700–1788) Une Épisolière Anglaise du XVIIIè Siècle*. Paris: L'Harmattan.

Kerhervé, Alain (ed.) (2009) *Polite Letters: The Correspondence of Mary Delany (1700–1788) and Francis North, Lord Guilford (1704–1790)*. Newcastle: Cambridge Scholars.

Kerhervé, Alain (ed.) (1763) *The Ladies Complete Letter-Writer*. Newcastle: Cambridge Scholars, 2010.

Kirkham, Margaret (1983) 'The Austen Portraits and the Received Biography', in Todd, Janet (ed.) *Jane Austen: New Perspectives*. New York: Holmes and Meier, pp. 29–38.

Lang-Peralta, Linda (1997) '"Clandestine Delight": Frances Burney's Life-Writing', in Coleman, Linda S. (ed.) *Women's Life-Writing: Finding Voice/Building Community*. Bowling Green, : Bowling Green State University Press, pp. 23–41.

Lee, Hermione (2005) *Body Parts: Essays in Life-Writing*. London: Chatto & Windus.

Le Faye, Deirdre (ed.) (1995) *Jane Austen's Letters*. Oxford: Oxford University Press.

Letters from Mrs Delany to Mrs Frances Hamilton from the Year 1779 to 1788 (1820). London: Longman.

Levy, Michelle (2008) *Family Authorship and Romantic Print Culture*. Basingstoke: Palgrave Macmillan. doi:10.1057/9780230590083

Llanover, Lady (Augusta Hall) (1861–62) *The Autobiography and Correspondence of Mary Granville, Mrs Delany* (6 vols). London: Bentley.

Lord, John (1886) *Beacon Lights of History. Volume 7: Great Women*. New York: Fords, Howard and Hulbert.

MacArthur, Elizabeth J. (1990) *Extravagant Narratives: Closure and Dynamics in the Epistolary Form*. Princeton: Princeton University Press.

de Man, Paul (1979) 'Autobiography as De-facement', *MLN*, 94, pp. 919–30.

Marcus, Laura (1994) *Auto/biographical Discourses*. Manchester: Manchester University Press.

Mezei, Kathy (2005) 'Domestic Space and the Idea of Home in Auto/biographical Practices', in Kadar, Marlene, Warley, Linda, Perreault, Jeanne and Egan, Susanne (eds) *Tracing the Autobiographical*. Waterloo: Wilfred Laurier University Press, pp. 81–95.

Milne, Esther (2010) *Letters, Postcards, Email: Technologies of Presence*. New York: Routledge. doi:10.4324/9780203862155

Mullan, John (2001) 'Malice', *London Review of Books*, 23(16), pp. 20–3.

Nokes, David (1997) *Jane Austen: A Life*. London: Fourth Estate.

Nussbaum, Felicity (1989) *The Autobiographical Self: Gender and Ideology in Eighteenth-Century England*. Baltimore: John Hopkins University Press.

Peterson, Linda H. (1999) *Traditions of Victorian Women's Autobiography.* Charlottesville: University Press of Virginia.

Peterson, Linda H. (2003) 'Collaborative Life Writing as Ideology: The Auto/biographies of Mary Howitt and Her Family', *Prose Studies*, 26(1), pp. 176–95. doi:10.1080/0144035032000235873

Porter, Charles A. (1986) 'Foreword to Men/Women of Letters', *Yale French Studies*, 71, pp. 1–14.

Plummer, Ken (2001) *Documents of a Life 2: An Invitation to a Critical Humanism.* London: Sage.

Regis, Amber K. (2019) 'Un/making the Victorian Literary Biography', in Bradford, Richard (ed.) *A Companion to Literary Biography.* Chichester: Wiley-Blackwell, pp. 63–86.

Renza, Louis A. (1977) 'The Veto of the Imagination: A Theory of Autobiography', Reprinted in Olney, James (ed.) *Autobiography: Essays Theoretical and Critical.* Princeton: Princeton University Press, 1980, pp. 268–95.

Ritchie, Anne Thackeray (1883) *A Book of Sibyls.* London: Smith Elder.

Ritchie, Anne Thackeray (1913) 'A Discourse on Modern Sibyls', *Pamphlet 24.* London: English Association.

Rossetti, William Michael (ed.) (1908) *The Family Letters of Christina Georgina Rossetti with Some Supplementary Letters and Appendices.* London: Brown Langham.

Sabor, Peter (2012) 'Journal Letters and Scriblerations', in Cook, Daniel and Culley, Amy (eds) *Women's Life Writing 1700–1850: Gender, Genre and Authorship.* Basingstoke: Palgrave Macmillan, pp. 71–85. doi:10.1057/9781 137030771

Sanders, Valerie (1989) *The Private Lives of Victorian Women.* Hemel Hempstead: Harvester.

Sanders, Valerie (1996) '"Fathers' Daughters": Three Victorian Anti-Feminist Women Autobiographers', in Newey, Vincent and Shaw, Philip (eds) *Mortal Pages, Literary Lives: Studies in Nineteenth-Century Autobiography.* Aldershot: Scolar Press, pp. 153–71.

Showalter Jr., English (1986) 'Authorial Self-Consciousness in the Familiar Letter: The Case of Madame de Graffigny', *Yale French Studies*, 71, pp. 113–30.

Simon-Martin, Mertxell (2013) 'Barbara Leigh Smith Bodichon's Travel Letters: Performative Identity Formation in Epistolary Narratives', *Women's History Review*, 22(2), pp. 225–38. doi:10.1080/09612025.2012.726112

Smith, Margaret (ed.) (1995, 2000, 2004) *The Letters of Charlotte Brontë* (3 vols). Oxford: Oxford University Press.

Smith, Margaret (2012) 'The Brontë Correspondence', in Thormählen, Marianne (ed.) *The Brontës in Context.* Cambridge: Cambridge University Press, pp. 115–22. doi:10.1017/CBO9781139028066

Smith, Sidonie (1987) *A Poetics of Women's Autobiography: Marginality and the Fictions of Self-Representation.* Bloomington: University of Indiana Press.

Smith, Sidonie (1995) 'Performativity, Autobiographical Practice, Resistance', in Smith, Sidonie and Watson, Julia (eds) *Women Autobiography Theory: A Reader.* Madison: University of Wisconsin Press, 1998, pp. 108–15.

Stanley, Liz (1992) *The Auto/Biographical I: The Theory and Practice of Feminist Autobiography.* Manchester: Manchester University Press.

Stanley, Liz (2004) 'The Epistolarium: On Theorizing Letters and Correspondences', *Auto/biography*, 12, pp. 201–35.

Stanley, Liz (2013) 'Documents of Life and Critical Humanities in a Narrative and Biographical Frame', in Stanley, Liz (ed.) *Documents of Life Revisited: Narrative and Biographical Methodology for Twenty First-Century Critical Humanities*. Farnham: Ashgate, pp. 3–14. doi:10.4324/9781315577869

Stanley, Liz, Salter, Andrea and Dampier, Helen (2012) 'The Epistolary Pact: Letterness and the Schreiner Epistolarium', *a/b Auto/Biography Studies*, 27(2), pp. 262–93. doi:10.1080/08989575.2012.10815380

Styler, Rebecca (2017) 'Josephine Butler's Serial Autobiography: Writing the Changing Self through the Lives of Others', *Life Writing*, 14(2), pp. 171–84. doi:10.1080/14484528.2017.1291267

Summerfield, Penny (2013) 'Concluding Thoughts: Performance, the Self, and Women's History', *Women's History Review*, 22(2), pp. 345–52. doi:10.1080/09612025.2012.726120

The British Letter-Writer: Or Letter-Writer's Complete Instructor (1760). London: J. Cooke.

The Complete Letter-Writer Containing Familiar Letters on the Most Common Occasions in Life (1776) 5th edn. Paterson: Edinburgh.

Thomas, Katie (2012) *Postal Pleasures*. Oxford: Oxford University Press.

Tomalin, Claire (1997) *Jane Austen: A Life*. London: Viking.

Uglow, Jennifer (1987) *George Eliot*. London: Virago.

Uglow, Jenny (1993) *Elizabeth Gaskell: A Habit of Stories*. London: Faber and Faber.

Uglow, Jenny (2004) 'Manuscript Moments', in Bostridge, Mark (ed.) *Lives for Sale*. London: Continuum, pp. 181–5.

Walford, Lucy Bethia (1892) *Twelve English Authoresses*. London: Longman.

Webb, Eugene J., Campbell, Donald T., Schwartz, Richard D. and Sechrest, Lee (1966) *Unobtrusive Measures: Nonreactive Research in the Social Sciences*. Chicago: Rand McNally & Co.

Whitehill, Jane (ed.) (1932) *Letters of Mrs Gaskell and Charles Eliot Norton 1855–1865*. Oxford: Oxford University Press.

Whyman, Susan (2009) *The Pen and the People*. Oxford: Oxford University Press.

Winkworth, Susanna (1883) *Letters and Memorials of Catherine Winkworth. Volume 1*. Clifton: Austin.

2 The Diary and Letters of Madame D'Arblay (1842–46)

Women's Life Writing and Family Considerations

The preservation and survival of personal papers affected the representation of women in their own words within the community of life writing. The initial examination of women's lives emerging from letters explores that process of creating lives from a letter archive in two publications of the mid-nineteenth century. The two variants are the selected letters of Frances Burney in her *Diary and Letters* edited by Charlotte Barrett and Elizabeth Gaskell's *Life of Charlotte Brontë*. Chapters 2 and 3 set out the case for the Barrett-Gaskell model of women's lives told through letters.

The model of a woman writer's letters as life writing was created by the impact of publication and responses to it. This chapter, therefore, looks at the collection and trajectory of Burney's letters and the credo set out by her *Memoirs of Dr Burney*. It then uses examples from the published letters to explore five elements that compose the model. The appearance of the *Diary and Letters* made public areas of letter writing that had been privately conducted since correspondence began but were openly and apparently rapaciously deployed in the interest of self-image. Letters were presented as a type of currency and used for trading. The editing process created a fear of withheld or ulterior correspondence that undermined the complete record and openness of communication with both correspondent and audience. Letters gave women the potential for self-narration and for dramatising themselves in the lives of others. There arose the possibility that letters had been recomposed, reordered or fictionalised all along. Finally, there was the sinister prospect that the letters had been written at the time with publication in mind. It is these factors in Burney's *Diary and Letters* of trading, withholding, self-narration, fictionalisation and prior intent to publish that will inform and inflect women's letters as life writing in the later nineteenth century.

In making a readable narrative out of Burney's letters, the author, editor and publisher helped to create a model for the publication of letters as life writing that betrayed the tension between the life lived and the life represented by letters. The public/private dimension was particularly apparent in the negotiation of the space to write a life that was balanced between the two spheres. Burney's fame was dependant on her writing but her life had to be exemplary of womanhood. The focus on her Court experiences in Volumes 3, 4 and 5 of the *Diary and Letters* became a substitute for domestic life before her late marriage to General D'Arblay. As a writer, therefore, she had to be rescued from her own fame in order to be able to write about it.

The Burney Collection

The modern edition of the journals and letters has been produced at the Burney Centre in 25 volumes. Burney's *Diary and Letters* published between 1842 and 1846 was reduced for publication from a vast collection. Although the seven volumes of Barrett's edition have significant omissions and elisions, they are still voluminous enough to make overall analysis complex. The manuscript, as Burney herself noted, was '[c]urtailed and erased of what might be mischievous from friendly or Family Considerations' (Ellis 1889, p. 1). The original publication was vilified in reviews that were already setting up the terms on which other women's published letter writing would be received and based. Thomas Macaulay in the *Edinburgh Review* (1843) linked the diarist with Jane Austen, and the family of Mary Delany were already alert to their potential misrepresentation in Burney's narrative. Foremost among the critics at the time was John Wilson Croker writing in the *Quarterly Review*. His response to Burney's *Memoirs* of her father (Croker 1833; Benkovitz 1959) and to the *Diary and Letters* ten years later (Croker 1842; Shattock 1989, p. 67; pp. 146–7) was to set the tone for both Burney's own task of writing and for that of women's letter writing in print for the decades to come.

The original catalogue of the Burney family correspondence compiled in preparation for the modern *Journals and Letters* tracks the accumulation of papers and the early editing originally done in conjunction with Dr Burney (Hemlow, Burgess and Douglas 1971, pp. x–xvii). He set a precedent by destroying his second wife's papers in November 1797 including his own letters to her that she had preserved. Burney's sister Susan wrote to Burney on 28 November 1796: 'his sole occupation has been the heartrending business of examining & destroying old letters the records of affection & happiness with his two vanished partners – his own he says he has destroyed without mercy' (Olleson 2012, p. 282). The death of Susan in 1800 brought back to Frances the journal letters of her youth and her days at Court. At Dr Burney's death the trunk used to house the papers was taken to France and initially lost in the aftermath of the Napoleonic Wars before being restored to the D'Arblays in Bath in 1816 (Hemlow, Burgess and Douglas 1971, p. xi). Even after Burney's review and reduction of her vast hoard of material in the last 20 years of her 87-year life, 10,000 Burney documents have been identified by the Burney Centre at McGill University. When threatened with their loss, Burney described the documents in a letter to her son dated 31 March 1815 as 'my Letters of all my life!' (Hughes 1980, p. 83).

Burney's letters followed numerous routes to the trunk despite passing initially along a trajectory that took them out of the writer's keeping. Burney's modern editor, Joyce Hemlow, observes that 'it was customary in the letter-writing ages to return at the deaths of recipients of letters complete packages of the same, neatly docketed and tied, to the senders or writers' (Hemlow, Burgess and Douglas 1971, p. xvii). A law of 1813 decreed that letters belonged to their senders despite appearing to be addressed and thus gifted to a recipient (Thaddeus 2000, p. 188). This situation would later obstruct Elizabeth Gaskell in her use of letters in *The Life of Charlotte Brontë* as she explained to George Smith in a letter dated 15 November 1856 (Chapple and Pollard 1966, pp. 420–21). Brontë's letters were inherited and thus copyrighted to Brontë's widower, Arthur Bell Nicholls. Burney had already been thwarted in seeking to memorialise her own father through his celebrity correspondents who still owned the letters she inherited in 1814.

When editing her own work, Burney had decided that her journals should initially appear to have been addressed 'To Nobody', and an introductory preface to this effect was included in the printed *Diary and Letters* by careful chronological rearrangement (Delafield 2012, pp. 31–2). Burney spent time away from her family on visits, at Court and in France, and she wrote journal letters to be shared among her sisters, her father and family friends including Samuel Crisp and Frederica Lock. Her writing fulfilled domestic responsibilities for communication and provided a space in which to practise her writing and self-narration. The focus on Burney herself noted by critics of the *Diary and Letters* at the time resulted from the quest to justify her fame exacerbated by the use of celebrity material, as well as the sense of being overwhelmed by the collection extant by the 1830s. Dr Burney's burning of his correspondence was not the first bonfire to take place. In fact, the element of preservation and editing was itself preserved in Volume 4 of the *Diary and Letters* as reported in a jointly addressed journal letter of July 1788 when Burney was serving at the Court of George III. Burney reported that a courtier named Fairly had argued with her that no one would read letter collections 'in future times': 'those times brought their own letters and avocations, and all such hoards were as generally useless as they were frequently hazardous'. In the journal letter of the time addressed to her sister Susan and her 'dearest friends' and now edited by her niece Charlotte, Burney appeared to take Fairly's advice to heart. She described a resolution: 'to take a general review of my manuscript possessions, and to make a few gentle flames, though not to set fire to the whole' (Barrett 1842d, pp. 208–9). It is notable that Burney and her editor preserved the discussion with Fairly against other considerations more than 50 years later. Fairly described the horror of public exposure if (or perhaps when) the letters circulate more widely at Burney's death: 'Think but how they will be seized; everybody will try to get some of them; what an outcry there will be! Have you seen Miss Burney's letters? Have you got any? I have a bit! And I have another! and I! and I! will be the cry all around' (p. 208).

The sense of editing and control but also panic at the vastness of the collection was made apparent. There is ample evidence that many of Burney's papers did make various bonfires over the course of her life. Her acquisition and accumulation are features of a letter collection that continues to be reproduced and catalogued 175 years after her death. Fairly's assessment of the hazards of the letter hoard haunted Burney in her role as family memorialist, and his warning reappeared in print and thus as biographical fact. This is, in turn, complicated by the very fact that Fairly was himself a fictionalised representation of Colonel Stephen Digby, eligible widower and object of Burney's unrequited love. Burney's reported protest that 'I assured him that I kept none dishonourably–none that I was bid to destroy' (Barrett 1842d, p. 208) was in part a riposte to the cautious relatives who had already responded both to the publication of the *Memoirs of Dr Burney* and to the advertised publication of the *Diary and Letters* (Hemlow, Curtis and Douglas 1972, pp. xlvi–vii).

Burney the correspondent survived her three sisters and of course her father, and then her husband. The journal letters she composed for Susan and their elder sister Esther were returned to her 'hoard' and the correspondence of her deceased son was added in 1837. In a letter dated 20 April 1838 to her remaining sister Charlotte Broome and her daughter Charlotte Barrett, she described the 'killing mass of constant recurrence to my calamity' (Hemlow, Douglas and Hawkins 1984b, p. 954). The reply to this letter is footnoted in the modern edition of the letters. On 26 April 1838, less than five months before her own death, Charlotte Broome was worried about Burney's peace of mind 'yet, I dare not advise you to Burn them, for fear you should *repent*'. Broome was concerned that 'these M.S:S' might 'get in to the possession of any friend who is in the *habit* of publishing, & dealing with Booksellers' (p. 954). She concluded, therefore, that burning was the only safe option in a further letter of 15 May (p. 954).

Fairly's 'Have you got any? I have a bit! And I have another!' would seem to have been prophetic. Burney was caught between twin goals of education and privacy when faced with the 'hoards', and her part in making sense of the papers was fuelled by family and valuation questions that emerged within the published version of 1842–46. Recovery of the original texts which is ongoing may be suitable for a contextual positioning of the Burneys but the reclamation and retrieval of every document provides material for a life and not the life itself. The problem for Burney, and subsequently for Barrett, was that the context for publication was Burney's fame as an author and as a courtier. By the time the papers were available, however, the lives and duties of women were seen to be in conflict with the public expression of Burney's private life. The publicity and response to her *Memoirs of Dr Burney* also caused Burney to exercise caution on her own account, and, subsequently, other players in the *Diary and Letters*, such as the family of Mary Delany, took fright over Barrett's inherited enterprise as editor.

Burney's *Memoirs of Dr Burney* (1832)

The *Diary and Letters* has followed a complex publication and transmission process discussed in the modern editions of Burney's journals and identifiable in the context of Burney's own life and authorship. Barrett as editor had to deal with the anticipation of those whose lives and letters would be included but also with the anxiety arising from the previous publication of the *Memoirs* that had translated itself into Burney's editing of her collected papers. The early volumes of the *Diary and Letters* were reviewed in the quarterlies not only for themselves but in the light of Burney's *Memoirs of Dr Burney* published in 1832. The tracked provenance of the letters has been undertaken in the modern edition but Burney herself discussed her methods both in her memoir of her father and in the preserved documents that formed the *Diary and Letters*.

The *Memoirs* appeared in three volumes in 1832 and was already negotiating a path through the use of letters as life writing, a negotiation that would both illuminate and undermine Burney's later project. Readers of the earlier work were made aware that Burney's own collection of letters had already been amassed because she used them as part of her biography of her father. The full title of the work, produced after much delay and discussion between Burney and her surviving sisters, was *Memoirs of Doctor Burney Arranged from His Own Manuscripts, from Family Papers and from Personal Recollection by His Daughter Madame D'Arblay.* The title itself became a paratextual message with Burney's own name prominent on the title page in larger type than the listed evidence with the word 'arranged' creating a narrower bottleneck in much smaller type. The evidence presented was much interpreted and overlaid by Burney's other objectives and there are various theories to account for the processes that took place (Thaddeus 2000, 180–202). Claire Brock suggests that Burney used the *Memoirs* to 'reiterate her own story' (Brock 2006, p. 135). Burney insisted that her father was not competent to deal with his own material towards the end of his life as the result of a stroke and that these were 'abridged, or recollected, not copied Memoirs' (Burney 1832c, p. 384). The contemporary interpretation was that Burney had written her own life into that of her father and there are many passages where this seems to be the case including a lengthy account of the publication of *Evelina* in Volume 2 (Burney 1832b, pp. 123–70). The account of her father's death came, apparently, from one of her own letters written to her husband in April

1814, dramatised along with the briefer reaction of devoted manservant George (Burney 1832c, 428–33).

Janice Farrar Thaddeus attempts to contextualise Burney's approach to the *Memoirs* by explaining that Burney discovered 12 trivial and dull notebooks and that she burned material because she was disappointed. Thaddeus suggests that she was 'simply revising her father into the sort of man he wanted the world to remember' (2000, p. 187–8). Burney found herself using up her valuable eyesight on this project that diverted her from her own papers. One significant factor was her need to disguise the fact that her elder sister Esther had been born out of wedlock (Thaddeus 2000, pp. 194, 196). Croker in his review would object to her 'habit of *novel-writing*' (1833, p. 125) and make five critical points that were to haunt the process of life writing. These were that this was her memoir; that it was she and not her father who deteriorated; that she had imposed her own view of her stepmother and not used Dr Burney's actual notebooks; and, crucially, that she had suppressed information about her age.

Memoirs of Dr Burney both announced Burney's intentions and gave notice of potential future deployments of letters as life writing. On the left-hand facing page, and therefore preceding the title page, was an 'Advertisement', ostensibly from the publisher of the work, Moxon. It explained that a fourth volume containing Dr Burney's 'correspondence' had been postponed until 'it can be rendered more complete'. This was owing to the 'dearth' of available material, and 'the Biographer' entreated the loan of letters owned or inherited 'where there seems no objection to their meeting the public eye' (Burney 1832a, p. ii). These would be 'restored to their owners, with the most grateful acknowledgements' (Burney 1832a, p. ii). The collection of her father's papers inherited by Burney contained unfinished memoirs and letters received by Dr Burney: letters that could technically be reclaimed by their authors and the family of those correspondents. In effect, Burney could only publish family letters, including those from herself, of course, to buttress her account of Dr Burney.

In her 'Preface, or Apology' to the *Memoirs* Burney put herself forward as 'Editor and Memorialist', burdened with the expectations of family and friends. She corrected herself in the opening line when she described '[t]he intentions, or rather, the directions' of her father which had appointed her to the 'sacred duty' of publishing his Memoirs, delayed by her grief at the time and changes of circumstances since his death in 1814 (Burney 1832a, p. v). The Preface was about her inability to write and her separation from her 'manuscript materials' indeed at threat to her own life but

> [n]ow... that...she finds herself sufficiently recovered from successive indispositions and afflictions to attempt the acquittal of a debt which has long hung heavily upon her mind, she ventures to re-open

her manuscript stores, and to resume, though in trembling, her long-forsaken pen.

(p. vi)

The grandiloquent and rather self-centred style that Burney cultivated in the latter part of her writing life was all too evident. In the body of the memoirs, she referred to herself in the third person as 'his second daughter' and as 'the Editor', 'the Memorialist' and 'the Biographer'.

In her 'Apology', Burney suggested that the life of an eminent man should not pass unrecorded but also that she was qualified to record that life, not just as his daughter and confidant but because she 'possesses all his papers and documents' (Burney 1832a, p. viii). She reinforced her accreditation as memorialist with a reference to generic boundaries: 'biography, from time immemorial has claimed the privilege of being more discursive than history' (p. vii). She thus justified herself in seeking 'to diversify the plain recital of facts' (p. vii) with her own memories but without ever digressing from the facts and opinions of her father although she then admitted that Dr Burney was not actually present in some of the scenes recounted: 'The accounts are not rigidly confined to his presence, where scenes, or traits, still strong in the remembrance of the Editor, or still before her eyes in early letters or diaries, invite to any characteristic details of celebrated personages' (p. viii). She worried, quite rightly as it transpired, about this 'personal obtrusion' and begged for 'apparent egotisms' to be pardoned in the interests of education for the 'living curiosity of the youthful reader' (p. viii). She contradicted herself in redefining her father as both private and as a man who rose from humble beginnings to eminence as a man of letters and head of his profession 'by means and resources all his own' (p. ix). It already seemed far from true that this 'history must necessarily be simple' (p. viii) and this opening rhetorical device clearly began the negotiation for her own life in letters as both private and eminent.

Burney also drew attention immediately in her edition to the potentially fictional nature of the life and the letters by using as an epigram to the *Memoirs* one verse from her anonymous dedication of her own novel *Evelina* published in 1778. The publication of the novel would itself contextualise the first volume of Burney's *Diary and Letters* in 1842 as discussed below. In 1832, this relocated poem as epigram effectively conflated all her reasoning for being her father's 'Editor and Memorialist'. The dedicatory poem 'To — —' had consisted of five four-line verses to the 'author of my being' from which she quoted:

O could my feeble powers thy virtues trace
By filial love each fear should be suppress'd;
The blush of incapacity I'd chace,
And stand–Recorder of Thy worth!–confess'd.

(Burney 1832a, p. iii)

On the title page of the *Memoirs*, this verse was renamed 'Anonymous Dedication of Evelina, to Dr. Burney, in 1778'. The redirection of the poem represented a contorted process of rewriting since the novel was originally published without her father's knowledge or approval. It was also another circumstance that served to undermine the integrity of the *Memoirs* and of subsequent life writing. If this text had been rearranged and revisited in a new context, then the letters might have been rearranged too.

Burney seemed to have been expecting to revise a nearly completed memoir when she inherited the papers, and she discussed this with her sister Esther in a 'double letter' or 'pamphlet' dated 25–28 November 1820, at which point the idea of writing appears to have been originally abandoned until 1828 (Hemlow, Douglas and Hawkins 1984a, pp. 183–97). She announced to her nephew Charles Parr Burney, eventual inheritor of the Charles Burney papers, 'I am liberated' on 27 July 1832 (Hemlow, Douglas and Hawkins 1984b, p. 759). The paragraph on private life and self-help, however, broadly reflected the opening of the autobiographical 'Introduction' to the *Memoirs* that followed on from the 'Apology'. It was apparently Dr Burney's own account of his life 'copied from a manuscript memoir in the Doctor's own handwriting', a fragment of only a thousand words (Burney 1832a p. x). Burney's further note here explained that her father made a number of attempts to write such an account and that she has used various similar documents in the compilation of the *Memoirs*. Reflecting her own trials in recovering information for the work, she unselfconsciously called the autobiographical account the 'minute amplitude of this vast mass of matter' (p. xvi).

The process of composition of the memoirs can be partially recovered from the modern *Journals and Letters* although even the editors of volume 12 of the twentieth-century edition note that Burney's time was employed in the *Memoirs* rather than her own letter writing between 1828 and 1832 (Hemlow, Douglas and Hawkins 1984b, p. 1007). The earlier letter from 1820 recovered for the modern edition demonstrates how Burney was forced to confront the nature of her father's papers four years after being reunited with her lost trunk two years after the death of General D'Arblay. It is evident that her sister Esther to whom Burney wrote did not think the papers would make any money, and Burney concluded, 'authorship & emolument are at this moment very obtuse'. Burney was frustrated at not being able to write because of all the reading or 'decyfering' she must do: 'my dear Father has kept, unaccountably, All his letters, however uninteresting, ceremonious, momentary or unmeaning'. Her father had sorted his manuscript papers 'but destroyed not a line, not even an invitation to dinner', and yet, Burney further bemoaned: 'Can any one read such names, & not conclude that the Press would cover them with Gold?' (Hemlow, Douglas and Hawkins 1984a,

p. 193). In the light of Croker's response to Burney's project, it is not surprising that this letter would not appear in the *Diary and Letters*.

The *Diary and Letters*

In fact very few pages of the *Diary and Letters* were devoted to the publication of the *Memoirs*. After Volume 5 appeared in early 1843, the publisher Colburn severely abridged the available publication space by reducing the number of volumes from ten to seven, and further editing delayed the last two volumes until 1846. Barrett, however, did reproduce a letter written to Esther in August 1823 in which Burney told her sister that 'innumerable papers... for reasons prudent, or kind, or conscientious, have been committed to the flames' (Barrett 1846b, p. 373). Barrett included a brief paragraph of her own about an 'attack (in a periodical publication) upon [Burney's] veracity' countered by Dr Johnson's belief of Burney's absolute truthfulness (Barrett 1846b, p. 378). This commentary was a severely compacted version of Burney's response to her critics. The debate about fact and fiction, public and private was, however, rekindled by the inclusion of a supportive letter from Robert Southey to Alexander D'Arblay. Southey wrote in March 1833 '"Evelina" did not give me more pleasure when I was a schoolboy, than these memoirs have given me now' (Barrett 1846b, p. 378).

Across the seven volumes of the *Diary and Letters*, there were over 1,200 documents to be edited and Barrett's editorial choices laid her open to criticism in the 1840s on at least two counts. The first was that of violating the diary-letter-journal's generic status as a private document; the second was that of self-congratulation and aggrandisement on Burney's behalf. For the life to be seen as exemplary, the sociable family correspondence made public through fame had to be domesticated again. For publication, Burney and her editor Barrett reinforced a sense of immediacy by using the term 'diary'. It was in this way that a woman's account of her own life might be authorised as a private though not as a printed text. The diary element of the *Diary and Letters* was difficult enough to contain for her critics but was at least framed in the context of being written 'to Nobody' or, at the multiple boundaries of journal writing, 'to Miss Nobody'. The letters that dramatised Burney as a person and gave her a self to write about became more conflicted.

The public/private, eminence/domestication tensions were indicated at the very boundary of the *Diary and Letters* when Volume 1 launched immediately into a diary entry for the year 1778:

> This year was ushered in by a grand and most important event! At the latter end of January, the literary world was favoured with the first publication of the ingenious, learned and most profound Fanny Burney! I doubt not but this memorable affair will, in future times,

mark the period whence chronologists will date the zenith of the polite arts in this island!

(Barrett 1842a, p. 1)

The prior account of the publication of *Evelina* had been substituted by Barrett's 'Introductory Memoir' that summarised Burney's life to the point of first publication. The *Early Diaries* covering this period had already been sacrificed in the interests of economy and would not appear until 1889, edited by Annie Raine Ellis. In the context of her actual life, Burney had in fact been seeking an opportunity to communicate her success using the domestic form of a letter, asking her sister Esther on 1 October 1777 for an invitation 'to spend the Day' to which she added: 'Write a Note that I may make public' (Troide 1991, p. 287). This content reflected a more detailed inflection of the letter form and its circulation. There were letters for keeping secret and letters for reading aloud. In addition, the earlier diary and letters not yet published would have demonstrated how Burney set herself up as a family chronicler using a mock heroic tone. She wrote for instance on 20 February 1774, 'But for my Pen, all the adventures of this Noble family might sink to oblivion!' (Troide 1991, p. 4). The development of and authorisation for this tone adopted in writing within the family were not presented at the publication stage in 1842. Without a context for the printed version, page 1 Volume 1 of the *Diary and Letters* presented a stark announcement of the event that made Burney's life publicly accessible at that one key instant of fame. Barrett claimed co-editorship because she was a reader of the full texts (Delafield 2012, p. 34), and it has been observed that Burney's 'egotism was unduly magnified by Barrett's editorial decision' (Thaddeus 2000, p. 213). The decision taken by Burney, by her editor niece and/or by the publisher to open the first published volume with the 'grand event' of *Evelina* may indeed have dictated the apologetic tone that women's life writing in letters would have to adopt for more than 50 years afterwards.

Barrett described the *Diary and Letters* as 'a journalising memoir' (Barrett 1842a, p. viii). Burney's own allusion to a memoir as more than history is part of her editor's brief but the documentary evidence in 1842 was more clearly a response to the impact felt from the *Memoirs*. Burney kept her 'Diary' and wrote journal letters for over 60 years, and her writing reflected the traditions that authorised women's writing projected into the public sphere: namely household record, spiritual autobiography, family chronicle and travel journal (Delafield 2009, pp. 9–11). Julia Epstein suggests that 'the privacy of the epistolary form offered Burney a protected textual space' (1986, p. 165) but that protection was removed by the publishing impulse. Barrett negotiated with the new 'memoir' audience by asserting in her 'Introductory Memoir' that Burney's letters were 'originally intended for no eye but her own' (Barrett, 1842a, p. xxx). In printing the letters for public consumption, Barrett called for the 'eye... of indulgent friendship' (xiii) suggesting that the new reading public would read the letters as the original correspondents did. Barrett's agenda of domestication in tension with Burney's fame, however, undermined any suggestion that the letters could merely be a sisterly communication.

Barrett's edition also presented a rationale for the letter as a vehicle for the publication of an exemplary life. In the August 1823 letter to Esther about the *Memoirs* that appeared in the *Diary and Letters*, Burney proposed to destroy 'all letters that may eventually do mischief, or that contain nothing of instruction or entertainment' in order, she claimed, to 'save my own executor the discretionary labours'. She added: 'I should hold it wrong to make over to any other judgment than my own the danger or the innoxiousness of any and every manuscript that has been cast into my power' (Barrett 1846b, p. 373). This statement protected Barrett from suggestions that she had made her own choices of material, although research has proved that Burney's executor had inherited Burney's methods and was active in destroying and obscuring letters during the editing process (Hemlow, Cecil and Douglas 1972, pp. xliv–lv). In a letter publicly re-read in 1846, Burney believed that letters could thus become 'real conversations' because they would not be vulnerable to re-reading by posterity although clearly that re-reading was now taking place. She reminisced to Esther about Samuel Crisp's view that to 'dash away whatever comes uppermost' makes a letter more valuable to its reader. In a possible allusion to the theft in 1812 and publication in 1814 of Nelson's letters from Lady Hamilton, she added: 'How little, in those days, did either he or I fear, or even dream of the press!... Now everybody seems obliged to take as much care of their writing desks as of their trinkets or purses' (Barrett 1846b, p. 373).

This was a letter that had to work hard in Barrett's cause because of the publisher's curtailment of the *Diary and Letters*. In it, Burney commended her correspondent ''tis a real sister's letter' (Barrett 1846b, p. 372). Given the usual aim of the *Diary and Letters* to polish syntax and smooth expressions, this phrase was designedly retained as part of the image-making of the domestic woman. Barrett also tried to reclaim her aunt from the very circumstances of her own fame when bringing the edition to a close in Volume 7: 'These Journals and Letters may show the merits and peculiarities of her individual character, and the bright example she gave in the most important relations of her life' (Barrett 1846b, p. 383). Barrett concluded in person that 'these memoirs' confirmed the testimony of General d'Arblay that Burney's private life represented 'the best and most valuable parts of her character' (p. 385). The words of a dead husband were called into play as evidence of the domestication of the author but Barrett did not resist a reference to the public fame of her aunt since this was 'no slight praise when given to the Author of Evelina, Cecilia and Camilla' (p. 385). Barrett's contortions closed the volume with a statement that drew attention both to the domestic and private elements of Burney's life but also introduced the word 'memoir' with its potential to echo the *Memoirs of Dr Burney*, and she also reintroduced the sense of potential fictionalisation by returning to Burney as an author.

In these contortions, Barrett continued to respond to the reviewing environment. Croker had written in 1833: 'Madame D'Arblay... conceals from her readers, and perhaps from herself, that it is her *own Memoirs* and *not* those of her father that she has been writing' (pp. 106–7), and he had renewed his campaign by yoking the early volumes of the *Diary and Letters* with the *Memoirs* as a 'strange display of egotism' (Croker 1842, p. 243). After extensive quotation from the *Diary and Letters* he concluded: 'talking so much, she says so little' (p. 287). The unedited unfolding letters were ostensibly written for private reading. They were also edited to justify the transgressive acts of being a novelist and of rebelling against the appointment at Court. They had every right to centre on the self until, that is, they were reclassified as life writing.

Editing and reviewing apart, the letters were appearing in the conditioned environment of publishing. Henry Colburn limited the length of the final text as well as its potentially inflammatory contents. He also sought to position the *Diary and Letters* as a document that recounted the workings of the Court. The endpaper of Volume 1 described the *Diary and Letters* in February 1842 as 'Now in the course of publication, uniformly with Miss Strickland's "Queens of England" in about 6 monthly volumes'. This was an attempt to make the Burney volumes part of a very different series designed to enhance a purchaser's book shelf in their shared uniformity. Colburn's copywriter drew attention to Burney's resolution to keep a journal made in 1768 despite the fact that the *Diary and Letters* commenced in 1778: 'the results of such a resolution are now to be given to the world precisely as they left the hand of the writer (the omission required by personal and family considerations being alone excepted)'. The advertisement continued:

> The CORRESPONDENCE which will form another portion of this publication and will take its place chronologically with the DIARY, will include besides a large number of Madame D'Arblay's own letters, a selection from those addressed to her by the various distinguished literary and other persons with whom she was intimate.
> (Barrett 1842a, endmatter)

The *Diary and Letters* was positioned as a work of fact, accuracy, family consideration, chronological arrangement and value in the context of other correspondents. The later advertisement for Volume 6 at the end of volume 7 situated it with other biographical works such as the 'Letters and Despatches of Nelson', the 'Memoirs of Hester Stanhope', Walpole's 'Reign of George II' and Strickland's ninth and latest 'queen of England'.

'Miss Burney's Diary' headed the page with the usual reference to 'the author of "Evelina", "Cecilia" &c.' but there then followed a long list of 'noble and distinguished personages' who featured in the sixth volume from the King and Queen to 'Miss Betterton, &c. &c', and Colburn urged subscribers to complete their sets 'without delay, to prevent disappointment' (Barrett 1846a, endmatter). Burney was therefore presented simultaneously as being both a literate witness to events at Court and the author of novels that were written in the form of letters.

Letters as Life Writing: The Model

The foregoing discussion has begun the contextualisation in the *Diary and Letters* of five elements that constitute the evolving model of published letter collections: trading, withholding, self-narration, fictionalisation and prior intent to publish. The suggestion of the role of letters as traded currency is ostensibly an innocent one borrowed from the very language of domestic communication. Burney wrote to her sister on October 12 1779:

> As you say you will accept memorandums in default of journals, my dear Susy, I will scrawl down such things as most readily occur to my remembrance, and when I get to the present time, I will endeavour to be less remiss in my accounts.
>
> (Barrett 1842a, p. 126)

The following year from Bath, Burney wrote 'so many packets do I owe you' (Barrett 1842a, p. 190). This is the preserved language of household accounting and daily recording but the trading and valuation of letters became distinctively apparent both in the *Memoirs* and across the whole package of compilation and advertising that was Barrett's edited work.

   The fear that withheld or ulterior correspondence would undermine completeness and veracity was often present and preserved within the published texts. Burney's journal entries were actually written on small tablets that she kept about her person and these were later transcribed or re-edited as packets or standalone accounts. The diary, as it was termed, was often written up after the event, especially during Burney's five years at Court (Clark 2012). Burney wrote in September 1787 'my memorandums of this month are so scanty, that I shall not give them their regular dates' (Barrett 1842c, p. 441). The loss of 'dates' within the letters contributes to the sense that her record has a reflective quality and makes the generic instability of the letter as life-writing apparent. In Volume 5 sometime after 19 March 1789, she wrote: 'The rest of this month I shall not give by daily dates but by its incidents' and again, for April, 'I shall abbreviate this month also of its chronological exactness' (Barrett 1843, pp. 16, 20). There are also conspiracies within letters that appear to withhold the full story. Burney wrote to Susan from London on 2 April 1783: 'I will resume my journal – in which there is a gap that will make my accounts, for some time at least, fully intelligible only to yourself'. To the 'coterie' who will be her audience, she wrote, 'my little obscurities will be as useful and amusing as my copiousness' (Barrett 1842b, p. 261). In the same month she negotiated a revised and withheld narrative when she wrote to Crisp, 'Susan who is my reader, must be your writer' (Barrett 1842b, p. 263).

Judy Simons contends that Burney's isolation within a hostile environment is part of her self-image (1990, p. 36), and this isolation created both a catalyst for self-narration and a place for herself in the lives of others. In the midst of reports of praise and blame directed at herself, Burney countered the criticism brought against her at the time: 'I have always feared discovery, always sought concealment, and always known that no success could counterbalance the publishing my name' (Barrett 1842a, p. 80). Writing from Court, she distinguished her genres: 'Having now journalized for one complete week, let me endeavour to give you, more connectedly, a concise abstract of the general method of passing the day, that I may only write what varies' (Barrett 1842d, p. 27). Barrett summarised this as 'domestic details' in her chapter heading to Part 1 of Volume 3 (1842c, p. 5) and Croker used the term 'domestication in Queen Charlotte's family' in his review of Volumes 1–3 (1842, p. 260).

The possibility of re-composition was ever present and highlighted in the printed text by rows of asterisks that indicated elisions. The process of composition and compilation, and the narrative occasion for the writing of the journals and letters were regularly discussed and their provenance thus highlighted in the life-writing cycle. In 1779, Burney addressed 'my dear Susy' in order to 'recollect the most particular circumstances that have happened, journal fashion, according to the old plan' (Barrett 1842a, p. 80). Burney also meditated on the intention to record and used the retrospective position that the diary tradition afforded her. Thus, she could legitimately communicate on a journey using the travel journal mode in May 1779: 'Once more, my dearest Susy, I will attempt journalising, and endeavour, according to my promise, to keep up something of the kind during our absence, however brief and curtailed' (Barrett 1842a, p. 103). It was also made clear that Burney had intervened in the life at a further retrospective moment and that her text anticipated the outcome of letters apparently arranged in order. Susan had helped to persuade a reluctant Dr Burney to allow Frances to marry General d'Arblay in 1793, and a 'Memorandum' dated 7 May 1825 was retained by Barrett although it was clearly added during Burney's editing phase: 'never, never was union more blessed and felicitous; though after the first eight years of unmitigated happiness, it was assailed by many calamities, chiefly of separation or illness, yet still mentally unbroken' (Barrett 1843, p. 249). It was to this memorandum that Burney could add her new name of 'F. D'Arblay' reiterating not only her authorship of the *Diary and Letters* but also her concealed editorship.

Burney's novel *Evelina* had demonstrated how the fictional use of the epistolary form could be accomplished, joyous and flirtatious. The authorial achievement that made her life interesting and exemplary for the reader of her *Diary and Letters* suggested, however, that her own letters might be fictitious and untrue. The factual letters have apparently been written to form a narrative. This letter writing could only represent an exemplary life if it had emerged from an unfolding unedited experience to legitimise the appearance of letters in print. Fiction has made it possible, and even probable, that lives recovered from letters will appear less true.

In addition, the possibility that letters have been written with publication in mind arose and this was a more serious concern within the lives of women of the nineteenth century. This was despite the fact that their role as a correspondent could be vindicated by their role as family chronicler, spiritual autobiographer or travel journalist. Burney had a life to write about as author and as Court attendant that was given a new domestic context by motherhood although authorship remained an underlying and significant feature. One final example gives a sense of how Burney positioned her letter-life-writing self. It was a letter that would also have formed one of the packets returned to the trunk at the death of Dr Burney. On 10 July 1796, Burney began a semi-public journal letter to her father:

> If I had as much time as of matter, my dear father, what an immense letter I should write you! But I have still so many book oddments of accounts, examinations, directions, and little household affairs to arrange, that with baby-kissing included, I expect I can give you today only part the first of an excursion which I mean to comprise four parts.
>
> (Barrett 1846a, p. 54)

This simple opening, preserved by Burney-Barrett for the much-edited published version, created the image of women's letter writing in all its contradictions and negotiations. The four-part excursion was likely to have been compiled from memoranda kept during the composition of Burney's novel *Camilla* that was about to be published. Burney gave an account of a visit to Windsor to present the King and Queen with copies of the novel. In recording this publishing-worthy event, she created the myth of not having time to write that was the fate of all female correspondents and 'journalists', and she maintained the status of letter record among all the household activities that she must profess to her father and to her public.

Julia Epstein suggests that Burney's journals and letters become a 'generic hybrid' (1986, p. 173), although the instability of the various letter forms tends to defeat life-writing intent in terms of a narrative thread. Lorna Clark draws attention to the 'undigested' nature of the collected documents so that 'a coherent narrative is no longer possible' since Burney's 'life spills over the narrative that tries to contain it' (2001, pp. 285, 296). In the *Diary and Letters*, the letter form with its suggestions of fictionalisation, trading and secrecy was intended to contain the life. An act of self-narration has allowed Burney to present herself as the heroine of her own life, but this process was paradoxically undermined by publication because of new Victorian objectives and the publisher's targeting of his market. The letter collections to come would have to accommodate the response to Burney's self-narration and the suspicions it cultivated.

Bibliography

Barrett, Charlotte (ed.) (1842a) *The Diary and Letters of Madame D'Arblay. Volume 1: 1778–1780.* London: Henry Colburn.

Barrett, Charlotte (ed.) (1842b) *The Diary and Letters of Madame D'Arblay. Volume 2: 1781–1786.* London: Henry Colburn.

Barrett, Charlotte (ed.) (1842c) *The Diary and Letters of Madame D'Arblay. Volume 3: 1786–1787.* London: Henry Colburn.

Barrett, Charlotte (ed.) (1842d) *The Diary and Letters of Madame D'Arblay. Volume 4: 1788–1789.* London: Henry Colburn.

Barrett, Charlotte (ed.) (1843) *The Diary and Letters of Madame D'Arblay. Volume 5: 1789–1793.* London: Henry Colburn.

Barrett, Charlotte (ed.) (1846a) *The Diary and Letters of Madame D'Arblay. Volume 6: 1793–1812.* London: Henry Colburn.

Barrett, Charlotte (ed.) (1846b) *The Diary and Letters of Madame D'Arblay. Volume 7: 1813–1840.* London: Henry Colburn.

Benkovitz, Miriam (1959) 'Dr Burney's Memoirs', *Review of English Studies*, n.s.10, pp. 257–68.

Burney, Frances (1832a) *Memoirs of Doctor Burney, Volume 1.* London: Moxon.

Burney, Frances (1832b) *Memoirs of Doctor Burney, Volume 2.* London: Moxon.

Burney, Frances (1832c) *Memoirs of Doctor Burney, Volume 3.* London: Moxon.

Brock, Clare (2006) *The Feminization of Fame, 1750–1830.* Basingstoke: Palgrave. doi:10.1057/9780230286450

Chapple, John A.V. and Pollard, Arthur (eds) (1966) *The Letters of Mrs Gaskell.* Reprint, London: Mandolin, 1997.

Clark, Lorna (2001) 'The Diarist as Novelist: Narrative Strategies in the Journals and Letters of Frances Burney', *English Studies in Canada*, 27(3), pp. 283–302.

Clark, Lorna J. (2012) 'Dating the Undated: Layers of Narrative in Frances Burney's *Court Journals*', *Lifewriting Annual*, 3, pp. 119–39.

Croker, John Wilson (1833) 'Memoirs of Dr Burney', *Quarterly Review*, 49, pp. 97–125.

Croker, John Wilson (1842) 'Diary and Letters of Madame D'Arblay, Vols I, II, III', Quarterly Review, 70, pp. 243–87.

Delafield, Catherine (2009) Women's Diaries as Narrative in the Nineteenth Century Novel. Reprint, London: Routledge, 2016. doi:10.4324/9781315233536

Delafield, Catherine (2012) 'Barrett Writing Burney: A Life among the Footnotes', in Cook, Daniel and Culley, Amy (eds) Women's Life Writing 1700–1850: Gender, Genre and Authorship. Basingstoke: Palgrave Macmillan, pp. 26–38. doi:10.1057/9781137030771

Ellis, Annie Raine (ed.) (1889) The Early Diary of Frances Burney (1768–1778). Volume 1. London: Bell.

Epstein, Julia (1986) 'Fanny Burney's Epistolary Voices', The Eighteenth Century, 27(2), pp. 162–79.

Hemlow, Joyce, Burgess, Jeanne M. and Douglas, Althea (eds) (1971) A Catalogue of the Burney Family Correspondence, 1749–1878. New York: New York Public Library.

Hemlow, Joyce, Cecil, Curtis D. and Douglas, Althea (eds) (1972) The Journals and Letters of Fanny Burney. Volume 1: 1791–92. Oxford: Clarendon Press.

Hughes, Peter (ed.) (1980) The Journals and Letters of Fanny Burney. Volume 8: 1815. Oxford: Clarendon Press.

Hemlow, Joyce, Douglas, Althea and Hawkins, Patricia (eds) (1984a) The Journals and Letters of Fanny Burney. Volume 11: 1818–1824. Oxford: Clarendon Press.

Hemlow, Joyce, Douglas, Althea and Hawkins, Patricia (eds) (1984b) The Journals and Letters of Fanny Burney. Volume 12: 1825–1840. Oxford: Clarendon Press.

Macaulay, Thomas Babington (1843) 'Diary and Letters of Madame D'Arblay', The Edinburgh Review, 76, 523–70.

Olleson, Philip (ed.) (2012) The Journals and Letters of Susan Burney. Farnham: Ashgate. doi:10.4324/9781315556444

Shattock, Joanne (1989) Politics and Reviewers; The "Edinburgh" and the "Quarterly" in the Early Victorian Age. Leicester: Leicester University Press.

Simons, Judy (1990) Diaries and Letters of Literary Women from Fanny Burney to Virginia Woolf. Basingstoke: Macmillan.

Thaddeus, Janice Farrar (2000) Frances Burney: A Literary Life. Basingstoke: Macmillan. doi:10.1057/9780230288324

Troide, Lars E. (ed.) (1991) The Early Journals and Letters of Fanny Burney. Volume 2:1774–1777. Oxford: Clarendon Press.

3 The Life of Charlotte Brontë (1857)

Family Considerations and the Written Life

Charlotte Barrett wrote herself out of Burney's *Diary and Letters* but was discreetly present in her framing introduction and in other interpolations. Elizabeth Gaskell used her presence in *The Life of Charlotte Brontë*, and in Brontë's actual life, to refine a definition of the woman as writer and to defend Brontë from accusations of coarseness. The *Life* offered a model for letters as life writing developed along different lines. One major difference was that Gaskell discussed her selection methods within the text, making clear her own role in the choice of representative passages. A letter collection was deployed to write a life using linking passages of greater length and discursiveness. In fact, Gaskell used her own letters to reflect on the biography she was undertaking and, unlike Barrett, was keen to include herself in the pages of her work. With the help of Brontë's correspondence, Gaskell effectively conspired to make another letter writer the heroine of her own life. Barrett was qualified to edit as niece and executor; Gaskell was qualified as a fellow writer and contemporary.

The Gaskell model was based on the establishment of biographical and autobiographical credentials and the creation of a narrative shape from available evidence. The model shared with Barrett's edition the elements of trading and withholding, of self-narration and fictionalisation. Gaskell's *Life* introduced a narrative of recovery and duty, also explored by Barrett, and used Brontë's own words within a new frame. The letter form was used by Gaskell to present a woman within the context of nineteenth-century life writing. Where Gaskell's own letters were her evidence, there were further textual transmissions into new contexts that will be discussed below. This chapter assesses the 'duty narrative' of Brontë's letters to her old schoolfriend Ellen Nussey and the positioning of Brontë's own words in the *Life*. The chapter then looks at the shaping of the narrative and the transmission of Gaskell's letters into the biographical text.

Elizabeth Gaskell's *Life of Charlotte Brontë* was commissioned in 1855 by Brontë's father Patrick with the cautious co-operation of her husband Arthur Nicholls. Gaskell had, of course, formed her own judgement of life at Haworth and was anxious to promote Brontë as a writer in the context of sacrifice and domesticity. In the *Life*, preserved documents guided the narrative with Gaskell steering them as Burney had disastrously failed to do. Gaskell relied heavily on some 370 partially censored letters loaned by Nussey, although over 500 letters to Nussey are now extant and held by the Haworth Museum. Where the biography addressed the 'two parallel currents' (Peterson 2006, p. 223) of Brontë's life, Gaskell's choice of source or correspondent took her in specific directions. Gaskell omitted or removed vital elements of Charlotte's life in part because another friend, Mary Taylor, had destroyed Brontë's correspondence on her (that is Taylor's) departure for New Zealand. When a letter from Taylor to Gaskell herself furnished a conclusion to the *Life*, this was further evidence of how the community of life writers had mapped letters onto the course marked out by the biographer.

Recovery and the 'duty narrative'

It has been suggested that Gaskell's was a work of recovery and fictionalisation. Harold Nicolson described the *Life* as 'an excellent sentimental novel replete with local colour... it is a story but it is not history' (1933, p. 128). Carolyn Heilbrun believes that Gaskell restored Brontë as a woman and made her safe (1988, p. 22), and Alexis Easley suggests that the *Life* was 'a politicized form of literary recovery' (2004, p. 103). Gaskell's *Life* mined and extracted letters accumulated on research trips to Haworth and Brussels, and from others arriving in packets acknowledged in Gaskell's own correspondence (Chapple and Pollard 1966, p. 372). We know, for instance, that she even persuaded Constantin Heger, Brontë's 'professor' in Brussels to extract for her parts of the four letters his wife retrieved from their wastebasket. Three, dated 24 July 1844, 24 October 1844 and 8 January 1845, had been torn up (Smith 1995, pp. 355–60, 369–71, 377–80) but the fourth (18 November 1845, pp. 433–8) remained intact and was not extracted by Heger/Gaskell. These letters were sewn back together in 1845, printed in *The Times* newspaper on 29 July 1913 and now appear online in the custody of the British Library. At the end of August 1855, Susanna Winkworth wrote to her sister Catherine, friend of Gaskell and latterly confidante of Brontë: 'I am glad to hear that her quest for material has been most successful, and I really think that now she will make a capital thing of the "Life" and show people how lives ought to be written' (1883, p. 501). Despite 'family considerations' and family sponsorship, Gaskell chose to follow a particular line or series of arcs through her narrative. This line was largely recovered from and reinforced by the letters of one correspondent, Nussey.

Gaskell's approach to her biography or memoir determined that *The Life of Charlotte Brontë* was about letters because it was letter evidence that she sought and recovered in her researches of 1855–57. She aimed to present Brontë in her own words as much as possible. Gaskell also wished to write a 'life in relation' (Culley and Styler 2011) and presented herself as a correspondent as a means of authorising and supporting her own intervention and interpretation. She found a very willing collaborator in Ellen Nussey, the 'pious and devoted magpie' (Stevens 1972, p. 1) who had collected Brontë's letters for 24 years and was one of the joint instigators of the biography. Gaskell could set aside 'family considerations' to an extent because she was using Brontë's own words, her own letters and a correspondence with someone who was not a family member. At the same time she was looking for a particular shape for the *Life*. This shaping countered some of the life-writing problems of indigestible collected letters like those of Burney but brought its own issues of bias and selectivity. There was also a third correspondence that emerged unwittingly from the letters, that of Brontë with her own fictional and epistolary personae. This complex construction of identity both informed and destabilised the *Life*.

In order to shape her material, Gaskell read original manuscript letters recovered before the later indiscriminate dispersals of the nineteenth and twentieth centuries. As described in the 7 November 1854 letter to Nussey (Barker 1997, p. 395), Brontë's letters did indeed 'fall into many hands' despite Nicholls's initial efforts to retain control. He was ambushed over copyright by the publisher George Smith during the composition of Gaskell's *Life* as discussed in letters from Gaskell to Smith dated 22 November and 6 December 1856 (Chapple and Pollard 1966, pp. 422–3). Nicholls was then regularly harassed by Ellen Nussey and finally capitulated when the journalist and collector Clement Shorter visited him in 1895. In her account of the letters' transmission, Margaret Smith, modern editor of Brontë's collected letters, admires Gaskell's dogged pursuit of her subject with 'direct access to MSS and the fact that she had charmed so many correspondents into yielding up their treasured letters' (Smith 1995, p. 31). A historian of the life of Arthur Nicholls sees Gaskell's quest in a rather different light when he describes her on one of her visits to Haworth being 'intent on literary loot' (Adamson 2008, p. 89). Bizarrely, although consistent with her own passion for autographs (Parker 2009), Gaskell contributed to the subsequent dispersal of 'loot'. In 1861, for instance, she offered up her letter from Brontë of 18 June 1851 for auction in support of the Sanitary Commission (Smith 1995, p. 32; Smith 2012, pp. 117–21). Another letter, written to a Mrs Spencer in late 1856, is now in Princeton University Library and in it Gaskell offered to reconsider giving this letter away once the *Life* was written. She wrote that all her notes and short letters from Brontë had been 'weeded out for the purpose of autographs' but that she was keeping the 'long & characteristic letters... for the purposes of biography' (Chapple and Shelston 2000, p. 163).

Linda Peterson describes the extant Nussey and lost Mary Taylor letters as 'points of origin for the duty narrative' (2005, p. x). Gaskell wrote to Nussey of Brontë on 6 September 1855, 'she was one to study the path of duty well' (Chapple and Pollard 1966, p. 871). The penultimate paragraph of the *Life*, quoting from Taylor's letter to Gaskell of 18 January 1856, opened, 'She thought much of her duty' (Peterson 2006, p. 370), and, in her discussion of women of letters, Peterson concludes that '[duty] trumps professionalism' (2009, p. 148). The duty narrative in letters had to be composed to recover Brontë's life from accusations of coarseness and unwomanliness. Life-writing instability or hybridity, as demonstrated in Chapter 1 and in the example of Burney, had exposed Brontë to accusations of coarseness in the first place. She had exploited editing and life writing through fiction when she subtitled *Jane Eyre* 'An Autobiography edited by Currer Bell' (1847) for the first edition. In the novel, a gender-unspecific editor was ostensibly responsible for the selective appearance of a woman's life in print, and the *Quarterly Review*, following on from Croker reviewing Burney (1833, 1842), once again targeted the writing of a woman

Identity was at the heart of many reviews of *Jane Eyre* because of the unknown author and her pseudonym. Elizabeth Rigby, the anonymous reviewer in 1848, reviewed the novel *Vanity Fair* by an identifiably male author alongside *Jane Eyre*, and yoked her comments to the 1847 report of the Governesses Benevolent Institute ([Rigby] 1848). In the *Quarterly*, Rigby thus reviewed the fictional governess created from Brontë's real-life experiences and positioned this fictionalised 'autobiography' alongside a report about real governesses. In the review, the character of Jane Eyre was also likened to Richardson's epistolary heroine Pamela because Jane addresses Rochester as 'master' ([Rigby] 1848, p. 164). This comparison allied the character of the author with forms of life writing and epistolary fiction, raising the problem of authorial identity that Gaskell would explore within the *Life*. Rigby deplored the 'coarseness of language and laxity of tone' and now famously concluded that the author – if a woman – had 'long forfeited the society of her own sex' (1848, pp. 163, 176). When Gaskell wrote her riposte to Rigby in Volume 1 Chapter 3 of the *Life*, it was immediately contextualised by an account of the sufferings of Brontë's sister Anne. This included a passage likening Charlotte to Christ on the cross with references also to the parable of the Pharisee and the Publican (pp. 242–3). These biblical references countered the perceived profanity of the sisters' texts. As Rigby had invoked real governesses, so Gaskell used Brontë's actual life experience to make Charlotte apparently immune to the reviewer's remarks. For the reader of the *Life* in 1857, she was further insulated and 'numbed to all petty annoyances by the grand severity of Death' (Peterson 2006, p. 242).

Gaskell later claimed to be 'withholding nothing' and countered the 'coarseness here and there in her works' with more evidence of harshness in Brontë's life and 'her strong feeling of the duty of representing life as it really is, not as it ought to be' (Peterson 2006, pp. 342, 346). At the time of writing, Gaskell felt the need to counter the coarseness accusation more strongly because she had seen the manuscript of *The Professor* and discussed it with Smith in August 1856 (Chapple and Pollard 1966, pp. 403–5). In September, she wrote to Emily Shaen, sister of the Winkworths, that the novel had 'little or no story; & disfigured by more coarseness, – & profanity in quoting texts of Scripture' (p. 410). With Smith, she also considered whether the novel should appear before the *Life* in the furtherance of her recovery project, and her letters at this time were generally open about her concerns that the fictionalisation of Constantin Heger should add to the problems of Brontë's reputation (pp. 412–7).

As a counterpart to the recovery process, it was notable that the men who featured, such as Heger and also James Taylor, George Smith and Arthur Nicholls, had to be renovated from within Brontë's actual life in order to appear in Gaskell's written *Life*. In the reshaped evidence, marriage proposals such as those of Taylor and George Nussey were played down, and the relationship with George Smith was made more professional, probably by the publisher himself (Jones 1984). There were manuscript changes to the one surviving letter to Mary Taylor that, ironically, Gaskell described as 'safe' in October 1856 when it circulated to W.S. Williams, reader at Smith Elder (Chapple and Pollard 1966, p. 883). As a happily married man, Smith was particularly keen to de-emphasise his role in the incident narrated by the Taylor letter of Brontë and her sister Anne arriving in London to prove their identity. His amendments depersonalised the event so that the visit would seem to be to the publisher Smith Elder as an entity (Peterson 2006, pp. 231–2). Male relatives were tackled more brutally in line with their environmental impact on Brontë's character. The representation of Patrick Brontë was based on earlier information supplied partly by Charlotte herself as discussed in Gaskell's letter to Catherine Winkworth of 25 August 1850 (Chapple and Pollard 1966, pp. 123–6) but also by Lady Kay-Shuttleworth, as Gaskell explained to her friend Charlotte Froude on the same day (pp. 128–9). Linda Peterson, editor of the *Life*, notes that Gaskell covered Brontë's feelings about Heger and her near breakdown by relocating the more explicable anxiety over Branwell from 1845 to 1843 (2006, p. 417, notes 379, 385).

This task of recovery subsequently exposed Gaskell to criticism. In an article in the *Edinburgh Review*, James Fitzjames Stephen wrote that Brontë 'greatly abused the license of her art' in presenting Lowood in *Jane Eyre* and he then accused Gaskell of being 'an avenging Deity' who had produced 'a highly wrought drama' in the *Life* (1857, pp. 155, 156). Stephen aligned Gaskell with Brontë by raising concerns about the fictionalisation of the *Life*, adding that 'Mrs Gaskell... cannot discharge from her palette the colours she has used in the pages of "Mary Barton" and "Ruth"' (p. 155). Without naming either of the two novelists, Dinah Mulock Craik also took Gaskell to task in an article in *Chambers's*

Edinburgh Journal entitled 'Literary Ghouls: A Protest from the Other World'. Craik suggested that the *Life* was written 'tenderly and wisely... but – it ought never to have been written at all' (1858, p. 116). As Dinah Mulock, Craik published her best-selling novel *John Halifax Gentleman* in 1856 and had outgrown her status, in a letter to Maria James of 29 October 1851, of Gaskell's 'nice little friend' (Chapple and Pollard 1966, p. 167). During her quest for Brontë's letters to the poet and critic Sydney Dobell, Gaskell told Smith in September 1856 that Charlotte had dropped the correspondence when Dobell 'suggested some bosh about her and Miss Mulock's being "kindred stars"' (Gaskell, *Letters*, September 1856, 414). In 'Literary Ghouls', Craik described biographers as 'resurrectionists of modern times' (1858, p. 113) and the unnamed Brontë was identifiable from the quotation 'Am I going to die', paraphrasing Charlotte's last words presented by Gaskell in the penultimate chapter of the *Life* (Peterson 2006, p. 368). Craik announced that publishing a life was not consonant with 'real womanly feeling' and summoned up the spirit of Brontë herself whose letters had been 'printed... and published for the amusement of every careless or sarcastic eye' (1858, p. 116). The publishers of *Chambers's Journal*, however, added their own postscript, pointing out that biography was a 'popular and important department of literature' (p. 116). The editor both named Gaskell and yoked her contribution to the established model of letter-based life writing: 'our Boswells will still be read with a luxurious feeling of enjoyment and admiration, and our Gaskells will still command our interest and our tears' (p. 117). This would seem to suggest that despite the article, *Chambers's* readers were being encouraged to think the recovery a success.

'Charlotte's own words'

Gaskell emphasised the authority for her text by drawing attention to the use of Brontë's own words. During Anne Brontë's terminal illness, a letter of 12 April 1849 was prefaced: 'I take Charlotte's own words as the best record of her thoughts and feelings during all this terrible time' (Peterson 2006, p. 249). The editorial policy of extracting was noted at the introduction of the correspondence with Margaret Wooler, Bronte's headmistress and employer: 'Acting on the conviction which I have all along entertained, that where Charlotte Brontë's own words could be used, no others ought to take their place, I shall make extracts from this series, according to their dates' (p. 185). Gaskell retained greetings and adieux to demonstrate Brontë's adherence to convention so that the letters themselves were part of duty and normality. She was careful to describe her work as a *Life* so that the incompleteness of the letters did not seem to be prominent; she was making a life out of the letters rather than positioning her subject in any broader historical context. In using Charlotte's own voice, the exemplarity of Brontë as author was posited within the framework of duty and family ties which was also the form used in women's spiritual autobiography and in travel diaries presented through journals or journal letters. The letter form influenced the *Life* in other ways through the conduct manual, through the tailored persona of the correspondent and through Gaskell as a correspondent herself.

The modern edition of the *Life* (Peterson 2006) notes the use of over 270 letters of which 152 were written to Nussey. Of other friends, there were 13 letters to Margaret Wooler, seven to Laetitia Wheelwright and three to Emily Brontë. A further 56 were those to Smith Elder, its proprietor George Smith and the readers James Taylor and W.S. Williams. Nine were letters of business to Aylott and Jones about the publication of the sisters' poems. There were 13 letters to Gaskell herself, eight to G.H. Lewes and four to Sydney Dobell. Gaskell used Brontë's own words to create moments of drama and to reinforce the evidence of her biographical stance. Sometimes only small sections were extracted and in extreme cases letters were run together.

Each of the two volumes of the *Life* comprised 14 chapters. Brontë's letters closed 16 of the 28 chapters and became increasingly part of the shaping rationale in Volume 2. In Volume 1 Chapter 7, Gaskell interjected, 'let Charlotte explain' (p. 87) and at the end of Chapter 14, she announced that the description of Branwell 'shall be by Charlotte herself, not by me' (p. 181). The volume closed, as Linda Peterson has noted (2006, pp. xix, 425, note 463, 2009, p. 132), on the theme of tragedy leading to triumph with a letter about the failure of the *Poems* and reference to the subsequent 'Biographical Notice' of Brontë's sisters who were still living at this point in the *Life* (Peterson 2006, p. 191). In Volume 2, all but the two final chapters were closed by Brontë's own words. She was dead by the end of Chapter 13 where her last words were reported, and Mary Taylor's letter to Gaskell was substituted in the final chapter. In this second volume, Brontë's letters were organised to act as conclusions to narrative sequences and this process emphasised internal patterns and arcs. Chapter 5 began by announcing that 'life at Haworth was so unvaried' that 'the postman's call was the event of her day' (Peterson 2006, p. 279). At the end of Chapter 3, Brontë wrote to Nussey or 'E', 'I write to you freely' in a letter originally dated 14 July 1849 (p. 256). For Chapter 4, Gaskell glossed 'noiseless daily duties' in her own coda to a letter about Thackeray (p. 269). Several chapters ended with discussions of books in letters to W.S. Williams (19 March 1850, p. 278) and James Taylor (5 September 1850, p. 292), and several others reinforced the theme of isolation in the midst of fame highlighted by the later chapters. In Chapter 9, on 8 July 1851 Brontë wrote that she depended on George Smith's letters (p. 214); in Chapter 10 she could do no visiting according to a letter to Nussey dated 11 May 1852 (p. 331) and she wrote to George Smith on 6 December 1852 that she could only venture forth 'papa's health permitting' in Chapter 11 (p. 341).

In the process of using Brontë's own words, Gaskell also used Charlotte's 'Biographical Notice' of 1850 to supplement the letters and to explain the origin of the sisters' volume of poems (Peterson 2006, p. 182). There are only three surviving letters from Emily and five from Anne to provide any account of their own experiences, and, in some ways, Nussey was allowed in the *Life* to become a substitute sister and observer before Gaskell's involvement with Charlotte. Nussey was, for instance, elided with the 'Notice' in the account of Emily's death (pp. 238–41) and was also allowed to hijack the text with her account of the visit to Scarborough where Anne died (pp. 252–4). At the time, however, Nussey was not privileged to know about the literary efforts of her friends, a situation that should perhaps have rung alarm bells for the biographer. Nussey later claimed she always knew about publication even though it was not openly discussed, and in the text of the *Life* it was suggested that Anne Brontë gave away the secret about their poetry appearing in magazines (p. 186). Through Charlotte's 'Notice' in the context of the *Life*, readers could be reminded that *Wuthering Heights* and *Agnes Grey* were published 'on terms somewhat impoverishing to the two authors' (p. 208). The 'Notice' also provided information about the origins of *Jane Eyre* in Smith Elder's constructive rejection of *The Professor*, a novel that was 'accepted nowhere' (pp. 202, 210). Brontë's explanation of *The Tenant of Wildfell Hall* was that Anne thought it her 'duty to reproduce every detail' (p. 231) and this exonerated Gaskell in her own depiction of the demise of Branwell.

The use of letters that omitted the fact of authorship was not the only concern in the Nussey letters as evidence of the life. Citing Hannah More and Rosemary Bodenheimer, Peterson observes that the Nussey correspondence was weighted towards an 'epistolary period of life' for a woman of the early nineteenth century, and so was part of a project of improvement based on conduct books (2006, p. ix). In her biography of the family, Juliet Barker suggests that the correspondence began as a 'school exercise' (1994, p. 181). Barker differentiates between the two correspondents, seeing Nussey as the future 'emotional prop' and Mary Taylor as an intellectual stimulus (p. 182). In April 1850, for instance, Taylor wrote to Brontë about *Shirley*: 'You are a coward and a traitor. A woman who works is by that alone better than one who does not' (Stevens 1972, p. 94). In other words, the Nussey correspondence was about using letter models and not always about personal interaction.

The *Life* demonstrates how Gaskell mined the standard elements and conduct advice of the letters to support her themes and agenda. In May/June 1852, Brontë offered Nussey advice in coping with an unknown trial. For Gaskell, the context was a visit to Filey, during which Charlotte visited Anne's grave in Scarborough. '*That* duty, then, is done', Brontë wrote to Nussey on 6 June, and this phrase was retained in the *Life*. Brontë also insisted on being 'utterly alone' (Peterson 2006, p. 332), although Ellen would have joined her. In what appeared to be her next letter, Brontë agreed that she had improved but could not stay away long enough for a complete renewal of health, and she criticised a mutual friend for her style of describing her late 'precious, sainted father' (16 June 1852, p. 332). There was here an indication of a trade in letters since Ellen had enclosed the letter of the friend (Emma Sherwood), which Brontë now returned (Peterson 2006, p. 464, note 441). This representation of herself to Ellen was important both to the relationship at the time and to the compartmentalisation of Ellen as a correspondent but also, of course, to Gaskell's ongoing case. The incident was juxtaposed with Patrick Brontë's further illness, from which Ellen must be kept for Brontë-Gaskell to maintain that sense of full dutifulness and self-immolation. Brontë did not comment on Ellen's 'last' but reached once more for the conduct manual with an extract that Gaskell retained after a published ellipsis: 'Submission, courage, exertion, when practicable, – these seem to be the weapons with which we must fight life's long battle' (12 August 1852, p. 333).

At the same time, the repetition of letter manual elements would be avoided if other themes were to be highlighted. Gaskell used a letter dated 11 February 1834 to conclude that the winter 'was particularly wet and rainy, and there were an unusual number of deaths in the village' (Peterson 2006, p. 81). This supported her theory of the diseased and dreary existence in Haworth. The actual letter to Nussey dated 11 February 1834, however, began in letter manual style, 'My letters are scarcely worth the postage' and read very like a correspondence based on models with an irony probably not appreciated by Ellen at the time. Towards the middle Brontë concluded, 'According to custom I have no news to communicate' (Smith 1995, p. 125) but then explained to Ellen that their 'mutual correspondence' was designed to gain intelligence and to remind them of their 'separate existences', Charlotte in her 'wild little hill village' and Ellen 'surrounded by society and friends' (p. 126). Brontë finally congratulated herself in the manner of the letter manual on having 'very cleverly contrived to make a letter out of nothing' (p. 126).

It is essential to ask how much a life has been shaped by the survival of letters and by letters to a single recipient: one who was a correspondent but not necessarily a recipient of autobiographical fact. Brontë moved out of Nussey's orbit, and Ellen saw herself and her relationship with Charlotte as rivalled both by Brontë's career and, later, by her marriage. At the end of both volumes of the *Life*, there were manoeuvres to preserve Ellen as a witness at key moments despite her initial ignorance of the Brontës' authorship and her disapproval of the match with Nicholls. In terms of Volume 1, Marianne Gaskell wrote on behalf of her mother on 11 September 1856 to ask Nussey for information about the publication of the sisters' poems in 1846 (Chapple and Pollard 1966, pp. 882–3). At this point in the ultimate text of the *Life*, Ellen was included but anonymised to protect her family from publicity over their financial problems. The advice given in Brontë's letter dated 10 July 1846 was, however, too apposite to exclude because it recommended the choice of the most self-sacrificing path. Gaskell introduced it by saying: 'To whom it was written, matters not; but the wholesome sense of duty – the sense of the supremacy of that duty which God, in placing us in families, has laid out for us, seems to deserve especial regard in these days' (Peterson 2006, pp. 189–90). The letter was originally written just after the publication of the sisters' poems and Brontë told her unknown and unknowing correspondent that 'the right path' of staying at home with her mother 'is that which necessitates the greatest sacrifice of self-interest'. 'I recommend you to do what I am trying to do myself' (p. 190) was its choreographed conclusion, but the *Poems* unmentioned in the letter then recurred immediately in the *Life* at the end of Volume 1.

The rest of this duty letter was glossed over because it included a denial to Ellen that Brontë was engaged already to Nicholls who was here retrospectively renovated by Gaskell, just before the end of Volume 1, as a Jacob serving his time for Rachel. In Volume 2, this necessary omission becomes ironical for the modern reader since both Nussey and Gaskell would find communication difficult owing to the presence of Nicholls in the chain of correspondence. In life, Gaskell told a number of her correspondents that communication between her and Charlotte had lapsed, writing to Geraldine Jewsbury on 21 July 1854 (Chapple and Pollard 1966, p. 303), John Greenwood on 4 April 1855 (p. 336) and George Smith on 4 June 1855 (pp. 346–7). There was also a gap in the correspondence with Nussey near the time of the marriage despite Nussey's eventually being a bridesmaid, and Peterson notes that letters to Laetitia Wheelwright, a friend from the Brussels days, stood in during this period (2006, p. 472, note 541). Nussey disapproved of Nicholls's courtship and there is no surviving correspondence between 23 June 1853 and 1 March 1854. Given that marriage was part of the duty being emphasised, Gaskell then had to fall back on other rather trite statements when she began the shaping of her ending. We know, for instance, from subsequent editions of letters that Brontë wrote on 27 July 1854 from Cork to their mutual friend Catherine Winkworth, an Anglican, addressing the letter to Gaskell's home. On honeymoon, Brontë's un-poetical husband has allowed her to be alone with the crashing waves of the Atlantic Ocean, albeit under a rug. In the letter to Winkworth that Gaskell must have known about at the time given her part in its transmission via her Manchester address, Brontë commended Arthur's 'protection which does not interfere' as 'a thousand times better than any half sort of pseudo-sympathy' (Smith 2004, p. 280). Covering this period in the *Life*, Gaskell commented rather that '[h]enceforward the sacred doors of home are closed upon her married life' (Peterson 2006, p. 364) but it was, of course, Gaskell who closed them. To Winkworth at the time,

Brontë added that she would be indulgent as necessary to her husband and then launched into her view of Dickens's treatment of Gaskell over the serialisation of *North and South* in *Household Words*, a situation discussed frequently in Gaskell's correspondence but no longer fitting in terms of timing for the sombre and clearly signalled ending of the *Life*.

Gaskell and Letters

The reader of the 1857 *Life* had already been able to read Charlotte's 'Notice' in the reprinted edition of *Wuthering Heights*. The 'Notice' in the *Life* was a reminder of Brontë's ownership of the memory of her sisters, and Gaskell's own shaping was here foreshadowed as she developed her more extended and complex account. Brontë initially proposed in 1850 'a few lines of remark' (Letter to W.S. Williams, 29 September 1850, p. 293) and described this to Nussey as 'a *sacred duty*' (3 & 23 October 1850, p. 293). In a letter to Smith, Gaskell too described the commissioning of the *Life* as 'this grave duty laid upon me' (18 June 1855, p. 349) although by late October 1855 it had become 'too long for any prefatory notice' (p. 372) which had been the form of Brontë's memorialisation of Anne and Emily. In the course of Gaskell's quest to gain access to Smith's own material, the 'Sketch' on 10 October 1855 would become a 'Memoir' by the twentieth (p. 371).

The *Life* demonstrates how Gaskell deployed pre-conceived, pre-written narrative arcs that she had already rehearsed and revisited in letters of her own. Gaskell's reordering of material emphasised the authorship emerging from domestic duty, contextualised by the Brontës' living conditions and by the social deprivation that excused morbidity. It was the life within a context that explained the alleged 'coarseness' of the novels. Gaskell wrote to George Smith on 4 June 1855: 'the more she was known the more people would honour her as a woman, separate from her character as an authoress' (Chapple and Pollard 1966, p. 347). She described to an unknown correspondent on 23 August 1855, 'a drama of her life in my own mind' (p. 369). To Eliza Fox on 27 August 1850, after her first meeting with Brontë, Gaskell was already speculating: 'the wonder is to me how she can have kept heart and power alive in her life of desolation' (Chapple and Pollard 1966, p. 130). Gaskell was working out her narrative in a letter to Lady Kay-Shuttleworth of 7 April 1853 when she wrote that Brontë's 'life sounds like the fulfilment of duties to her father, to the poor around her, to the old servants' (p. 229). Comparing *Ruth* with *Villette* in the same letter, Gaskell contrasted the novels in order to introduce the morbidity theme: 'she puts all her naughtiness into her books, and I put all my goodness. I am sure she works off a great deal that is morbid *into* her writing, and out of her life' (p. 228). She wrote to Christian Socialist John Ludlow on 7 June 1853: 'her only way of relieving herself is by writing out what she feels' and 'somehow she only writes at her morbid times' (Chapple and Shelston 2000, p. 90). Towards the end of her task of writing the *Life* in autumn 1856, Gaskell had reduced her narrative arcs to a single sentence in a letter to Emelyn Story in Rome: 'Her circumstances made her faults, whilst her virtues were her own' (Chapple and Pollard 1966, p. 416).

Linda Peterson suggests that Gaskell 'quotes responsibly' from the letters (2009, p. 136) but the biographer also weaves the letter evidence into retrospective judgement and personal feedback. Gaskell's thesis can be illustrated in Volume 1 Chapter 7 where a retrospective overarching sweep of evidence was used to present the narrative arc using a letter to Ellen in 1832, her own personal interaction with Brontë after 1850 and the privilege of hindsight in 1857. Gaskell here brought herself into the life long before their first meeting: 'In after-life, I was painfully impressed with the fact, that Miss Brontë never dared to allow herself to look forward with hope... the pressure of grief... had crushed all buoyancy of expectation out of her' (Peterson 2006, p. 78). Gaskell insisted that Brontë's trust in God sustained her. She claimed the letters provided evidence that Brontë's hopelessness was constitutional or perhaps caused by grief at the loss of her elder sisters combined with bodily weakness. In Chapter 7, on 21 July 1832, Brontë replied to Ellen that: '[a]n account of one day is an account of all' (p. 78) following a conduct book request for an account of her days since leaving school. At this point in Gaskell's account in the *Life*, an unnamed drawing master has given the three sisters the tools 'to express their powerful imaginations in visible forms' (p. 78), and drawing and walking 'Charlotte told me' were her pleasure and relaxation (p. 79). In 1832, 'they never faced their kind voluntarily, and always preferred the solitude and freedom of the moors' (p. 79). The sisters might not have had the strength to get to a waterfall on their walks and may have avoided the village out of shyness but of course they never shirked their duties as Sunday-school teachers 'even after [Charlotte] was left alone' (p. 79) which was in May 1849. Duty, recovery and creativity are reinforced through letter evidence and personal interaction in a brief paragraph.

For the *Life*, Gaskell named herself as author on the title page of a piece of writing for the first time, and this was at Patrick Brontë's request because she was known to be an author and a woman. He wrote on 16 June 1855: 'I should expect, and request that you would affix your name, so that the work might obtain a wide circulation, and be handed down to the latest times' (Barker 1994, p. 782). Gaskell enclosed this letter in her letter to George Smith of 18 June describing 'this grave duty laid upon me' (Chapple and Pollard 1966, p. 349). Patrick wrote fatefully on 12 January 1856, during the research and writing period of the *Life*: 'few facts, and incidents, you have of a biographical nature... you must draw largely on the resources of your own mind' (Barker 1994, p. 787). The family choice of a novelist as biographer would, however, fuel those accusations of fictionalisation.

Gaskell announced that the *Life* was intended to present 'a right understanding of my dear friend' (Peterson 2006, p. 16), and Linda Hughes and Michael Lund suggest that 'Gaskell's sympathies and authorial voice are presented throughout the biography in dialogue with Brontë's' (1999, p. 124). This dialogue emanates from correspondence and collaboration although Deirdre d'Albertis sees the writing of the *Life* as a 'disguised form of literary competition' that was generated within Gaskell's 'divided mind' on working and home duties (1997, pp. 20, 161). Gaskell imported herself and her family into Brontë's life from the outset. She was a 'dear friend' at the beginning of Volume 1 Chapter 2, and 'my husband' appeared in anecdotal evidence of the Yorkshire rural character later in the same chapter (Peterson 2006, pp. 16, 19). In real time, Gaskell spent three days with Brontë in the Lakes in August 1850 and four days at Haworth from 19 September 1853. Brontë paid three visits to Manchester: a few days in June 1851, a week in April 1853 and four days in May 1854 prior to her marriage. The significant 'luminous cloud' letter that preceded Gaskell's Haworth visit included references to Gaskell's daughters Marianne, Meta, Florence and Julia, retained for publication as 'M. and M.', 'F. and J.' (pp. 353–4). The Gaskells were being portrayed as a substitute family within the recovery project.

Gaskell's life was thus entwined in Brontë's life and *Life* in a variety of ways. She featured in the life lived to the moment and discussed her interaction with her material during the writing process. It is clear that the biography was shaped textually from accounts supplied in Gaskell's own letters some of which she used in the *Life*. Gaskell repeated misinformation supplied by Lady Kay-Shuttleworth, hostess at Briery Close, on their overlapping visit to the Lakes in the letter written to Catherine Winkworth in August 1850. In the *Life*, Gaskell explained:

> If I copy out part of a letter, which I wrote soon after this to a friend, who was deeply interested in her writings, I shall probably convey my first impressions more truly and freshly than by amplifying what I then said into a longer description.
>
> (Peterson 2006, p. 287)

After her visit to Haworth in September 1853, Gaskell wrote, 'At the risk of repeating something which I have previously said, I will copy out parts of a letter which I wrote at the time' (Peterson 2006, p. 354). This is a letter to an unknown recipient describing life at Haworth although the *Life* is the only source for it (Chapple and Pollard 1966, pp. 247–50). Gaskell concluded after revisiting this letter 'I understood her life the better' (Peterson 2006, p. 356), and it is implied that greater understanding of herself in the life of Brontë and of her own letter within the *Life* was achieved first by the visit and then by the act of copying that produced a kind of secondary correspondence.

It has also been suggested that Gaskell's correspondence had an earlier intermediate life and that her letters were part of the context into which she was writing her riposte to reviewers such as Elizabeth Rigby. Gaskell must have either kept a draft of her 25 August 1850 letter (Chapple and Pollard 1966, pp. 123–6) or recalled it for the *Life*. She may even have kept a copy with a view to publication since near-extracts from the letter appeared in an obituary in *Sharpe's London Magazine* that was published in June 1855, some three months after Brontë's death ('A Few Words' 1855). Hughes and Lund discuss the context of this article (1999, pp. 124–30) and describe the letter as 'very lightly edited' for publication. Juliet Barker makes Gaskell 'responsible' (1994, p. 780) although Linda Peterson suggests, in conjunction with Margaret Smith, that a writer known to Catherine Winkworth called Frank Smedley was the author of the piece (2006, p. ix). Although their tone was very different, the texts of letter and article contained overlapping information and inaccuracies, and a second letter to an unknown correspondent that was also quoted directly within the obituary ('A Few Words' 1855, p. 342) has been included in Gaskell's own collected letters on this evidence alone (Gaskell, *Letters*, 127). This is an additional form of letter transmission in which the *Life* written as a riposte has come to inform letter sequencing in the biographer's own life. Gaskell's involvement represents a complex set of communal actions since the publication of the *Sharpe* article was also part of Nussey's reasoning for proposing a biography to Nicholls and Patrick (Barker 1994, pp. 780–81). The communication of letters in public has become the catalyst for a *Life* itself written out of private letters made public.

For the *Life* in 1857, however, Gaskell was apparently making letters into evidence that could be trusted because of its contemporaneousness, freshness and spontaneity. In reality, Gaskell's view of Brontë was conflicted at the time as demonstrated by her own letters. She told Eliza Fox in August 1850 that Charlotte was 'quiet sensible unaffected with high noble aims' (Chapple and Pollard 1966, p. 130) and she avoided analysing *Jane Eyre* in the *Life* because it was a book now 'high and safe on the everlasting hills of fame' (Peterson 2006, p. 217). Gaskell pretended in the *Life* that she was not part of the curiosity over Bronte's identity when *Jane Eyre* was published (p. 217) although she herself wrote to Anne Shaen, sister of the Winkworths' brother-in-law, on 24 April 1848 that it was 'an uncommon book. I don't know if I like or dislike it. I take the opposite side to the person I am talking with always in order to hear some convincing arguments to clear up my opinions' (Chapple and Pollard 1966, p. 57). Also hidden was her own panic at comparisons between their work as novelists. Gaskell reported in the *Life* that she asked for a delay in the publication of *Villette* to give her novel *Ruth* a 'start', quoting Brontë's letter of 12 January 1853 (Peterson 2006, p. 343) but Peterson notes that Brontë represented this in a letter to Nussey of 19 January 1853 as a pitiful request (p. 467, note 482). Gaskell chose rather to observe, 'It is with a sad, proud pleasure I copy her words of friendship now' (p. 343).

Two examples outside the Nussey correspondence demonstrate the further manipulation of presence and identity within the Brontë-Gaskell text. In both cases, Brontë was consciously representing herself for the correspondent using a complex portrayal of her identity as woman and author. In both cases, Gaskell the friend has become Gaskell the champion and biographer with power over the mechanism of the letter within her text. The community of life writing was expanded first into a short series of letters to Sydney Dobell, and secondly into Brontë's brief correspondence with Robert Southey that sets up a context within other letter collections.

The first letter to Sydney Dobell concluded Volume 2 Chapter 8 of the *Life*. On 8 December 1850, Brontë had sent Dobell a copy of the second edition of *Wuthering Heights* – a novel he had favourably reviewed in September 1850 on the assumption that the Bells were only one author and thus that Currer and Ellis Bell were one person. This new edition of *Wuthering Heights* contained the 'Biographical Notice' that differentiated the three sisters and tried to explain Emily's creativity and power. In the letter of 1850, and despite his mis-identification, Brontë thanked Dobell for the 'noble justice' rendered to Emily who was beyond 'human praise and blame'. She described herself as 'a plain country parson's daughter' but signed the letter 'with a full heart. C. Brontë' (Peterson 2006, p. 301). She was the daughter, the grieving sister and the identifiable, and now named, published author. The further letter to Dobell in Volume 2 Chapter 13 also spoke to identity and authorship but was relocated out of sequence to the chapter of the *Life* in which Brontë died. This second letter of 3 February 1854 was specially cultivated by Gaskell to emphasise Brontë's continuing duty to her father and to cover her own absence from Charlotte's life. According to Gaskell, the letter

> develops the intellectual side of her character, before we lose all thought of the authoress in the timid and conscientious woman about to become a wife, and in the too short, almost perfect happiness of her nine months of wedded life.
>
> (p. 358)

The letter retained its value as Brontë's own words despite the 'bosh' written by the correspondent himself.

The exchange of letters with Southey, two from each side, ranged more widely. Early in 1837, at the age of 20, Charlotte had written to the Poet Laureate Southey enclosing at least one poem. When Southey replied on 12 March 1837, he recalled her to her 'proper duties', telling her now famously that 'Literature cannot be the business of a woman's life, and ought not to be' (Peterson 2006, p. 100). Brontë's interpretation of her first letter to Southey with its 'crude rhapsody' appeared in her second letter dated 16 March. Her reply was ostensibly positioned as part of the narrative of submission but, in context, read not merely as the voice of a subservient daughter but also betrayed her underlying bitterness in response to this 'consecrated' (p. 101) letter from him. Brontë' referred three times to 'duty' or 'duties'. She wrote that the sight of the letter and the mere honour of having corresponded would help her to suppress her ambition: '[S]ometimes when I'm teaching or sewing I would rather be reading or writing; but I try to deny myself' (p. 101). Gaskell completed the picture by inserting into the *Life* Southey's rather naïve and avuncular reply that interpreted Brontë back to herself as subservient and included an invitation to the Lakes (p. 102). This incident was also, however, reframed in time to reflect naming and identity since Gaskell then claimed that she was with Brontë in the Lake District (Peterson 2006, p. 100) when Cuthbert Southey requested the letter back for inclusion in the *Life and Correspondence* of his father. It would be reclassified there as 'Literary Advice to a Lady*' with a note defining Brontë as '*now well-known as a prose writer of no common powers' (Southey 1850, p. 327). In the background, Gaskell would have been familiar at the time with the earlier volumes of the Southey publication. According to a letter to her friend Eliza Fox of 26 November 1849 that survives only in typescript, Gaskell had read Cuthbert Southey's rationalisation of the role of 'making my father his own biographer' through letters, a process discussed initially in Cuthbert's Preface to Volume 1 (Southey 1849, p. vi), although parts of her letter have been re-dated to February 1850 (Chapple and Shelston 2000, p. 90). Southey crossed generic and trans-generational boundaries of life writing when he then suggested that this was a 'work consistent with itself throughout in its autobiographical character' (Southey 1850, p. 394). When Brontë wrote to Southey in 1837 under her own name, he assumed in his reply that this was a pseudonym. Southey the memorialist in 1850 removed Brontë quotations from the letters of his father but showed no sense of irony that 'literature is not the business of a woman's life'.

Volume 1 Chapter 8 in the *Life* thus presented a complex negotiation about the Southey letter that also included the claim of Gaskell's own presence. The two novelists met first in August 1850 although Brontë had written to Gaskell as Currer Bell on 17 November 1849 identifying herself as a woman (Smith 2000, p. 288). When Gaskell mentioned 'Southey's memoir' in the Fox letter dated ten days later on 26 November 1849, it was in conjunction with a triumphant reference to the identity of the author of *Jane Eyre* and *Shirley* (Chapple and Shelston 2000, p. 90). In this letter, Gaskell also mentioned Dr John Epps, now known to have been a homeopathic doctor consulted by Charlotte in her own name about her dying sister Emily and now discoverable through a further surviving letter to W.S. Williams (20 December 1848, Smith, 2000, p. 155). Gaskell had made herself part of the quest for named authorship in 1848 and repositioned herself within the identity puzzle when 1837 was recollected in 1850 to be packaged for the *Life* in 1857.

In the penultimate chapter of her biography, Gaskell later had to write herself back out of the text. She also had to disguise the fact that she had lost touch with Brontë after her marriage because of the gap in ideology between herself as a Unitarian and Nicholls as an Anglican although, of course, she did approach Richard Monkton Milnes on 29 October 1853 about a possible appointment for Arthur (Chapple and Pollard 1966, pp. 252–3). This gap in beliefs and in correspondence produced further manoeuvring. According to the *Life*, the women apparently parted at Haworth in September 1853 for the last time, despite the 1854 pre-marriage visit to Manchester, intending, according to Gaskell, to renew their visits 'frequently' (Peterson 2006, p. 358). After a further visit by Brontë to Margaret Wooler followed by a letter, Gaskell explained that in drawing 'nearer to the years so recently closed, it becomes impossible for me to write with the same fullness of detail as I have hitherto not felt it wrong to use' (p. 358). This was not just out of a duty to 'family considerations' but actually because of the marriage. Despite its usefulness as home duty for the purposes of biography, the union with Arthur produced ideological distance in life, and this reconstruction of events extended to the distortion of some final facts. Gaskell re-dated and re-timed Brontë's death so that it appeared to have occurred on 'Easter morning' (p. 369) rather than on the actual day which was the Saturday before Palm Sunday. This was part of drama and fictionalisation within the recovery project.

Gabriel Helms suggests that Gaskell 'the biographer subordinates the letters to serve her intention' (1995, p. 369) but this was a multi-faceted process. The method of adapting Brontë's letters made them fictional because they were incorporated into Gaskell's 'duty narrative'. This narrative had also to shoulder the effects of the single correspondent, the recovery project and the real-life letters of a conflicted biographer. Mary Taylor wrote to Gaskell on 30 July 1857 that the book was 'a perfect success, in giving a true picture of a melancholy life' (Stevens 1972, p. 132) but by then Gaskell was revising. In a letter to Nussey of 28 January 1858, Taylor thought the third edition 'mutilated' because of the revisions regarding Branwell's Lady Scott, the Cowan Bridge School and Harriet Martineau (Stevens 1972, p. 134). 'I am almost merry in my bitterness', Gaskell wrote to Nussey on 16 June 1857 as she revisited her text (Chapple and Pollard 1966, p. 454). Despite her reservations about Brontë's subject matter, Gaskell had adopted the personae of champion and biographer and revisited her correspondence within the *Life*. She told Nussey, 'I weighed every line with all my whole power & heart, so that every line should go to it's great purpose of making *her* known and valued' (p. 454). Gaskell may only have utilised 13 letters from Brontë to herself but she was writing a life in a dialogue or correspondence with her biographical subject and in their own words. Recovery, duty and identity are thus elements of the life-writing model. As Gaskell's letters were referenced within Brontë's, the biographer's life was re-valued within the life of her subject. It was Gaskell with whom Mary Taylor corresponded by proxy on the final page of the *Life* of Charlotte, and in this way Gaskell could round her characterisation of Brontë's – and her own – 'divided mind'.

The composition of the *Life* had its own drama. Within a month of Brontë's death Margaret Wooler was writing to Nicholls: 'There is something particularly revolting in the bare idea of those communications being laid open to the public eye which were intended only for the eye of a confidential & sympathizing friend' (Barker 1994, p. 779), and into this scenario entered Elizabeth Gaskell. Wooler's remark is a reminder of Charlotte Barrett's Introduction to Frances Burney's *Diary and Letters*, demanding 'no eye but that of indulgent friendship' (1842a, p. 3). The preservation and deployment of letters, their timing and textuality, are part of the progress of the letter into life writing, as is the role of the biographer as narrator of a life shaped by many currents: by presence and absence, by family, by collector, by longevity and changing fashion. The next four chapters explore the logistical trajectory of writing, editing and shaping within the Barrett-Gaskell model in four further letter collections. The appreciation of women's authorship among women, their families and their circle of correspondents, including reviewers, produces scales of value for the letters as texts. There are concerns to be addressed about the nature and survival of guarded and unguarded correspondence, and how far this can contribute to a written life: a life shaped communally from the original act of recording.

Bibliography

Adamson, Alan H. (2008) *Mr Charlotte Brontë: The Life of Arthur Bell Nicholls*. Montreal: McGill Queen's University Press.

'A Few Words about "Jane Eyre."' (1855) *Sharpe's London Magazine*, 6 (June), pp. 339–42.

d'Albertis, Deirdre (1997) *Dissembling Fictions: Elizabeth Gaskell and the Victorian Social Text*. Basingstoke: Macmillan.

Barker, Juliet (1994) *The Brontës*. Reprint, London: Phoenix, 1995.

Barker, Juliet (1997) *The Brontës: A Life in Letters*. London: Viking.

Barrett, Charlotte (ed.) (1842a) *The Diary and Letters of Madame D'Arblay. Volume 1: 1778–1780*. London: Henry Colburn.

Chapple, John A.V. and Pollard, Arthur (eds) (1966) *The Letters of Mrs Gaskell*. Reprint, London: Mandolin, 1997.

Chapple, John and Shelston, Alan (eds) (2000) *Further Letters of Mrs Gaskell*. Manchester: Manchester University Press.

Craik, Dinah Mulock (1858) 'Literary Ghouls: A Protest from the Other World', *Chambers's Edinburgh Journal*, 242 (21 August), pp. 113–7.

Croker, John Wilson (1833) 'Memoirs of Dr Burney', Quarterly Review, 49, pp. 97–125.

Croker, John Wilson (1842) 'Diary and Letters of Madame D'Arblay, Vols I, II, III', Quarterly Review, 70, pp. 243–87.

Culley, Amy and Styler, Rebecca (2011) 'Editorial: Lives in Relation', Life Writing, 8(3), pp. 237–40. doi:10.1080/14484528.2011.579047

Easley, Alexis (2004) First-Person Anonymous: Women Writers and Victorian Print Media, 1830–70. Aldershot: Ashgate. doi:10.4324/9781315255224

Heilbrun, Carolyn G. (1988) Writing a Woman's Life. Reprint, London: The Women's Press Limited, 1989.

Helms, Gabrielle (1995) 'The Coincidence of Biography and Autobiography: Elizabeth Gaskell's Life of Charlotte Brontë', Biography: An Interdisciplinary Quarterly, 18(4), pp. 339–59.

Hughes, Linda K. and Lund, Michael (1999) Victorian Publishing and Mrs Gaskell's Work. Charlottesville: University Press of Virginia.

Jane Eyre: An Autobiography edited by Currer Bell (1847). London: Smith Elder.

Jones, Marnie (1984) 'George Smith's Influence on The Life of Charlotte Brontë', Brontë Society Transactions, 18(4), pp. 279–85.

Nicolson, Harold (1933) The Development of English Biography. London: Hogarth.

Parker, Pamela Corpron (2009) 'Woman of Letters: Elizabeth Gaskell's Autograph Collection and Victorian Celebrity', in Goggin, Maureen Daly and Tobin, Beth Fowkes (eds) Material Women 1750–1950: Consuming Desire and Collecting Practice. Farnham: Ashgate, pp. 265–78.

Peterson, Linda H. (ed.) (2006) The Life of Charlotte Brontë. Volume 8 of Shattock, Joanne (ed.) The Works of Elizabeth Gaskell. London: Pickering and Chatto. doi:10.4324/9781351220149

Peterson, Linda H. (2009) Becoming a Woman of Letters: Myths of Authorship and Facts of the Victorian Market. Princeton: Princeton University Press.

Rigby, Elizabeth (1848) 'Vanity Fair–and Jane Eyre', Quarterly Review, 84 (December), pp. 153–85.

Smith, Margaret (ed.) (1995) The Letters of Charlotte Brontë. Volume 1. Oxford: Oxford University Press.

Smith, Margaret (ed.) (2000) The Letters of Charlotte Brontë. Volume 2. Oxford: Oxford University Press.

Smith, Margaret (ed.) (2004) The Letters of Charlotte Brontë. Volume 3. Oxford: Oxford University Press.

Smith, Margaret (2012) 'The Brontë Correspondence', in Thormählen, Marianne (ed.) The Brontës in Context. Cambridge: Cambridge University Press, pp. 115–22. doi:10.1017/CBO9781139028066

Southey, Charles Cuthbert (1849) The Life and Correspondence of Robert Southey. Volume 1. London: Longman.

Southey, Charles Cuthbert (1850) The Life and Correspondence of Robert Southey. Volume 6. London: Longman.

Stephen, James Fitzjames (1857) 'The License of Modern Novelists', Edinburgh Review, 106 (July), pp. 124–56.

Stevens, Joan (ed.) (1972) Mary Taylor: Friend of Charlotte Brontë: Letters from New Zealand and Elsewhere. Auckland: Oxford University Press.

Winkworth, Susanna (1883) Letters and Memorials of Catherine Winkworth. Volume 1. Clifton: Austin.

4 Autobiography and Correspondence of Mary Granville, Mrs Delany (1861–62)

The Family Letter Collection

On 3 July 1820, Madame d'Arblay née Burney wrote to her long-term friend and correspondent Georgiana Waddington concerning the letters of Mary Granville, Mrs Delany. Two of Delany's letters to Jonathan Swift had appeared in print in her lifetime (Hawkesworth 1766) and subsequently nine to Samuel Richardson (*The Correspondence of Samuel Richardson* 1804). Her letters to her friend Frances Hamilton (*Letters from Mrs Delany* 1820), to be published that year, were the subject of Burney's letter, and Burney observed soothingly, '*She*, who did not write for the press, can never be satirized that she did not prepare for it' (Hemlow, Douglas and Hawkins 1984, p. 165). The Delany family were, however, already anxious that their family member was being prepared for the press by Burney herself.

This chapter traces the interwoven life writings of Burney and Delany. The *Autobiography and Correspondence of Mary Granville, Mrs Delany* put into press by Waddington's daughter, Lady Llanover, was an attempt to recover Delany and her family from the perceived misrepresentations of Burney's *Diary and Letters*. With family and antiquarian objectives at the forefront, the impact of letter trading, royal anecdotes and recovery into domestic womanhood were nonetheless discernible. Llanover also effectively initiated a final correspondence with Burney and the life writing she had made public. The chapter begins by positioning the Llanover response through her mother's relationship with Burney. The Granville family had already attempted to influence the publication of the *Diary and Letters* in the 1840s as a response to Burney's memoir of her father published in 1832. In the 1860s, Llanover stepped into the argument, and the resulting debate can be recovered using the twentieth- and twenty-first-century publication of Burney's letters. The chapter then revisits Delany's appearance in Burney's life writing. It considers how Llanover used the dynastic technique of aligning Delany with two sets of ancestors in order to assert control over her great-great-aunt's life and tangentially that of her mother Waddington and her grandmother Mary Port. The chapter explores the issues of direct ripostes to Burney as well as the wider view of Llanover's objectives when putting her venerated relative into the marketplace through the medium of letters.

As a marker of Delany's identity, the letter was designedly unstable in the eighteenth century and Llanover's attempts to fix her ancestor's life and auto/biography for the nineteenth century effectively alienated Delany from her own correspondence.

Burney and Waddington

In light of the extended family history deployed by Llanover, the timescale of Delany's life in letters was effectively a sweep across several centuries, to include her autobiography in letters begun in 1740 onward to the publication and reviews of her *Autobiography and Correspondence* in 1861 and 1862. Delany was born in 1700 and the first surviving letter, to her sister Ann, is dated 29 November 1720 (Llanover 1861a, p. 57). The *Autobiography and Correspondence* began with a presumed piece of life writing about Delany's early years that Llanover used as Burney did her father's autobiographical writing in the *Memoirs of Dr Burney* (1832a, pp. x–xv). Llanover then explained that Delany undertook in 1740 to write her life in the form of letters to her friend the Duchess of Portland. Llanover additionally supplemented these retrospective accounts with the actual letters written by Delany to Ann as well as other letters circulating at the time, notably from their uncle Lord Lansdowne. In terms of timescale, these letters had already been referred to in the *Memoirs* of 1832 and the *Diary and Letters* of 1842–46 before reaching the *Autobiography and Correspondence*. Between 1815 and 1822, Llanover's mother Waddington had been attempting behind the scenes to recover her own letters for burning because of the indiscretions feared from publication. Delany's appearance in the press was, therefore, a complex negotiation between family pride and truthfulness in which letters were presented as evidence but also demonstrated their instability as a medium for life writing.

Georgiana Mary Ann Port married Benjamin Waddington in 1789 after having created a scandal by falling in love with Colonel Goldsworthy, a court official more than 30 years her senior. Burney and Waddington had met in the household of Mary Delany in 1784 and were in touch, latterly very sporadically, until 1824 (Hemlow, Burgess and Douglas 1971, p. 202). Their ongoing relationship can now be traced, from Burney's side at least, in Volumes 9–11 of the modern-day *Journals and Letters* (Derry 1982a, 1982b; Hemlow, Douglas and Hawkins 1984). Lady Llanover herself can even be glimpsed in the letters exchanged by the two women. On 22 August 1817, Burney described 'the bright Augusta' as Waddington's 'sole care, & sole solace' (Derry 1982a, p. 614) after the marriages of her sisters Frances and Emelia Waddington and their removal to Italy. After Emelia's death, when Llanover was aged 17, Burney suggested in a letter dated 12–19 November 1819 that Augusta's 'extreme youth should rather make her spared from effusions of too poignant, & too lasting affliction' (Hemlow, Douglas and Hawkins 1984, p. 145).

There seems at some point to have been a suggestion from Burney that she should play a part in editing a more extensive work about Delany who was Waddington's great-aunt. Waddington was informally adopted by Delany and living with her in the later 1780s. She could have been aware of their joint life-writing activity since the task of editing began during Delany's lifetime as revealed in the *Memoirs* and the *Diary*. Remembering this, Burney wrote to Waddington on 12–15 March 1792 about papers being used by Delany's nephew Court Dewes for a biography in *Biographia Britannica* since she (Burney) annotated the original text (Hemlow, Cecil and Douglas 1972, p. 130; note 4). The 'Delany' entries in the *Biographia*, an eighteenth-century collective biography, made Delany subsidiary to her husband Patrick. The Delanys were included because of their association with Swift, and Dewes was expansive on the topic of Delany's flower mosaics that had come into his possession (Dewes and Keates 1793, p. 90). Latterly, these mosaics passed to Waddington and then Llanover and are now in the British Museum. Dewes was also clear that Delany's 'moderate spirit' and quiet way of life (Dewes and Keates 1793, p. 90) ensured that she was not a dependant on the Duchess of Portland or the Royal Family, a subject that exercised the Delany family after the publication of the *Memoirs*. Burney's relationship with Waddington, recoverable from within the one side of their correspondence still extant, illustrates all the issues of trading, withholding and self-narration in Barrett's published edition, and this provides a background narrative to Burney's own attempts at writing Delany's life.

The situation arising in the 1840s over the *Diary and Letters* was ongoing from 1815 when Burney started to elide the investigation of her father's papers with those of her long-term correspondent Waddington. In the letters now recovered for the modern *Journal and Letters*, Burney argued on 3 July 1820 that she could not deal with any Delany papers:

> with what propriety could *I* make the attempt–I, who, – but for my annihilating miseries, should ere this have published a selection of the Correspondence with Memoirs of the Life of my dearest Father – a task delegated to me by my family.
> (Hemlow, Douglas and Hawkins 1984, p. 163)

General d'Arblay had died on 3 May 1818 but Emelia, Waddington's fourth daughter, had also since died on 12 April 1819. Of Waddington's six daughters born between 1790 and 1802, only Burney's goddaughter Frances living in Rome with her husband the future Baron Bunsen and Augusta, the future Lady Llanover, now survived. Waddington had begun her campaign for the return of her own letters following the death of Charles Burney in 1814. She was fearful of revelations about the Port family, about her own obsession with Colonel Goldsworthy and about a suspected attachment between Burney's son Alex and her daughter Frances following a visit in July 1815 (Derry 1982a, p. 42, note 5). There has recently even been some suggestion that Lady Llanover was herself disappointed in the attentions of the young d'Arblay (Skinner 2014, p. 15, note 4). On 17–19 August 1816, Burney wrote evasively: 'You again desire me to burn all your Letters... I would much sooner return them to you, little as I should like to part with them' (Derry 1982a, p. 181). By 22 August 1817, she agreed that '[a]s soon... as I can assemble my papers, I will commit all that are the memorials of your long friendship for me, to the flames' or at least send the packets back (Derry 1982b, p. 613). Read at this distance such letters seem to convey a veiled threat. The letters are valid as documents even without their corresponding replies, and the documents present information that can still be repeated in answers to letters now destroyed. The work of the Burney Centre has proved that letters may never be recalled and even their destruction cannot guarantee the concealment of their contents.

There was clearly a mass of papers that had been lost and recaptured during Burney's time in Europe and that Burney continued to avoid returning. In July 1821 she actually quoted from her own will to reassure Waddington that Alexander will return 'unread and unexamined' anything remaining in her (Waddington's) handwriting among the 'immense hoards' (Hemlow, Douglas and Hawkins 1984, p. 237), and in 1822 the letters were finally returned and destroyed (Hemlow, Cecil and Douglas 1972, p. xxii, note 3). Burney's proposed memoir of her father was still nearly ten years off but the terms of engagement between the two women that would later be invoked by Llanover had already been prepared.

Delany in Burney's *Memoirs* and *Diary*

As discussed in Chapter 2, Burney recorded her life as it was lived and tried to give that life a shape through journals composed for her father and sisters. The narrative then took on a new context when she came to act as the editor of her vast resource of family papers from the 1820s onwards. In trying to record her father's life in her *Memoirs of Dr Burney* published in 1832, she attracted waves of criticism for allowing her life to predominate over his. The Granville family were incorporated into the *Memoirs* through Delany's acquaintance with Dr Burney in Volume 2 and Llanover's later objections were founded on Burney's depiction of Delany and her representation of their relationship. Burney would use the same documents 20 years later to write about Delany in the *Diary and Letters*.

In Volume 2 of the *Memoirs*, the Burneys have lost the acquaintance of Hester Thrale on her remarriage but 'some solace opened to Dr Burney

for himself, and still more to his parental kindness for this Memorialist'
through 'a beginning intercourse with *the fairest model of female excel-
lence of the days that were passed*, Mrs Delany' (Burney 1832b, p. 300).
It was explained that these were words used by Edmund Burke who 'en-
ergetically esteemed' Delany and a footnote added that she was 'Daughter of John Granville Esq. And niece of Pope's Granville, the then Lord
Lansdowne, "of every Muse the friend"' (Burney 1832b, pp. 300, 301).
Burney also claimed that her own mentor Samuel Crisp was 'a favourite
with her [Delany's] bosom friend, the Dowager Duchess of Portland'
and Burney brought together the literary connections within this circle
by proposing to refer to a letter of her own in order to describe her first
meeting with Delany:

> As this venerable lady still lives in the memoirs and correspondence
> of Dean Swift, an account of this interview, abridged from a letter
> to Mr Crisp, will not perhaps, be unwillingly received as a genuine
> picture of an aged lady of rare accomplishments and high bred man-
> ners, of olden times.
>
> (Burney 1832b, p. 302)

Dr Burney remained offstage during this incident in his life, leaving his
daughter to be 'the happy instrument of this junction'.

For the Delany family, Burney was highly presumptuous in using
these connections and invoking documents as evidence. 'Mrs Delany'
was the running header for a number of sections of the *Memoirs* drawing attention to Delany's fleeting involvement in Dr Burney's life (Burney
1832b, pp. 300–14, 367–70; Burney 1832c, pp. 45–67). Delany provided
Dr Burney with a dictated account of the opera singer Anastasia Robinson
and other information for Burney's *Memoir of Handel* 'by the desire of the
King himself' (Burney 1832b, pp. 367, 381). Frances Burney quoted from
her own letters to her sister Susan including one dated 18 July 1783 in the
text where she reiterated Delany's resemblance to their maternal grandmother and exclaimed: 'How truly desirable are added years, where the
spirit of life evaporates not before its extinction' (Burney 1832b, p. 369).
Towards the end of Volume 2, one of Delany's letters was quoted in such a
way as to make a Burney letter appear to come from the Queen. The quotation read 'Your affectionate Queen, CHARLOTTE' laid out as if it were
the end of the letter to Susan (Burney 1832b, p. 398). Despite this cavalier
visual presentation of correspondence, Burney told her sister in this same
sequence that Delany 'entrusted to me her collection of letters' (Burney
1832b, p. 398). Burney then introduced 'her beautiful great-niece' with the
first of three identical footnotes carrying on into Volume 3 and describing
the companion as 'Miss Port, now Mrs Waddington of Llanover House'
(Burney 1832b, p. 398, 1832c, pp. 57, 91).

Burney was appropriating royal and literary connections, threatening revelations from correspondence and presuming to present Llanover's own mother within this life of an organist-composer. On her arrival at Court, Burney announced that 'her lovely great-niece [footnote] flew out with juvenile joy to hail the approaching residence of the Memorialist so near to the habitation of her aunt' (Burney 1832c, p. 91). Burney presented herself as a substitute for the Duchess of Portland in Delany's life (p. 93) but also seemed to imply that Delany was financially dependant on her late friend: 'though from the Duchess no pecuniary loan was accepted by Mrs Delany, unnumbered were the little auxiliaries to domestic economy which her Grace found means to convey' (p. 50). Dr Burney was once again absent from his life when he spared Frances from being his amanuensis so that she could comfort Delany on the Duchess's death. Here the potential for documentary contamination and misrepresentation recurred since Burney was 'empowered to relieve some of [Delany's] cares by being entrusted to overlook, examine and read her letters and manuscripts of every description; and to select destroy, or arrange the long-hoarded mass' (Burney 1832c, pp. 53–4). Burney spoke of herself in the third person as daughter of Dr Burney when she continued: 'She even began revising and continuing a manuscript memoir of the early days of Mrs Delany; but as it could be proceeded with only in moments of unbroken *tête à tête*, it was never finished' (Burney 1832c, p. 54). Delany had also received back the letter-based autobiography sent to the Duchess.

In 1832, members of Delany's family were thus alerted to the representations of Delany and of her great-niece Georgiana, also known as Mary, who was Llanover's mother and Delany's companion during the last years of her life. Hearing of the publication of Burney's *Diary and Letters*, Georgiana insisted on being anonymised in the text. Her designation as 'Miss P––' or 'Miss ****' throughout, however, echoed the 'Mr B––' of Richardson's *Pamela* and signally failed to conceal her presence and identity. On the one hand, there seemed to be something to hide and on the other a hint of potential fictionalisation.

In the second volume of the *Diary and Letters* published in 1842, Burney revisited her meeting with Delany on 19 January 1783. During December 1782, she had written to Susan about reports from Sir Joshua Reynolds and Edmund Burke that Delany and her friend the Duchess of Portland had been reading and re-reading her novel *Cecilia* (Barrett 1842b, pp. 192–3, 195). On 23 December, Burney saw Delany's geranium collage at Mrs Walsingham's and on 27 December, Hester Chapone asked if Burney was aware that 'Swift's Mrs Delany' was among her 'unknown friends'. Burney continued: 'There, Miss Susanna, there, daddy, the <u>Old Wits</u> have begun the charge! This was very pleasant to me indeed, for if they have curiosity as well as I, we shall all have some end to answer in meeting' (Barrett 1842b, p. 216). At Chapone's on 30 December, Burney admired a picture of Delany, and Chapone engineered the meeting that was introduced by Burney with the words: 'And now for Mrs Delany' (Barrett 1842b, p. 249). The modern *Early Journals* have recovered the full text of this letter/journal in which Burney continued: 'How fertile in adventures for my Susy has this spring proved! A Journal could never be more worth keeping in such a sort of life as ours' (Troide and Cooke 2012, p. 283). The recovered text shows clearly the retrospective rewritten character of the journals and a relish for writing that would only have reinforced Llanover's concerns of a relationship exploited.

By 7 July 1783, she was 'sweet Mrs Delany, whom I love most tenderly' (Barrett 1842b, p. 272) and on 8 January 1784 a 'venerable and excellent old lady' (p. 298) who can be kissed. This entry in Burney's journal was juxtaposed with an almost cursory reference to spending the previous afternoon with Dr Johnson. In a letter on 3 January 1785 to Waddington as 'Miss ****' or 'M––' soliciting her sympathy on Johnson's death, Burney presumed to describe her friend as 'your and my beloved Mrs Delany' (p. 342) and 'our all-amiable Mrs Delany' (p. 343). Delany was part of letter trading when Burney described her as 'revered' in a letter to Susan dated 25 August 1785 (p. 349). A letter to Frederica Locke a few days afterwards on 29 August 1785 mentioned Burney's access to letter collections, later disputed by Llanover. Burney wrote that '[s]he is employing me, when able, to look over her papers: 'tis to me a sacred task, for she cannot read what she is trusting me with' (p. 350). Delany was losing her eyesight in the last years of her life. On 25 November 1785, Burney wrote to her sister that the Duchess of Portland was 'a very Susan to her' (p. 357), another upstart statement equating one of the wealthiest women in the land with Susan who had married Molesworth Phillips, a Major in the Royal Marines, on 10 January 1782.

This 'looking over' of correspondence continued during Burney's time at Court which began on 17 July 1786 with Volume 3 of the *Diary and Letters*. On 16 August 1786, Burney described a life of 'slavery' (Barrett 1842c, p. 116) 'sitting dumb and unnoticed' (20 August 1786, p. 123) and later spending '[a] day... of nothing but dress and fatigue' (16 August 1787, p. 428). She also claimed that Delany 'tells me every occurrence of her long life, shews me all her letters, confides to me all her own papers' (1 September 1786, p. 133). Her long journal letter dated 6 October 1786 described the autobiography written for the Duchess of Portland 'in the form of letters, and with feigned names' (p. 182) that had been returned to Delany, 'that dear and very extraordinary lady' (p. 182), at her friend's death. Burney wrote about this 'secret' to her extended journal-letter community: 'In recalling them to her, she... related so many interesting anecdotes belonging to the times, which being known already to the Duchess, she had not inserted, that I proposed filling up the chasms, and linking the whole together' (p. 182). The *Memoirs* had, of course, indicated that this biographical work would remain unwritten but at the time Burney proposed to 'complete with the help of these letters, a history of her whole life' (p. 183). Despite regular interruptions even from the King, Burney announced, 'we proceeded in the memoirs pretty well through the infantine past' (p. 184), and the two women learned to provide themselves with 'double employment' when they were engaged in selecting or burning the letters, including those of Swift and Arthur Young, 'preserving only such as were ingenious, with possible hazard to the writers and their family' (p. 183).

The publication of Volume 3 of Burney's *Diary* including these claims would have caused alarm in the Granville family. Barrett headed Part 1 of Volume 4: 'The New Year – Character of Mrs Delany' (Barrett 1842d, p. 1) and the older woman's picture formed the frontispiece despite the fact that Delany died a quarter of the way through the volume. In the context of the Burney family's being mentioned in the published letters of Johnson (p. 15), Burney reported 'reading [Delany's] memoirs' in January 1788, and mentioned Delany's 'purity of prudence' in avoiding dangers in her earlier life (p. 17). In April 1788, however, Burney wrote: 'I have scarce a memorandum of this fatal month... the ever-remembered sacred scene that closed the earthly pilgrimage of my venerable, my sainted friend' (p. 130). This timing of Burney's writing and its evidence for her record demonstrate her methods of writing up her journal letters. After the intervention of the Warren Hastings trial, Burney had written in March that she had been seeing her friend in town 'by every opportunity; and received from her at Easter a letter written in her own hand, full of all the spirit, affection, fancy and elegance with which she could have written at twenty-five' (p. 130). Burney's words were written with retrospective knowledge of Delany's death and a later annotation produced in print would have exacerbated the threat to the Granvilles: 'Dear, precious, invaluable lines! how shall I preserve and love them to my latest hour!!' (p. 130).

Delany's 'Autobiography' and the Granville/ Dewes Dynasty

The cumulative effect of this account of Delany's final years drew the Granville family into a contest over life writing and the evidence of letters. At the age of 17, Delany had been forced into marriage with a man more than 40 years her senior for the sake of family connections but once widowed she had lived an independent life for 20 years before marrying an Irish clergyman in her early forties. Delany's own family had not supported her in the marriage to Patrick Delany but needed to reclaim her as a favourite at Court and confidante of the wealthy Duchess of Portland.

Augusta Hall, Lady Llanover (1802–96) published the papers of Mary Delany, her great-great-aunt, in six volumes in 1861 and 1862. There were two series of three volumes each and the intervening period between the two helped to stoke Llanover's ire against both Burney and the reviewers. Although 20 years had passed since the appearance of *The Diary and Letters of Madame D'Arblay*, the texts and letter evidence continued to interact with one another as this chapter demonstrates. The *Autobiography and Correspondence of Mary Granville, Mrs Delany* included not only Delany's views of Burney but a veritable torrent of abuse from the editor whose family now regarded Burney as an upstart social climber and collector of celebrity contacts. Responses to the *Autobiography* in the early 1860s included the views of Margaret Oliphant in *Blackwood's Edinburgh Magazine*, and among Charlotte Barrett's own untranscribed papers in the British Library is a draft review of Llanover's edition. These and other articles also revisited the reception of Burney's published *Diary*. Llanover could neither maintain her editorial neutrality nor hide family panic about times in a previous century spent in the company of Burney, the upstart daughter of a music master. The Bee of Gwent, as she became known through her work on Welsh culture, revealed more than she intended, however, in trying to reverse the Granville family out of its involvement with the Burneys.

Llanover's recovery of Delany took place as part of a family project in which Delany's prudence, privacy, talents and heredity must be represented within the letter form. Burney's efforts had not only presented certain facts about Delany but had also proved that the letter as life writing was public, open to accusations of boastfulness and likely to promote women above their station. Llanover's path was thus more difficult than she seemed to have appreciated and reviews of her work were almost universally critical over prolixity, failure of editing and sermonising within the surrounding text. Llanover's text was partly connecting narrative but it also attempted to explain and justify the letters as they were originally written. There were many footnotes about family connections and descent that Llanover invoked to replace Delany within the circle she would have graced in life. Delany herself was set aside in the rush to claim kinship with the noblest families in the land. Her family had been thwarted by the death of Queen Anne in 1714. They then sold their daughter in marriage to the highest bidder and subsequently bickered over the absence of a settlement from Delany's first husband Alexander Pendarves who died in 1725. The family disapproved of Mary's second marriage to Patrick Delany and at his death in 1768 Delany became even closer to the Duchess of Portland, recipient of the 'Autobiography'.

Llanover began her task by announcing that as 'Editor' and descendant of Delany's sister, Ann Granville, 'it was a duty to her memory to give these MSS to the world, the simplicity of which, together with the fact of their never having been intended for public perusal, will disarm the severity of criticism' (Llanover 1861a, p. ix). Family duty, remembrance and unplanned communication were highlighted within the Barrett-Gaskell model. Mary Granville was firmly defined as 'the eldest daughter of Bernard Granville, son of Bernard, the second surviving son of the celebrated Sir Bevil Granville' (p. vii). This Sir Bevil was a Royalist hero of the Civil War who died at the Battle of Lansdowne in 1643, and Llanover could also name an ancestor drowned at the sinking of the Mary Rose in 1545. Within a few lines Delany herself was fading from view in the welter of hereditary information.

It was claimed that 'the materials for a very complete record of her life and times have been supplied' from Delany's two unfinished manuscripts and her collected letters (Llanover 1861a, p. vii). Llanover used the brief fragment referred to by Burney that mentioned meeting Handel (pp. 1–6), and she also included an account of the singer Anastasia Robinson provided for Dr Burney (pp. 72–5). As editor, however, Llanover was already challenging Burney's involvement in the text of this account by explaining that the fragment was 'dictated to a confidential amanuensis' (p. vii). The 'Autobiography' that followed consisted of 18 letters written to the Duchess of Portland, and furnished the account noted by Burney of Delany's life up to 1733. Interwoven 'to render the chain of events more complete' were other family letters 'in their proper order of dates' (p. viii) so that the autobiography appeared to occupy over 400 pages of Llanover's first volume whereas there are only 70 pages of manuscript. As the 'Autobiography' opened, Llanover made the case for its accuracy at the same time as needing to indicate that Delany did not value the letter collections Burney had referenced in her publications. The recollections in the letters of 1740 were to be corroborated by 'the other letters to and from her family, which are introduced where they are contemporaneous, but which Mrs Delany did not herself collect, or consequently refer to' (p. 6).

Llanover used the medium of letters despite the fact that it appeared to follow the Burney model of applying family documents to life writing. Delany had, to some extent, chosen it for her in the choice of letters for the 'Autobiography' and the 'life and letters' approach to exemplary lives was clearly prevalent in the mid-nineteenth century. Llanover dignified the Delany documents as 'autobiography' and 'correspondence' in opposition to the more homely 'diary and letters', although ironically the evidence of Delany's control over her letters had already come from accounts in the *Diary and Letters*. It is notable also that the works of Burney and Delany would have been classified originally within the hybrid category of the court memoir described by Amy Culley as an elision of insider and documentary accounts within life writing (2012, p. 134). Delany's letters now form the second volume of *Memoirs of the Court of George III* (Kerhervé 2015). At the time, the original advertising for Burney's *Diary and Letters* emphasised the court material and the full title of Llanover's edition was *Autobiography and Correspondence of*

Mary Granville, Mrs Delany with Interesting Reminiscences of George the Third and Queen Charlotte: the title emphasising Delany's role within the royal circle.

Llanover's genealogical sermonising tone was intended to bolster Delany's suitability for the attentions of the Queen and the Duchess of Portland and so to contest Burney's claims of mutual sociability. Llanover added further gravitas with her allusions to the ancient line of the Granvilles although she found it difficult initially to excuse her great-grandmother Ann from the dynastic pursuit of her husband. Llanover had accepted a dynastic marriage herself and also needed to exploit the connection as part of her Burney vendetta. Despite the lack of evidence for Delany's support of the match between Ann and John Dewes at the time, Llanover added a note about the propriety of Ann's choice:

> Thus it was that the beautiful and gentle Ann Granville married Mr Dewes, whose descent was as ancient though not quite so illustrious as her own, and whom she preferred, with a moderate fortune, to the numerous admirers who had previously been rejected because their principles did not keep pace with their estates.
>
> (Llanover 1861b, p. 93)

This section would be quoted almost verbatim by John Dewes's great-great-grandson in his *History of the Granville Family* (1895, pp. 453–5). Roger Granville's father Bernard Dewes changed his name to Granville following an inheritance in 1827, and Roger used papers collected by his father to trace the Granville family back to Edward I to whom they are doubly related through the marriage of Catherine daughter of Lord Abergavenny to the High Sheriff of Devon in the sixteenth century (pp. 474–5).

The accumulation of ancestry in 1861 reinforced Llanover's disapproval of the presumed acquaintance of Frances Burney with Delany. Llanover also included a long footnote in Volume 2 of *Autobiography and Correspondence*, linking great-grandfather John, Delany's brother-in-law, to the 'ancient' Dewes family stretching back to Otho des Ewes of the Duchy of Guelderland in the Netherlands and his descendant Gerard des Ewes, a lord of Kessel (Llanover 1861b, p. 90). Llanover was able to trace the family to England in the reign of Henry VIII from a joint ancestor, Adrian d'Ewes. Adrian was three times great-grandfather to John Dewes and great-grandfather to the seventeenth-century antiquarian and baronet Symonds d'Ewes. *The Autobiography and Correspondence of Sir Simonds D'Ewes, Bart during the Reigns of James I and Charles I*, published in two volumes in 1845, helped Llanover to differentiate the letter writing of Delany from that of the upstart Burney. The papers of d'Ewes had appeared contemporaneously with

Burney's *Diary and Letters,* and they were also published by Llanover's publisher Bentley. Llanover alluded to the work in her own choice of title for Delany's *Autobiography and Correspondence,* and the statement of Symonds D'Ewes's nineteenth-century editor strengthened Llanover's claims that Delany was innocent of any acts of intentional life writing. James Orchard Halliwell announced, 'The knowledge that it was not intended for the press ensures its greater authenticity as an historical work' (1845, p. ix).

The D'Ewes autobiography was presented as having been composed from a diary whereas Delany's was composed from the 18 customised letters sent to the Duchess of Portland. These seem to have been written with the intention of forming a basis for the promotion of their friendship through which Delany arranged a narrative of the self. In the face of such first-person evidence, Llanover chose to present the letters as a reinforcement of the family connection and a quaint example of bygone manners despite the sense of self and self writing. This selfhood was, of course, contrary to the notion of nineteenth-century domestic womanhood. Kerhervé in his recent study has described Delany's autobiography as 'entre fiction et idéalisation' (2004, p. 26), and Delany gives her 'characters' fictional names such as 'Gromio' for her husband Alexander Pendarves and 'Averno' for his estate at Roscrow in Cornwall (Llanover 1861a, p. 35). Her suitor Lord Baltimore was 'Herminius' and her second husband Dr 'Dessario' (p. 296). The Duchess was called 'Maria', although her given name was Margaret Cavendish, and Delany signed herself Aspasia. The classical Aspasia was an outsider or immigrant in fifth-century BC Athens who was mistress to Pericles the Elder although it seems unlikely that her role as mother to his illegitimate son was a reason for retaining this pseudonym in a publication of 1861. The title denoted a female scholar and was associated with the Bluestocking circles of the eighteenth century (Bigold 2013, p. 133; Ylivuori 2019). The letters were not designedly written for publication but neither were they innocent of arrangement and meaning within the cultivated sociability that produced this communal life writing.

The one-sided correspondence of the 'Autobiography' provided a narrative but also retained its episodic character including conventional appeals for the letter sequence to end borrowed from both letter manuals and the epistolary novel. The 18 letters were embedded in family correspondence, mostly to Delany's sister Ann, and always headed 'Letter Number' with the subtitle 'Autobiography' to distinguish them from family record. Letter 1 concluded: 'I must take breath, and next post will pursue my subject. I hope you will consider how much your patience must suffer, repent of your commands and release me from my engagement' (Llanover 1861a, p. 9). The letters retained their markers of friendship, asking for putative replies as a convention for withdrawing or potential withholding. In Letter 5 Delany wrote 'your curiosity must be strong, if you can bear with patience another's long narration' (p. 32). At the end of Letter 16, Delany suggested that this was 'a very proper period' to bring 'my little history' to an end (p. 242). She was teasing her correspondent in a sophisticated epistolary construct. She wrote to the Duchess of her fear that the 'history' has not

> given you the entertainments and satisfaction you expected from it. If it has failed in those particulars, I hope it will at least convince you of the great confidence I have in your friendship, and how much I am your faithfully devoted ASPASIA.
>
> (p. 242)

Llanover seemed to take Delany's personal writing at face value without exploring the nature of the relationship between the two women. Having intervened early on to explain that Delany's first marriage was 'a very striking illustration of the complete disregard shown in marriage at that period to everything but the worldly settlement in life' (p. 32), Llanover tried after Letter 16 rather to explain the attentions of Lord Baltimore over some seven pages of a note in which she traced his family line in both directions (pp. 243–50). She then retired into the background to leave Delany's family to correspond with her in the intervening period covered by the 'Autobiography' up to 1733. Patrick Delany was introduced in Letter 17 some 50 pages later before another intervening gap of over a 100 pages at which point the final letter numbered 18 (pp. 411–13) led into a new chapter concerning Delany's correspondence with Swift. These letters had already put Delany into print (Hawkesworth 1766, pp. 228, 232), and Kerhervé lists the 13 letters dated between 29 May 1733 and 2 September 1736 written to Swift and used by Llanover (2005, p. 44, note 26). The last began: 'I receive too many advantages from your letters to drop a correspondence of such consequence to me' (Llanover 1861a, p. 569) but no further letters have survived. This correspondence joins with the letters to Ann and the 'Autobiography' to demonstrate how Delany was engaged in self-fashioning through manipulation of the letter-writing medium.

The subsequent volumes of the *Autobiography and Correspondence* continued with long footnotes and sequences of letters to and about Delany. Despite the firm family framework of the *Autobiography and Correspondence*, the identity of 'Mrs Delany' fluctuated from Mary Granville, to Penny Penny, Penelope Darves, 'our dear Pearl' (Llanover 1861b, pp. 247–8) and Aspasia. It was only latterly that she would become Burney's venerable angel. Llanover seemed unwilling to admit that survival as a woman with few resources was about role-playing in a way permitted by letter writing. Llanover rather employed her vast resources to elucidate family and social connections and to disconnect Delany and her family papers from Burney.

Riposte to Burney

It was in the second of the two series of Llanover's edition that the editor became clearly exasperated both with Burney and with critics of the 1861 volumes of the *Autobiography and Correspondence*. She had expected notice to be taken of inaccuracies in Burney's 1832 and 1842 accounts of Delany. The family were concerned about indiscretions and the apparent claims that Delany was supported financially by the Duchess of Portland. In the body of the text of Volume 4 of the *Autobiography and Correspondence*, Delany wrote on 27 January 1772 in a letter to Waddington's mother of receiving 'a perigot pie from the Duchess of Portland on the road, and potted rabbits' (Llanover 1862a, p. 407). This provoked an indignant retort from Llanover with almost no context at this stage in Delany's life:

> It is probable that Miss Burney, having on some occasion heard of similar Christmas presents mentioned in a similar manner, took it into her head to intimate, many years afterwards, that Mrs Delany was actually "maintained" by the Duchess of Portland! An imagination so evidently absurd that it would not be worth mentioning, excepting as a charitable endeavour to suggest a possibility of its having been a very ridiculous mistake instead of a wilful fabrication.
>
> (p. 407)

In Volume 6, the attack became more open when Llanover announced:

> It is here necessary to allude to the Diary of Madame D'Arblay, a subject particularly unpleasant to the Editor, who is very much averse to throwing discredit upon the dead, especially upon an individual who may have been known to persons still living.
>
> (Llanover 1862c, p. 125)

Barrett was, of course, still alive as were her sons Richard and Arthur along with Burney's nephew Charles Parr Burney and Susan Burney's granddaughter Minette Kingston and her husband Peter. Llanover continued to excuse herself by explaining that she had not intended to comment on 'the above-named authoress, whether under her maiden or her married name' believing that 'the obvious disagreement between the narrative in her "Diary" and the facts elicited from the original MSS published in the three first volumes of "The Autobiography and Correspondence of Mary Granville, Mrs Delany" would have been sufficient' (p. 125). Llanover wanted to believe in the naivety and simplicity of the life-writing process and that it was only Burney who was engaged in image-making. Reviews of the earlier volumes of the *Autobiography and Correspondence* had not uncovered any discrepancies and Burney was 'even quoted as if she had been an authentic and corroborative biographer, who had *honoured* Mrs Delany by *her notice*' (p. 125). Llanover devoted some four pages of diatribe to Burney. The first meeting between the two women, discussed above, was described as an account with 'scene and dialogue' (p. 126) and Llanover almost spat out her own sentences to declare Burney a 'writer of FICTION' who used 'pert and vulgar dialogue' (p. 127). Llanover invoked the authority of Croker (1833) with relief that his *Quarterly* review of the *Memoirs* could be described as 'just' (p. 126). A long footnote later to a letter dated 6 December 1783 explained that the Duchess of Portland paid no compliments to *Evelina* (p. 158), and Llanover described the diary of Miss Hamilton, governess to the Royal Princesses, as 'a refreshing contrast to the Diary of Madame D'Arblay' (p. 151).

There was a further sustained attack at the point in the *Autobiography and Correspondence* where Burney was appointed to her position at Court as recompense for Charles Burney's not being appointed Master of the Queen's band. Llanover claimed that Burney 'lost all consciousness of her actual or relative position. She lived in an ideal world of which she was, in her own imagination, the centre' (Llanover 1862c, p. 361). Llanover tried to gloss over Delany's part in an appointment that in reality served Delany's comfort and gave companionship to Georgiana, later Llanover's mother. Delany wrote to her niece Mary Port, Llanover's grandmother on 21 December 1785: 'Miss Burney... is indeed, a most valuable acquaintance, and on *Mary's account*, as well as my own, I am happy to have as much of her company as I can' (p. 325). '*Mary*' was the future Georgiana Waddington but Llanover added a note that this encounter was merely an opportunity for the Queen to assess Burney's capabilities as a reader. Since Delany's letters to Frances Hamilton (1820) were already in the public domain and could not be withdrawn, Llanover appended notes to letters commending Burney on her role at Court dated 3 July 1786 (pp. 365–6) and 17 May 1787 (p. 437). Producing an example of Burney's letter-writing style, Llanover added the comment that 'Miss Burney appears to have *begun* to emerge from the respectful self-abasement of her former style, and to appear more like her real self' (p. 241). Llanover asterisked Burney's 'happy occupation*' in the text of a Hamilton letter with the note that 'Miss Burney seems to have impressed Mrs Delany with the belief that she delighted in her office' (p. 437). Burney had revealed her dissatisfaction with her 'office' in the published *Memoirs* and *Diary* so that her treachery was now doubly in print. Mary Delany herself treated Burney with dignified sympathy, writing to Hamilton in Ireland, 'excellent as they are, her novels are her meanest praise. Her admirable understanding, tender affection and sweetness of manner, make her valuable to all those who have the happiness to know her' (p. 278). For Llanover no word could escape comment, however, and she protested in another footnote: 'For "admirable understanding" *talent* might be substituted; for "tender affection" a gentle sympathizing voice; and "for sweetness of manners" (*apparently*) timid and undeviating attention and respect to Mrs Delany' (p. 278).

Llanover seemed oblivious to the fact that she was undermining the value of correspondence as evidence by thus reinterpreting Delany's lack of observation, and in a further flourish, she produced eye-witness testimony of Burney's perfidy. During diary entries in the *Autobiography and Correspondence* for 1785, Llanover inserted letters from 1832 written by Anne Agnew to counter Burney's account of Delany in the *Memoirs*. Agnew, previously Anne Astley, was a 'waiting-woman' to Delany and esteemed to be a suitable witness 'in the full possession of her faculties', especially when she helpfully suggested in her own handwriting that 'authoresses take great latitude' (Llanover 1862c, p. 316). Agnew was specifically called upon to insist that Delany did not live on the Duchess of Portland's charity after being written out of her brother's will and that Delany's income was supplemented only by the justifiable generosity of the Royal Family (p. 317). Agnew also suggested that Burney could have had little opportunity to read any of Delany's letters despite Burney's claims of editorship intensified in the *Diary and Letters*. Llanover admitted that Agnew believed Burney's 'great regard' for Delany 'but that she was so in the habit of "*composing fictions*" in her novels, that she was not to be depended upon where she desired to work up an effect, or *herself* to produce an impression' (p. 320). The riposte, however, once again undermined the letter as evidence because of the need to re-sequence and to introduce retrospective testimony. Llanover suggested that Delany's use of the letter in the late eighteenth century was an antiquarian politeness but that Burney's was part of fiction.

The alternative documentary evidence of Delany's will in an Appendix at the end of Volume 6 brought Llanover's shrill commentary to its culmination. A tenth codicil to the will included a bequest to Burney of two medallions of the King and Queen and a copy of a painting done by Delany. Burney, it appeared, had been found out because she had quoted in the *Diary and Letters* from words addressed to 'esteemed friends' written on 22 February 1778 in the original will '*six years before Mrs Delany ever saw Miss Burney*!' (Llanover 1862c, p. 490). In Volume 4 of the *Diary and Letters*, Burney had used dramatic licence to appropriate the lines to herself because they accompanied the other copies of this same picture but she had also named Bishop Hurd as the original addressee of Delany's words. Burney also claimed to have had her choice of a mosaic flower and that a Quarto of Shakespeare was promised by Delany on her death bed (Barrett 1842d, p. 135) although Llanover denied the existence of these latter bequests. It is significant, however, that Llanover quoted from the original will because this suggested that Delany actually was indebted to the Duchess who was alive in 1778 when the will was originally made. The will stated that Delany would repay at her death a sum of £400 advanced to her by the Duchess to buy her house in London in St James's Place 'for which the Duchess had her bond' but 'would never receive the interest' (Llanover 1862c, p. 484).

The *Autobiography and Correspondence* was also in dialogue with the *Diary and Letters* through a 20-year-old review. Despite Llanover's exasperation with contemporary reviewers, she had pronounced Croker's 1833 review 'just' and his views in his 1842 *Quarterly* review were also happily in alignment with Llanover's particularly with regard to Burney's Court appointment and social status. Delany had been noticed by Croker in his review of Burney's *Diary* where he described her as a 'venerable relique of the days of Addison, Pope and Swift' (1842, p. 260) and Burney's 'private friend' (p. 264). Croker also pointed out that Delany had been 'made more generally known' by the publication of letters (p. 260), referring to the letters to Swift (Hawkesworth 1766) and Frances Hamilton (1820). On the subject of her appearance in the *Diary*, Delany was associated with what Croker described as the best part of the early volumes: namely their representation of the 'unaffected urbanity and condescension' of the Royal Family (p. 260) although he did discern that Burney's place at Court was for Delany's 'satisfaction' (p. 260). He had already suggested that the people in the *Diary* including Delany were only described for 'the glorification of Miss Fanny Burney' (p. 245). He suggested that Burney used Delany, however, to facilitate 'intercourse with her royal friends' (p. 260). Croker concluded, 'Miss Burney thought herself above her business, though we rather suspect she was really below it' (p. 260).

In the 1860s, Llanover's publication was not noticed either by the *Quarterly* or by the *Edinburgh Review* (Paston 1900, p. 283) in which Macaulay (1843) had been more supportive of Burney. The *Athenaeum*, however, provoked Llanover with a review of her first series that drew attention to her inexperience as an editor ('*The Autobiography and Correspondence of Mary Granville, Mrs Delany*' 1861, p. 11). Burney was invoked as a competing source and the text was nominated a 'diary' when the reviewer suggested that Llanover could have included 'the diary of the Court-life of Mrs Delany, which all readers desire to compare with little Burney; but which is now deferred to a fourth volume' (p. 11). The reviewer added: 'It is a reverence carried to such excess as to inflict great injury on some of the best materials ever put at the disposal of an editor for the illustration of social history' (p. 11). A few weeks later, the publisher Bentley nonetheless advertised the *Autobiography and Correspondence* in the *Athenaeum* for 9 March 1861 using judiciously edited quotations from a range of weekly publications including the *Saturday Review*: 'No more agreeable collection of miscellaneous gossip is to be found in biographical literature' ('The Books of the Season 1861, p. 340). He judiciously omitted the words 'On the whole' that began this sentence in the original and ignored its judgement that the first three volumes adopted 'the tone of an obsolete romance' without reaching the interesting period of Delany's residence at Court ('Autobiography of Mary Granville (Mrs Delany)' 1861, pp. 165, 166). Even with Bentley's pruning, however, family history was reduced to 'gossip' and the use of Delany's own words was undermined by that classification as 'biography'.

Reviews of the second series were more scathing. In *Blackwoods Edinburgh Magazine* in April 1862, Margaret Oliphant mused on the 'nature of female fame' in a piece entitled 'The Lives of Two Ladies'. The 'two ladies' were Delany and Hester Thrale Piozzi, and Oliphant finally declared the women, perhaps with some justification given her own circumstances, 'bright non-productives, possessors of a celebrity which neither genius nor labour has purchased' (1862, p. 423). The lives of two other women also emerged when Oliphant noted Llanover's 'passing onslaught upon poor Fanny Burney, that unlucky auto/biographist whom recent critics have cut to pieces so unsparingly' (p. 411). She observed, as has been demonstrated, that 'Mrs Delany's editress... occasionally pauses to mount a little pulpit of her own [and] comes in with amusing grandeur in her own person' (p. 409). Pointing out how Llanover contorts herself to insist that the Duchess of Portland could never have condoned Burney's novels, Oliphant suggested that it was Llanover who was the writer of fiction, having honoured 'the sisterhood [of female authorship] by almost joining it' (p. 411).

In its turn, *Fraser's Magazine* commented on the length of the work suggesting that more memoirs of this size could mean that 'the lives of the living would be entirely consumed in reading the lives of the dead' ('Mrs Delany; or a Lady of Quality in the Last Century' 1862, p. 448). The reviewer noted Burney's 'affectionate celebration of [Delany's] virtues and accomplishments' but was most entertained by the display of ingratitude and 'the flutter of irritated pride about Madame D'Arblay': 'It is insinuated that the blood of all the Granvilles was insulted by the intimacy between Mrs Delany and little Fanny Burney' (p. 455). Reference back to Croker's reviews was described in *Fraser's* as 'a piece of crowning spite against Madame D'Arblay' (p. 456), and the *Westminster Review* also drew attention to Llanover's revisiting the critical response to Burney's *Memoirs* and *Diary*. The reviewer found it difficult 'to disentangle the really pleasing characteristics of Mrs Delany from amid the mass of words with which they are here overgrown' and concluded resoundingly: 'if she is to be remembered at all in days to come, her reputation had better have been left even to the tender mercies of Madame D'Arblay' ('Mrs Delany' 1862, pp. 398–9).

Among the remaining papers of the Barrett family in the British Library is a letter to Charlotte Barrett that quotes from this review, rather judiciously omitting the word 'even' (Sharpe 1862, p. 226). Barrett's correspondent also mentions the *Fraser's* review and tells Barrett that 'the opinion of the world is all your way, the very ill nature of the hostile book, all helps to raise Mad[ame] D'Arblay' (p. 227). Aged 75, Barrett had by this time been a widow for nearly 20 years and had outlived three of her five children. The British Library papers also include the manuscript of a review of Llanover's *Autobiography and Correspondence*. A printed version of this review seems not to be extant but the letter quoting the *Westminster Review* article also discusses the publication of 'your article' (p. 226) around the same time. The manuscript piece likens Llanover to Mrs Wittiterly collecting distinguished visitors in *Nicholas Nickleby* ('Review of Delany Memoir' 1862, p. 43). It describes Llanover's approach to Burney as 'vixenish spite' towards one who had been a comfort to Mrs Delany in her old age (p. 42). The manuscript, quoted also by Kerhervé (2004, p. 33, note 114), suggests that Delany would be unknown 'had not the Memoirs of Madame d'Arblay come to light' (p. 10) but the disingenuousness of the claim that 'this reader skipped Mrs Delany' (p. 10) seems hard to credit if Barrett herself were the author of the draft review thus preserved and catalogued.

In 2009 and 2010, exhibitions of Delany works and memorabilia took place at the Yale Centre and Sir John Soane's Museum in London. The visual reinterpretation of Delany is part of Delany's recovery and recuperation from the effects of the *Autobiography*, and there are a number of layers to this revival of her circulating character. In an article to accompany the exhibition, Alicia Weisberg-Roberts explained that Delany's artistic skills were part of her rediscovered identity and that the paper collages of her 'Hortus Siccus' were 'a work through which she created herself' (2009, p. 10). Delany's paper-cutting skill was designed to cause art to replicate and exactly impersonate nature, and her collection was commended by scientists of the day including Joseph Banks and Erasmus Darwin (Hayden 1980, p. 158). Roberts sees it as a fault in biography that Delany's role at Court as a symbol of public virtue has come to overshadow her wider cultural role in 'influential circuits of Georgian Britain' (2009, p. 1). Positioning Delany as a court memoirist, Alain Kerhervé has also endeavoured to restore Delany to the canon of early modern epistolary writing by classifying her within a French model and expanding 'le corpus delanyen' (2004, p. 55). At the same time, the collective sociability of public life conducted through the salon was one of the features of the Bluestocking circle (Pohl and Schellenberg 2003, p. 11) and the letter as a gift took its place within material culture as a mark of friendship (Eger 2009, p. 110). In the autobiography in letters rearticulated for the Llanover edition, Delany 'created herself' for the Duchess of Portland, and letters functioned as a significant part of the network of Bluestocking friendships that the women shared. The flowers later also became an extension of the letter as life writing, with each image representative of friendship and a social network (Eger 2009, p. 136). The evolution of her visual and verbal sociability demonstrates that Delany in effect engineered her own reinvention and image-making throughout her long life, and these inventions resemble an epistolary collaboration on what Mireille Bossis has dubbed a 'methodological journey' (1986, p. 68).

On 27 August 1782, the Duchess of Portland wrote to Lord North on behalf of her friend and collaborator, 'I ought to apologize for the taking the pen out of Mrs Delany's hand' (Kerhervé 2009, p. 128). As part of their friendship, Delany and Margaret Cavendish, Duchess of Portland, collaborated in creativity and life writing, and yet Delany's *Autobiography and Correspondence* became part of a *post-mortem* of their friendship based on money and worldly favour. Llanover's attempt to recover Delany through letters for a Victorian readership produced a controlled antiquarian image that caused Delany to lose the multi-faceted identity she had cultivated in her own times. The re-ownership of the lives of both Burney and Delany was also over-written by the trend for celebrity accounts of the Court. It has been suggested that nineteenth-century publication destroyed Bluestocking networks (Pohl and Schellenberg 2003, p. 14), and Llanover's edition had a part to play in this. In terms of collaboration, Llanover could not admit that Burney had a role in Delany's image-making. Delany's role playing and self writing had to be neutralised because Burney could not be forgiven for putting herself into the marketplace and taking Delany with her.

Bibliography

'Autobiography of Mary Granville (Mrs Delany),' *Saturday Review*, 11 (16 February), pp. 165–7.

Barrett, Charlotte (ed.) (1842b) *The Diary and Letters of Madame D'Arblay. Volume 2: 1781–1786.* London: Henry Colburn.

Barrett, Charlotte (ed.) (1842c) *The Diary and Letters of Madame D'Arblay. Volume 3: 1786–1787.* London: Henry Colburn.

Barrett, Charlotte (ed.) (1842d) *The Diary and Letters of Madame D'Arblay. Volume 4: 1788–1789.* London: Henry Colburn.

Bigold, Melanie (2013) *Women of Letters, Manuscript Circulation and Print Afterlives in the Eighteenth Century.* Basingstoke: Palgrave Macmillan. doi:10.1057/9781137033574

Bossis, Mireille (1986) 'Methodological Journeys through Correspondences', *Yale French Studies*, 71, pp. 63–75.

Burney, Frances (1832a) *Memoirs of Doctor Burney, Volume 1.* London: Moxon.

Burney, Frances (1832b) *Memoirs of Doctor Burney, Volume 2.* London: Moxon.

Burney, Frances (1832c) *Memoirs of Doctor Burney, Volume 3.* London: Moxon.

Croker, John Wilson (1842) '*Diary and Letters of Madame D'Arblay, Vols I, II, III*', *Quarterly Review*, 70, pp. 243–87.

Culley, Amy (2012) '"Prying into the Recesses of History": Women Writers and the Court Memoir', in Cook, Daniel and Culley, Amy (eds) *Women's Life Writing 1700–1850: Gender, Genre and Authorship.* Basingstoke: Palgrave Macmillan, pp. 133–149. doi:10.1057/9781137030771

Derry, Warren (ed.) (1982a) *The Journals and Letters of Fanny Burney. Volume 9: 1815–1817.* Oxford: Clarendon Press.

Derry, Warren (ed.) (1982b) *The Journals and Letters of Fanny Burney. Volume 10: 1817–1818.* Oxford: Clarendon Press.

Dewes, Court and Keate, George (1793) 'Mary Delany', in Kippis, Andrew (ed.) *Biographia Britannica. Volume 2.* 2nd edn. London: Longman, Strahan & Co.

Eger, Elizabeth (2009) 'Paper Trails and Eloquent Objects: Bluestocking Friendship and Material Culture', *Parergon*, 26(2), pp. 109–38.

Granville, Roger (1895) *The History of the Granville Family.* Exeter: Pollard.

Halliwell, James Orchard (ed.) (1845) *The Autobiography and Correspondence of Sir Simonds D'Ewes, Bart during the Reigns of James I and Charles I. Volume 1.* London: Bentley.

Hawkesworth, John (1766) *Letters Written by the Late Jonathan Swift. Volume 2.* London: T Davies.

Hayden, Ruth (1980) *Mrs Delany: Her Life and Her Flowers.* 2nd edn. London: British Museum Press, 2000.

Hemlow, Joyce, Burgess, Jeanne M. and Douglas, Althea (eds) (1971) *A Catalogue of the Burney Family Correspondence, 1749–1878.* New York: New York Public Library.

Hemlow, Joyce, Cecil, Curtis D. and Douglas, Althea (eds) (1972) *The Journals and Letters of Fanny Burney. Volume 1: 1791–92.* Oxford: Clarendon Press.

Hemlow, Joyce, Douglas, Althea and Hawkins, Patricia (eds) (1984) *The Journals and Letters of Fanny Burney. Volume 11: 1818–1824.* Oxford: Clarendon Press.

Kerhervé, Alain (2004) *Mary Delany (1700–1788) Une Épisolière Anglaise du XVIIIè Siècle.* Paris: L'Harmattan.

Kerhervé, Alain (ed.) (2009) *Polite Letters: The Correspondence of Mary Delany (1700–1788) and Francis North, Lord Guilford (1704–1790).* Newcastle: Cambridge Scholars.

Kerhervé, Alain (ed.) (2015) *Memoirs of the Court of George III. Volume 2: Mary Delany (1700–1788) and the Court of King George III.* London: Pickering & Chatto.

Letters from Mrs Delany (widow of Doctor Patrick Delany) to Mrs Frances Hamilton from the year 1779 to 1788, Comprising Many Interesting and Unpublished Anecdotes of Their Late Majesties and the Royal Family, etc. (1820). London: Longman.

Llanover, Lady (Augusta Hall) (ed.) (1861a) *The Autobiography and Correspondence of Mary Granville, Mrs Delany. Volume 1.* London: Bentley.

Llanover, Lady (Augusta Hall) (ed.) (1861b) *The Autobiography and Correspondence of Mary Granville, Mrs Delany. Volume 2.* London: Bentley.

Llanover, Lady (Augusta Hall) (ed.) (1862a) *The Autobiography and Correspondence of Mary Granville, Mrs Delany. Volume 4.* London: Bentley.

Llanover, Lady (Augusta Hall) (ed.) (1862c) *The Autobiography and Correspondence of Mary Granville, Mrs Delany. Volume 6.* London: Bentley.

Macaulay, Thomas Babington (1843) 'Diary and Letters of Madame D'Arblay', The Edinburgh Review, 76, 523–70.

'Mrs Delany' (1862) Westminster Review, n.s. 21, pp. 374–99.

'Mrs Delany; or a Lady of Quality in the Last Century' (1862) Fraser's Magazine, 65, pp. 448–57.

Oliphant, Margaret (1862) 'The Lives of Two Ladies', Blackwoods Edinburgh Magazine, 91, pp. 401–23.

Paston, George [Symonds, Emily Morse] (1900) Mrs Delany (Mary Granville): A Memoir 1700–1788. London: Richards.

Pohl, Nicole and Schellenberg, Betty A. (2003) 'A Bluestocking Historiography', in Pohl, Nicole and Schellenberg, Betty A. (eds) Reconsidering the Bluestockings. San Marino: Huntingdon Library, pp. 1–20.

'Review of Delany Memoir' (1862) Barrett Collection 3702B, British Library, pp. 9–58.

Sharpe, Emily (1862) 'Letter to Charlotte Barrett', 9 April. Barrett Collection 3705, British Library, pp. 226–7.

Skinner, Gillian (2014) '"A Tattling Town like Windsor": Negotiating Proper Relations in Frances Burney's Early Court Journals and Letters (1786–87)', Eighteenth-Century Life, 38(1), pp. 1–17. doi:10.1215/00982601-2380007

'The Autobiography and Correspondence of Mary Granville, Mrs Delany' (1861) Athenaeum, 1732, 5 January, pp. 9–11.

'The Autobiography and Correspondence of Mary Granville, Mrs Delany' (1862) Athenaeum, 1784, 4 January, pp. 11–15.

The Correspondence of Samuel Richardson. Volume 4 (1804) London: Philips.

'The Books of the Season' (1861) Athenaeum, 1741, 9 March, p. 340.

Troide, Lars E. and Cooke, Stewart (eds) (2012) The Early Journals and Letters of Fanny Burney. Volume 5:1782–1783. Oxford: Clarendon Press

Weisberg-Roberts, Alicia (2009) 'Mrs Delany from Source to Subject', in Laird, Mark and Weisberg-Roberts, Alicia (eds) Mrs Delany and Her Circle. London: Yale University Press, pp. 1–19.

Ylivuori, Soile (2019) Women and Politeness in Eighteenth-Century England: Bodies, Identity and Power. Abingdon: Routledge. doi:10.4324/9780429 454431

5   *Letters and Memorials of Catherine Winkworth* (1883 and 1886)

A Life in Translation

Susanna Winkworth (1820–84), editor of the privately published *Letters and Memorials of Catherine Winkworth* (1883, 1886), lived her life alongside her sister Catherine (1827–78) and so was an almost exact contemporary of her auto/biographical subject. Susanna was also looking for a model to represent lives in letters, although not necessarily to challenge the representation of women's lives. The Winkworth sisters were peripherally but significantly involved in the preparation of Elizabeth Gaskell's *Life of Charlotte Brontë*, and although the text of *Letters and Memorials* was not widely circulated, it has become known because of its relevance to the lives of Gaskell and Brontë. Like Gaskell, Susanna utilised her own letters and wove her own words as editor into the 'memorials' of her family project. The Winkworths were, however, biographers in their own right through their work as translators, and published life writing offered the Winkworth sisters professional roles as middle-class women. Before the publication of Gaskell's *Life*, Susanna had translated, for Baron Bunsen, the *Life and Letters* of the German historian Barthold George Niebuhr (Winkworth 1852). Catherine wrote lives through hymns in her *Christian Singers of Germany* (1869) and translated Emma Poel's *Life of Amelia Wilhelmina Sieveking* (1863) and the *Life of Pastor Fliedner of Kaiserworth* (1867).

Letters and Memorials used the framework of Catherine Winkworth's life to present a family record in letters and linked narrative. The text bears many of the hallmarks of the life-writing model of the late nineteenth century outlined in Chapters 2 and 3. The Winkworth family is seen to be trading and withholding letters. Susanna's linking narrative focusses the reader's attention but her frequent use of ellipses to disguise more personal information draws attention to absences and omissions. The sense of duty emerges strongly from a flood of logistical arrangements and family gossip. The emergence of conduct information and a rationale for the life or lives represented is also strong. *Letters and Memorials* was a printed record of manuscripts no longer extant in which the family used their own words apparently re-fixed within a published volume. At the same time, Susanna's choices reveal themselves in the silenced voices and narratives that can now be correlated from other accounts including the letters of Gaskell and Brontë, and even the records of a private asylum. This chapter introduces the Winkworth family and then considers the model of letters in translation and the impact of contemporaneous family recording. The organisation of the private record re-sited family relationships and caused omissions and ellipses within the text. The chapter reviews the resultant public places within *Letters and Memorials*. These places are created by the mirroring of other lives within letters, specifically those of Gaskell and Brontë but also Dora Hensler, Alice Winkworth and Margaret Shaen.

The Winkworth Family

Susanna and Catherine Winkworth were the first and fourth daughters of the silk manufacturer Henry Winkworth and his first wife Susanna née Dickenson. Having moved from London, the family was initially based in the Ardwick area of Manchester and, from 1850, at Alderley Edge, a village in Cheshire. There were three other sisters, Emily born in 1822, Selina in 1825 and Alice in 1833, and also three brothers. Their mother died in 1841 and their father remarried in 1845. *Letters and Memorials* reflected the complex logistical arrangements that surrounded a family of the period with multiple caring requirements and, for the women, the need to manage a household while acquiring an education. Despite the family's size and variability in health, the Winkworths, like the Gaskells, acquired other wider and substitute family members whose lives also appeared in the account named for Catherine. When the family first moved to Manchester, for instance, Emily and Susanna remained in Islington in the household of their uncle, Thomas Winkworth. When Thomas's wife Sarah died in 1836, her children were cared for by their aunt, Eliza Winkworth who was Henry and Thomas's unmarried sister. Susanna went with Eliza to Mannheim in Germany in 1843 along with Thomas's three daughters (Winkworth 1883, p. 68). Selina and Catherine travelled to Dresden to join them in 1845. Thomas's second daughter Fanny married hurriedly in 1855 and emigrated to New Zealand (Winkworth 1883, pp. 505–6) but the couple were lost on a voyage to Melbourne in early 1857 (Winkworth 1886, p. 95). Thomas's fourth daughter Jessie lived in Shanghai in 1864 (Winkworth 1886, p. 427), and was mother to translator and biographer Catherine Winkworth Mackintosh who published lives of missionaries in the early twentieth century and translated the work of her uncle François Coillard (Coillard 1897; Mackintosh 1907; *Young Soldier of France* 1915).

Other aunts responded to other family crises including Mary from London, whom Susanna accused of using leeches too vigorously in one of Catherine's early illnesses (Winkworth 1883, p. 23), and also Selina and Eliza from Pembury, home of their grandfather Stephen Dickenson (p. 295). In *Letters and Memorials*, there are two Aunt Elizas and 'Aunt

E.M.W.' [Winkworth] (p. 118) must be distinguished from 'Aunt A.E.D.' [Dickenson] (p. 280). Another aunt Mary on their mother's side left two young sons, Clement and John Crispe, who were part of the new wider family. John was apprenticed to Henry Winkworth's company. He was 'like an elder brother to us' (p. 15) and attended Emily's wedding (p. 294) as well as ensuring the preservation of 'Aunt A.E.D.' in her home after the death of her brothers Stephen and Daniel Dickenson (p. 118). Clement featured less often and married in 1853, as Catherine wrote to her friend Eliza Paterson on 14 February: 'Engagements are all the fashion now. We have heard of eight or nine within the last ten days…our cousin, Clement Crispe, was married (more's the pity!) on Wednesday last' (p. 385).

Lives in Translation

Letters and Memorials made clear that the family was spread out across a number of households through the 50 years of Catherine's life. Roles within the family were shared and redeployed when split between London and Manchester and then in various locations where they were seeking 'to embody themselves in action' or otherwise to improve health or education. When Elizabeth Gaskell first wrote to Catherine, Catherine was in Southport for her health and there were letters from the Isle of Wight and from Malvern as well as European locations. Such separations, of course, produced letters as well as the likelihood of their preservation as a reminder of the absent author. Some of the letters' contents had to be doubly edited or translated both for the original and for the future readers. When Susanna was away in Bonn, for instance, Catherine wrote on 12 March 1851 that the Pembury aunts, Eliza and Selina Dickenson, were gossiping, making mittens and netting curtains at Alderley: 'Aunt Selina is always making a servant and Aunt Eliza a doctor of herself' with John Crispe in attendance (Winkworth 1883, pp. 278, 279). Susanna, however, had been to a ball and engaged in 'very sinful' (p. 279, note) dancing with the Prince of Prussia. Catherine reported that '[t]he Aunts have been bothering…to have your letter read to them, so I read all I could, and tried to conceal the long gaps left out in my reading, but in vain' (p. 279). Catherine continued: 'to my infinite amusement, the rank of your partner quite covers the sin of going to a ball and waltzing in their eyes. Besides, "his Uncle the King is so religious"' (p. 279). If letter reading was a hazardous practice in the company of aunts, it was nonetheless useful as a memorial of family life to be re-valued and revisited despite the additional gaps inserted by Susanna as editor. Catherine wrote to Emily, for instance, on 25 November 1851:

Fid's bark has brought me running down to see the letters […] On Sunday when Süschen was here, we had a grand reading of your letters aloud, after dinner, around the fire (omitting what we did not think edifying to Mamma, *e.g.* those dissertations on dress), and Papa observed two or three times, very emphatically, as he generally does over your letters: "Emily certainly writes remarkably good letters" [...].

(p. 316)

Catherine's reputation as a 'grave lady' noted by George Eliot in a letter to John Blackwood on 10 April 1859 (Cross 1885b, p. 72) was only somewhat relieved when Susanna retained for the future family readers her subsequent remark to Emily: 'Your dress information we *were* glad to have, especially to know how you look yourself; for as to the rest, I think it is very doubtful whether we shall ever have any occasion for ornaments in our hair again' (p. 316). This observation was followed in the text by another editorial ellipsis to compound the earlier letter-reading omissions. Letters in action and in retrospect were here demonstrating their potential to be withheld evidence.

Letters and Memorials was designed both to translate the shared family record of the Winkworths and to reframe the shared ambition of Susanna and Catherine to do something with their lives. On 12 June 1845, Catherine wrote to Susanna: 'Our whole life here is only a striving to express ourselves, to embody ourselves in action. We can scarcely conceive of such a thing as a passive life' (Winkworth 1883, p. 84). The sisters exchanged letters discussing their prospects in life and Catherine wrote to Susanna from Dresden on 9 March 1846 outlining the problems they faced as conservative middle-class single women with high-performing intellects:

> If I were a man, I would study till things got clear to me, and then I would speak and write; but being a woman, I shall never gather positive facts enough, or acquire the habit of thinking deeply and clearly, so as to be able to write, which is the only way in which a woman can express her thoughts, as she may not speak. I am, however, perfectly satisfied, since I am a woman, with my position in the world, I mean in the middle class of England; for I think that a woman there has more opportunity than in any other situation of getting correct ideas of life.

(pp. 103–4)

The letter professes to accept this inequality but the reasoning and philosophical debate across the volume belies the suggestion that the sisters were unable to think 'deeply and clearly'. As editor, Susanna preserved her own reply in which she dismissed two potentially respectable occupations for women: governess or novelist. She had already, however, explained the strict rules about suitable pastimes for the Winkworth children and that their reading matter was mostly religious. At an early age, Susanna devised the concept of a fairyland called 'All-Mood' (p. 13) and for the purposes of storytelling the younger children Catherine, Selina, William and Stephen had each adopted 'a continent and a kingdom of Natural History' in a manner now reminiscent of the young Brontës (p. 14). In 1846 she told Catherine: 'I would much rather get my living by writing novels with good principles in them than by being a governess, but for this, alas! I should never have talent, since I killed my childish imagination' (p. 108). A footnote here indicated that Susanna was discouraged from such storytelling by an aunt, presumed to be Eliza Winkworth, who discovered 'hidden manuscripts'. Susanna explained to the later family audience that she used mental arithmetic to 'stifle my unruly faculty' and to focus on religion (p. 109). The 1846 letter was, however, retrospectively dominated by Susanna's musing, 'I wonder if people ever get decently paid for translations' (Winkworth 1883, p. 108).

Susanna used the headline 'How to Find One's Proper Aims' to frame Catherine's letter of 9 March 1846 in which she differentiated the study of men from the study of women (Winkworth 1883, p. 103). This was a conduct-model letter, and on 27 March, Susanna in return practised her advice and letter-writing skills as sister and mother, observing that: the '*ultimate* object of all rightly-minded people must be to turn their existence to as great account as may be' (p. 104). She urged Catherine to find 'the *right* path' (p. 104) and lauded her talent of acquiring knowledge and of expressing herself before observing, 'I care more than I did about being fit to make myself independent' (p. 108) and posing the key question about translation as a livelihood (p. 108). Susanna acknowledged, however, the existence of 'external circumstances' over which they had no control (p. 105). She also devoted a significant proportion of the letter to her public duties for visiting the poor in a District and for teaching Sunday school that, she acknowledged in another footnote (p. 107), became more a part of her life when their father remarried. This occupation was then both preserved and juxtaposed with that final paragraph about translation and independence. Simon Morgan observes that middle-class women of the period could base their identity around 'civic virtue and public service' (2007, p. 5) which is what Catherine and Susanna did in the latter part of her life. For the family record, Susanna hedged independence from the new family home with the charitable works that would define the sisters' later lives.

In effect Susanna used *Letters and Memorials* to translate her advice to Catherine into the retrospective framework of their future lives. The letter survived for nearly 40 years to do this job and to suggest a narrative shape for their life writing. Lorraine Macknight has studied Catherine Winkworth's discovery of 'hymns as literature, theology and, unexpectedly, as livelihood' (2014, p. 42) which was the result of Susanna's proposal. Rachel Webster suggests that translation allowed the sisters to contribute to theological debate 'through unassuming literary forms' (2018, p. 34) and to commit to an orthodox Anglican position that rejected Unitarianism (p. 18). Life writing was also inextricably linked with the professional work of translation. The Winkworths' published works framed and re-sequenced daily life through prayers, hymns and sermons and a complex relationship developed between the original writer and the translation. The sisters' publications operated at a boundary between privacy and public education but as translators they both reinterpreted the hidden editor of the original text and were responsible for a uniformity of voice in the translated work they produced. As Susanne Stark points out, 'translation involves active moral decision-making' (1999, p. 41) and it was thus that Susanna's methodology in *Letters and Memorials* emerged from the sisters' translation work.

Catherine's translation of hymns and biographies as more accessible and possibly 'unassuming' forms of literature answered a need for respectable independence and intellectual stimulation for a woman in her position. The first series of her *Lyra Germanica* of 1855 had appeared in 23 editions by the end of the century with a second series extending to 12 editions (Lee 1900, p. 195) although her DNB entry dated the first series incorrectly (p. 194). In *Letters and Memorials*, Susanna translated a letter dated 30 May 1855 from Baron Bunsen about Catherine's work, commending 'the successful progress of her beautiful efforts' (Winkworth 1883, p. 494). After Bunsen suggested the addition of hymn tunes, Catherine's *Chorale Book for England* appeared in 1863 with music by William Sterndale Bennett and Otto Goldschmitt. Goldschmitt was the husband of the singer Jenny Lind with whom Catherine corresponded and theirs is one of the series of letters noted as missing in Susanna's preface to *Letters and Memorials* (p. vii). The hymnbook has been described in a study of Winkworth's translations as 'a facilitating and very portable cultural agent' (Macknight 2014, p. 42). The hymn like the letter is a shared and circulating communication, more so perhaps than the sermons of the Dominican John Tauler (*The History and Life* 1857) or the letters of a Prussian historian (Winkworth 1852) translated by Susanna. In her DNB entry, Elizabeth Lee described the *Lyra Germanica* as having 'translations [that] are always faithful, and at the same time poetical' (1900, p. 195). The hymns themselves in their original *Lyra Germanica* context also attracted commentaries and background information which suggest guided reading and thoughtful intervention by Catherine in her choices and representation of the German originals. A discussion of *Hymns Ancient and Modern* by Susan Drain (1989) gives some insight into the way translation within the model and constraints of a hymn was part of the intellectual milieu in which the Winkworth sisters operated. Drain quotes Catherine's approach to the revisions of a hymn for the burial of a child. Catherine explained in 1874 to the Committee revising *Hymns Ancient and Modern* that she had updated lines from the second series to read 'Lost awhile our treasured love, /Gained forever, safe above' (Drain 1989, p. 278). Catherine wrote on 15 July:

> in heaven we shall see how death itself even when it takes our best-loved treasure may prove a gain, if it makes us desire to reach the same place of reunion and happiness. I can't put that neatly into two lines but I give a slightly modified version.
>
> (p. 279)

Translation and condensed meaning were closely linked for inclusion in a text designed from the daily life of the Christian Year.

In their published works, the Winkworths were almost invariably permitted a 'Translator's Preface' in which they explained the bases on which the translated works had been reproduced in the English language. It has been suggested that their contributions would have been subordinate to the male voices in these publications (Stark 1999, p. 35) but this was not a wholly consistent feature of their works. Susanna was not named in the first volume of Niebuhr's *Life* (1852) but her name appeared in later editions and volumes. She wrote a 'Translator's Preface' to *Signs of the Times* (Bunsen 1856) and *God in History* (Bunsen 1868; Winkworth 1868) although for *God in History* she was framed by a preface in the form of a letter to Bunsen's son Henry from Arthur Stanley, Dean of Westminster. For *Theologica Germanica* (Pfeiffer 1854) and the sermons of John Tauler (*The History and Life* 1857), Susanna's translations were embedded within male prefaces by Charles Kingsley, and she was subordinated as a continuator of the *Life of Luther* (Kœnig 1855). Catherine was named on the title page of *Lyra Germanica* with equivalent status to her original authors although her name was misspelt as 'Catharine' in the 1855 first edition. Her life of Amelia Sieveking (1863), written by the German writer Emma Poel, was described as 'Edited with the author's sanction' as was Susanna's un-prefaced translation of *German Love* (Müller 1858) and Catherine's *Life of Pastor Fliedner* (1867). In 1871, Catherine 'selected and translated' *Prayers from the Collection of Baron Bunsen* and in her preface dated from Clifton on 3 June she referred to 'manuals of devotion' and to the context of her own hymn-writing vocation: 'good prayers, like hymns, will justify themselves by finding their own way to the hearts that want them' (1871, p. ix). Hymns and prayers were, perhaps, more palatable and 'unassuming' when 'written' by a named female translator or with the sanction of the original author.

The prefaces written by Susanna and Catherine read like letters, dated from their place of residence. The contents suggested a thoughtful appreciation of their task albeit a certain rigour towards their reading public. Their strictures highlighted also some of the features of letters as life writing: their privacy, their alteration when re-read in sequence and their potential for secrecy. Catherine described the hymns in *Lyra Germanica* as 'hymns, not sacred poems' although 'many of them may seem to English readers adapted rather to purposes of private than of public devotion' (*Lyra Germanica* 1855, p. xi). Letters too are private and not originally written as autobiographical constructs for public consumption. In *Christian Singers of Germany*, Catherine made clear that she had understood the exigencies of her art, recognising 'the disadvantage of being all translations from one hand' (1869, p. 4). She pointed out that the poems lost their 'variety of diction' originally identifiable through 'the date of composition or the individuality of the author' (p. 4). *Letters and Memorials* restored the voices of individuals but they were also integrated within the scheme of one author, Susanna.

Writing at Christmas 1867 in her preface to Bunsen's *God in History*, Susanna found herself subordinate to the Dean of Westminster but she also explained her aim 'to give as close a rendering of my author as the respective genius of the two languages admitted' (1868, pp. xv–vi). Her preference was to prioritise 'strict fidelity to the thought' over 'elegance of diction' (p. xvi). In *Letters and Memorials* too, Susanna tried to give a rendering of domestication and education but the frequent elisions also conveyed a sense of reticence where both fidelity and elegance had to be sacrificed to secrecy. In her edition of Tauler, Susanna had already explained that she wanted to share her own family experience of these sermons but had been concerned enough to omit passages obscure to the general reader and those referring to unacceptable 'Romish ritual'. Her selection guided by 'historical truthfulness' omitted Romishness but each chosen sermon was presented in its complete form (*The History and Life of the Reverend Doctor John Tauler* 1857, p. xii). She stood up for her own opinions and decisions in her 'Translator's Preface' dated 29 November 1856 where she concluded: 'for the light in which I regard these facts, I am alone responsible' (p. xx). As Stark points out, a translator is not 'a transparent figure' (1999, p. 23), and neither is the compiler of an edited letter collection.

A closer investigation of the Niebuhr *Life and Letters* clearly demonstrates that translation was not a neutral channel to life writing. The discussion here analyses Susanna's preparation for her own role in *Letters and Memorials* through her earlier approach to the hidden editor. Susanna explained in her memorial of Catherine that Gaskell knew Charles Bunsen socially and proposed to him the idea of her doing the translation of Niebuhr's letters. Bunsen (1791–1860) was a Prussian scholar and diplomat who was ambassador to London from 1842 to 1854, and the work of translation formed, according to Susanna, 'an important epoch to both Catherine and myself, being the occasion of my introduction to Bunsen, and, through him, to literary work which Kate at a subsequent period also undertook' (Winkworth 1883, pp. 169–70). Susanna extracted from her sisters' letters to demonstrate political interests and the ongoing discussion of a life in letters. Catherine wrote to their sister

Emily on 10 May 1849, explaining that Niebuhr's *Life* was 'composed almost entirely of his own letters, with just enough of his biographer's writing to make them comprehensible' (p. 181). Emily wrote to Susanna on 11 May 1849, after a trip to Hampton Court with Gaskell, 'Bunsen says the Life is divided into epochs, each chiefly filled up by Letters. That many of these might be advantageously omitted, and parts of the *"Kleine Schriften"* inserted' (p. 182). *Kleine Schriften* are essays or minor writings. Catherine then wrote to Susanna on 10 October 1849 after reading 'a good deal of Niebuhr': 'my fear is that you would want to extract too much and make his life too large' (p. 213).

In the eventual Preface to *Life and Letters* then, Susanna explained that she had made choices/omissions to avoid both repetition and the treatment of issues 'only of German interest' (Winkworth 1852a, p. viii), and this was in addition to the omission of intimate topics by the original editor, Niebuhr's sister-in-law, Dora Hensler. About a quarter of the new preface by Susanna was a direct (translated) quotation from Hensler who had removed some 'expressions of affection' and apologised for those retained 'unawares' (p. v). Hensler was presented in her own words as denying her own role as a learned editor: 'This aim is simply biographical; to communicate whatever can throw light upon his natural capacities and dispositions' (1852a, pp. v–vi). Winkworth initially followed Hensler in claiming that the life was 'chiefly composed of extracts from Niebuhr's letters' with short narratives to 'fill up the chasms they leave in his history,…prefixed to each of the periods in which it is divided' (p. v). At the same time she (the translator) also pointed out that the 'biographical notices' had been both abridged and expanded by her subsequent research (p. vii). Winkworth was distinguishing between the life written by Hensler and that researched by her in her translation. In the text, Hensler was described as 'supplying the place of a daughter' to her father-in-law, Professor Philipp Hensler, an early tutor of Niebuhr (Winkworth 1852a, p. 29). Susanna also seems to have thought of herself as an intellectual daughter to Bunsen. Many of the Niebuhr letters were addressed to Dora, a strong-minded decisive woman 'with deep feeling and no ordinary cultivation' (p. 30), and in Chapter 2 of the *Life and Letters* her relationship with Niebuhr was described in a rather contorted if not evasive manner. Dora was six years older than Niebuhr, 'a circumstance which prevented any shyness and restraint on her side while the unusual maturity of his character rendered him not too young to be a companion to her' (p. 30). Dora was depicted as someone who would be a reliable lifelong friend. In fact, in the course of her research, Susanna discovered that Niebuhr had wanted to marry Dora after the death of his first wife, Amalie, but that he eventually compromised by marrying, as his second wife, Dora's niece Margarethe (Winkworth 1883, p. 282). Susanna, in the guise of Dora, provided this tortured explanation of a companionship that would stretch across three volumes.

Susanna claimed that she had retained the balance and proportion of topics, although on a smaller scale than the original, but evidence in *Letters and Memorials* later demonstrated that this truncation was also caused by the pressure on time needed for the translation – a task shared with Catherine – and by the demands of the publishers Chapman and Hall. Catherine was involved by 8 January 1851, and wrote to Susanna compounding intellectual and domestic tasks: 'I reckon on not doing much needlework while I am with you doing Niebuhr' (Winkworth 1883, p. 267). By 9 May, Catherine was translating four pages in 2½ hours and cancelling a visit to the Shaens, Emily's in-laws, because the manuscript was needed by June: 'my not going to Crix will obviate the necessity of my hurrying with some needlework, and I can translate pretty fast' (p. 286). Sewing was never far away as a disguise for ambition but in *Letters and Memorials*, Susanna explained that she had moved on from merely translating and piecing together Hensler's German memoir. The 'simply biographical' letters had been superseded by their connecting narrative and 'the Biography was essentially an original work' (p. 287). When Chapman later asked her to prepare a second edition, Susanna reported to Catherine on 29 March 1852 that their friend John James Tayler, Unitarian minister and Professor of Manchester College, had told her 'the more I leave Madame Hensler and write for myself the better it is' (p, 282). In reporting Tayler's advice, Susanna was effectively preparing to be the future editor of Catherine's 'biographical' letters as an original hybrid work of auto/biography.

Contemporaneous Lives

Editing brought with it responsibility for balance and fidelity but the contemporaneous lives of the Winkworths were subject to realignment and omission. As a family record, *Letters and Memorials of Catherine Winkworth* was itself a letter to the future on the boundary between public and private writing. Susanna felt, however, that Catherine could not be adequately represented in public because several important series of letters had not been preserved (Winkworth 1883, p. viii) and so, as editor, she drew back from public printing. *Letters and Memorials* was privately printed and circulated initially only within the family although Volume 1 is now, of course, searchable online. This first volume was addressed by 'Your affectionate Aunt' 'TO MY NIECES AND NEPHEWS' and opened with an optional greeting left blank but printed 'Dear [...]' (p. ii). It was thus possible to personalise and gift the volume at the time of its original production but future survival and public circulation have now redefined and complicated Susanna's project. The recipient of the copy held in the University of California remains blank even pristine; the copy held by the British Library is addressed to 'Maggie' and signed 'Margaret Josephine Shaen April 15th 1883' in the same hand, presumed to be Susanna's. One copy has an identifiable recipient but another resides without a direction in a library more than 5,000 miles from its point of origin, and yet Susanna asked for honourable silence and conditional reading in her original preface addressed to 'Dear [...]':

> I now present this volume to you under the strict condition that you will keep it to yourself, and not lend or show it to any friend, however intimate; that is, not until my death, and then only with the consent of your Parents, should they survive. I depend upon your honour to observe this condition.
>
> (p. ii)

Given that a subsequent preface (pp. v–viii) was also addressed to the nieces and nephews, it would appear that these strictures were added later.

The potential readers from the next generation were the children of Susanna's siblings, Stephen, Selina and Emily. Stephen married 'a pretty little Miss Thomasson' (Winkworth 1886, p. 227), whose letters featured in Susanna's second volume, and they had two children, Mabel born in 1861 (pp. 269, 379) and Stephen (known as Steenie) born c. 1864 (pp. 471, 609, 668). Emma née Thomasson (1839–1909) and Stephen senior were members of the Alpine Club, and Emma was the first woman to climb the Jungfrau in Switzerland in 1863 (Winkworth 1886, pp. 399, 401; Lingard 2014, p. 5). Selina and her husband John Collie (Winkworth 1886, p. 96) had four sons: the eldest of whom, Harry (pp. 177, 308), was born in 1858 and emigrated to New Zealand. Their second son, Normie (pp. 287, 379), was sponsored by his Uncle Stephen at university and, as John Norman Collie (1859–1942), became a renowned chemist and mountaineer (Baly 1943). After Selina's only daughter Susan was born in 1861 (p. 328), Emily wrote to Agnes Sandars née Paterson on 10 April, 'What noble children Selina's are' (p. 343). By May 1858, Emily was mother to Margaret, William Godfrey (known as Freddie), Agnes (known as Lily) and Arthur (p. 199). After her last child, Frank was born in 1862 (p. 378), Emily was 'constantly living beyond her strength' (p. 390) and a 'suffering invalid' for the rest of her life (Shaen 1912, p. 67).

Of the 'parents' in Susanna's preface, Selina died in February 1885 and Stephen in 1886. Emily and her husband William Shaen both died in 1887. The majority of the backstops to the circulation of *Letters and Memorials* stipulated above had, therefore, been removed by 1887, within four years of the production of Volume 1. When the second volume appeared in 1886, it was overseen by Margaret, eldest daughter of Emily, whose copy of Volume 1 is now held in the British Library. For her later abridged version, *Memorials of Two Sisters*, Shaen consulted 'Miss Winkworth' (1908, p. viii), referring to the youngest Winkworth sister

Alice. Like Susanna and Catherine, Alice Winkworth remained unmarried and, in 1882, was elected to the Barton Regis Board of Guardians on which she served for 37 years (Martin 2002, p. 8). Alice also seems to have taken on her elder sisters' work with Clifton High School which, until 2013, offered the Alice Winkworth Scholarship. Margaret Shaen had other memorial responsibilities by 1908. Of Emily Shaen's children, the youngest Frank was close to death by 30 January 1879 and Margaret retained Susanna's letter to a family friend in the aftermath of Catherine's death: 'I fear we are losing the dear nephew whom she had gone to nurse [on her final journey to Monnetier]...a boy of 16, of singular promise, intellectually and morally, beautiful in person and in disposition' (Winkworth 1886, p. 705). Margaret's other brothers William and Arthur died in 1888 and 1890 respectively so that Susanna had ostensibly created a family record for a rapidly dwindling audience. In practice, however, the injunction to her original family readers provided short-lived insulation from licensed public scrutiny. In 1900, Elizabeth Lee could acknowledge in the Winkworths' DNB entry that she had consulted *Letters and Memorials* and used 'private information' meaning that knowledge of the existence of the text was already in circulation within 16 years of Susanna's death in 1884 (Lee 1900, p. 196).

If the identities of the future reading audience seem to have been fixed in Susanna's overarching letter to the future, roles within the family were more fluid at the time when *Letters and Memorials* was originally composed. This fluidity was reflected in modes of address preserved by Susanna in spite of her other omissions. Catherine, for instance, concluded a letter dated 24 June 1845: 'dear Mamma Sukey...Ever your affectionate child' (Winkworth 1883, p. 89), and Susanna addressed Catherine and Emily as 'My dear children' on 2 August 1849 (p. 195) and 'My dearest Children' on 20 September (p. 202) even though she was only two years older than Emily. It was not just maternal roles that were redeployed. Susanna wrote to Catherine on 24 March 1854 from Carlton House Terrace where she was working with Bunsen: 'You will think I am dead, or have forgotten my wife. Neither is the case. I am only so desperately busy day after day' (p. 432). Catherine then wrote to Susanna the next day:

> My dearest Susie,—I had by no means forgotten my husband but was waiting to know where to direct to him. Now, like a good wife, I will take care to tell no secrets, and have immediately scratched out all that part of your letter about politics to make sure.
>
> (pp. 435–6)

On 23 February 1855, Catherine again wrote to Susanna, 'I should have written before, as becomes a wifie' (p. 487). It may merely be that Susanna was acting the elder sister. Alternatively, these identities were perhaps being appropriated as markers for Susanna's professional role as translator of political German works and unofficial secretary to Bunsen as opposed to Catherine's more domesticated translation of the hymns in *Lyra Germanica*.

One significant omission amidst the 'scratched out' ellipses was that of the Winkworths' eldest brother Henry, born in 1823. Susanna's editorial choices suggested that after the death of nine-year-old Willy in 1839, there was only one brother, the younger Stephen, and from the first she described their cousin John Crispe as like an elder brother (Winkworth 1883, p. 15). Catherine idolised Willy and later wrote that she was haunted by 'his wasted form and pale spiritual face' (p. 76). On 5 January 1840, Catherine was still referring to 'brothers' in the plural (p. 29). It was during the immediate aftermath of Willy's death that slight evidence for the existence of Henry remained in Catherine's Journal printed in *Letters and Memorials* where she wrote about a conversation with '*A boy some years older than herself' suspected of 'an inclination towards Atheism' (p. 25). The nature of a conversation with 'X' away from home in Leamington makes it likely that this must have been a brother, Henry being four years older than Catherine. 'X' occurred again in the last entry for 1839 and on the very next page, on 12 January 1840. Catherine noted 'X. *sorrow*' (p. 29), only a few days later describing elusive hope within 'such a weary heart'; her word, at the age of 12, was 'illudes' (p. 30).

Henry Winkworth the younger has been traced to the records of the Ticehurst private asylum in Sussex where he was treated between 1845 and 1847 and discharged 'not improved' (Mackenzie 1992, pp. 128–9). Charlotte Mackenzie suggests that his treatment was too expensive for the family and that Susanna was paying doctor's bills during her time as Stephen's housekeeper in the 1850s (p. 101). The Winkworths' maternal grandfather Stephen Dickenson is also recorded as being in the asylum between March and May 1830 and again between March and October 1837 but he was apparently functioning as a farmer and deacon until his death in 1841. Susanna devoted several paragraphs to grandfather Stephen with her fond memories of 'these Pembury households' in *Letters and Memorials* where she chose to introduce the Kent family connections and their influence on their mother despite Catherine's lesser involvement with them compared with the three elder Winkworth sisters (Winkworth 1883, p. 5). By comparison, their brother Henry's mental health issues seem to have allowed him to be cared for at home but not to be discussed even in the privately printed volume for the family. It may be that a form of mania affecting his religion made his illness distressing. Nonetheless, his care would have added to the otherwise readily admitted round of sick visits and nursing that took its toll on the sisters' health and work capabilities. Emily was an invalid after the birth of Frank, and Susanna and Catherine were regular sufferers from unspecified but debilitating complaints. The letters contained much discussion of travel in pursuit of health together with a range of logistical arrangements to ensure that invalids were accompanied and cared for. The care described did not extend to any ostensible discussion of Henry although he was in their lives, and this omission echoes the situation of the younger George Austen who never featured in the letters of his sister Jane. The Austen-Leighs refer briefly to the Austens' third son as suffering from fits and being 'unable to take his place in the family' (1913, p. 20). There is other evidence that 'he grew up weak in intellect' but with financial support (Austen-Leigh 1942, p. 334), and Park Honan concludes that he was deaf and living in another household (1987, pp. 16, 24).

Letters and Memorials also had a problem with a family member who could be less conveniently forgotten in the form of Eliza Leyburn who became the Winkworths' 'new Mamma' in 1845 (Winkworth 1883, p. 81) and was known as 'Grannie' (Shaen 1908, p. 14) by the future readers of the family record. After the death of his first wife, Henry Winkworth had left the education of his children to Susanna as his eldest daughter and she explained in the connecting narrative of *Letters and Memorials* how she acted as his housekeeper and companion (Winkworth 1883, p. 42). In 1845, Eliza Leyburn became a threat to the sisters' autonomy but in *Letters and Memorials*, Susanna left commentary to the words of her younger sister Catherine, by this time aged 18. On 21 April 1844, Stephen's birthday, Catherine would describe her mother, who had now been dead for three years, as her 'best friend on earth'. 'My life is altered', she continued, 'altered from that hour; my sorrow put an end to my childhood, & I began to feel the solemnity of life' (p. 75). Only three months later, Catherine wrote of her shock at the marriage and the 'thought of a stranger taking the place of my dear dead Mamma', concluding, however, that the happiness of her father meant that it was her 'duty to do all I can to make the lady happy' (p. 78). A new chapter of *Letters and Memorials* began with the journal of 5 March 1845: 'Miss Leyburn, *i.e.*, my new Mamma comes home to-morrow; therefore this is the last day of this period of my life' (p. 81). On 23 March, Catherine added: 'we are all settling into our respective places. I hope & believe that we shall be very happy with our new Mamma, tho' she is very *different* from our *own* Mamma' (p. 81). Susanna then interpolated in square brackets '[Here ends the *Journal* for a considerable time.]' (p. 81), to be replaced by the joint diary of Selina and Catherine on their long trip to Dresden (1845–46). Susanna commented that 'Catherine always looked back to this period as an important epoch in her mental development' (p. 81), the implication being that this 'epoch' would unfold away from the newly re-formed family home. While visiting London prior to the removal to Germany, a letter dated 26 June 1845 from Catherine to Susanna provided proof of 'metaphysical questionings' but it revealingly concluded 'Goodbye my dear Mamma Sukey' (p. 89). Eliza Leyburn had doubly usurped the role of mother and a careful cropping of material allowed this criticism to remain within *Letters and Memorials* despite the dutiful behaviour that was mostly reflected in the remaining letters.

Eliza Leyburn was described in the later *Memorials of Two Sisters* as 'a lady of suitable age and much personal attraction' (Shaen 1908, p. 14) and much loved by her grandchildren, presumably including Margaret Shaen herself. Eliza Leyburn had made efforts to accommodate her stepdaughters. Catherine wrote to tell Emily on 31 October 1854 about reading Kingsley's philosophy lectures to Eliza 'secretly marvelling how much she understood'(Winkworth 1883, p. 470). Catherine, however, exclaimed revealingly to her sister 'What a change from the time when she came to us' (p. 470). Catherine's early Journal was omitted from Shaen's new version to be replaced by a retrospective passage written by Alice Winkworth, sole survivor of the stepchildren, who would care for Eliza until Eliza's death in 1893, aged 94. Alice was only ten years old at the time of her father's remarriage. The revised description in 1908 of Eliza's role in poetry recitals, games and handicrafts suggested that she was more comfortable with children and this level of achievement and aspiration would not have fitted with the earnest need for education of the elder stepdaughters at the time of the remarriage. Susanna's austere commentary and Catherine's eagerness to do her duty were replaced in *Memorials of Two Sisters* with an account that was milder but not much less cutting.

Gaskell and Brontë

Outside the widened circle of blood relations in Kent, London and Lancashire, *Letters and Memorials* also demonstrated that the Winkworths were seeking a substitute family within the new circles of education, religious enquiry and translation that embraced them. Clearly embedded within the sisters' lives and work were F.D. Maurice, the Shaens, Patersons, Martineaus, Taylers and Sattersfields. This section, however, traces the roles of Elizabeth Gaskell and Charlotte Brontë. Gaskell introduced Susanna to Bunsen and so was instrumental in her involvement with Niebuhr, whose translated life in letters preceded Gaskell's own *Life of Charlotte Brontë*. The discussion here focusses on the emergence of these two 'Lives' and the interweaving or mirroring of Gaskell's life within the Winkworths'.

The Gaskell and Winkworth families became intimate when the sisters were variously tutored by William Gaskell on the recommendation of Agnes and Eliza Paterson. *Letters and Memorials* is the only source for the earliest surviving letters from Gaskell to Catherine written in 1848, and in these Gaskell promoted herself for adoption by the family. Gaskell, who was 17 years Catherine's senior, wrote on 11 November: 'Do call me Lily, and never mind respect to your elders' (Chapple and Pollard 1966,

p. 62). In this letter, Gaskell called Emily and Selina 'my girls' and reveal-ingly appropriated the family while omitting to mention that she was the author of *Mary Barton*: 'I wish I had five sisters who were bound to love me by their parents' marriage certificate; but as I have not, I mean to take you for sisters and daughters at once' (p. 62). Among the 'five sisters', Gaskell associated Alice Winkworth with her own children but courted Emily, second sister to Susanna, as a friend. In May 1854, for instance, Gaskell bemoaned to her friend Mary Green the loss of a visit from Emily caused by an outbreak of scarlet fever: 'a visit I look forward to as one of the greatest pleasures of the year, from one year to another...I shall get a glimpse of her; that is all I am *so* sorry' (Chapple and Shelston 2000, p. 110). Gaskell wrote several long disquisitions on Florence Nightingale including one to Catherine dated 11–14 October 1854 (Chapple and Pol-lard 1966, pp. 305–10), and in *Letters and Memorials* on 30 October 1854 Emily recorded in a letter to Catherine 'a delicious letter from Lily—a regular folio' (Winkworth 1883, p. 468) which is the one dated 27 October 1854 (Chapple and Pollard 1966, pp. 316–21).

In her Preface, Susanna described 'the unreserve of sister-like inter-course' between Catherine and Gaskell. Catherine wrote more letters to Gaskell than to anyone else except Emily (Winkworth 1883, p. vii) and this appropriation of a family relationship may be an ongoing part of the tensions and 'family' divisions that emerge from the letters avail-able. Susanna's retrospective comments on Gaskell put her in a domestic context despite her success as a novelist: 'Her books, indeed were only written when all possible domestic and social claims had been satisfied' (Winkworth 1883, p. 128). Gaskell had been dead for 18 years in 1883, and the editors of Gaskell's letters suggest that Meta Gaskell destroyed her mother's Winkworth letters before *Letters and Memorials* was com-piled (Chapple and Shelston 2000, p. xii). Gaskell's daughters Marianne, Meta and Julia were still living and William Gaskell would only die in 1884. It has been suggested that the publication of the Niebuhr *Life and Letters* caused particular tension between Gaskell and Susanna in the mid-1850s (Uglow 1993, p. 276), and evidence of this relationship can be traced in the texts chosen by Susanna with the added benefit of letters from Gaskell to mirror the events of *Letters and Memorials*. Writing to Eliza Fox in London on 27 August 1850, Gaskell traced Su-sanna's immersion in 'German life' in Bonn (Chapple and Pollard 1966, p. 131), and on 17 November 1851, she wrote to Fox: 'Susanna W. keeps Wm busy at work correcting her proofs, for my dear! Niebuhr is on the point of appearing before the public! And poor Mary Barton gets more snubbed than ever as a "light and transitory" work' (p. 172). In May 1852, Gaskell's chosen correspondent was also Fox for the information that Susanna was 'cock a hoop about Niebuhr, she snubs me so, and makes such love to William he says "my life is the only protection he has"—else he *knows* she would marry him' (p. 190). Back within *Letters and Memorials*, Emily had previously written to Catherine from London on 7 May 1849 that 'Lily is deep in love with Mr Forster' (Winkworth 1883, p. 179) although it may be that Gaskell herself was the source of this information since it was accompanied by telling ellipses. In 1852, Gaskell decided, however, to marry Susanna to John Forster 'then I cd die in peace feeling my husband was in safety' (Chapple and Pollard 1966, p. 190). Susanna was perhaps too difficult as a substitute sister or daughter within Gaskell's circle although she featured regularly as a visitor and nurse. Alternatively, since Susanna was more often in Manchester house-keeping for Stephen and meeting Gaskell in person, the perceived rift may merely be exacerbated by the survival pattern of different sequences, as Susanna herself recognised in her reluctance to publish (Winkworth 1883, p. viii). For the sake of balance, it can now be observed that Gaskell was willing to recommend Susanna to the historian Leopold Ranke in 1853 as a woman 'whose general acquirements and amount of learning are such as are rarely possessed by a woman' (Chapple and Shelston 2000, pp. 88–9).

It was Catherine who accompanied Gaskell on her visit to Haworth seeking material for *The Life of Charlotte Brontë* as described in Gaskell's letter to her daughter Marianne of 27 July 1855 (Chapple and Pollard 1966, p. 364). Catherine would also go with Gaskell to Rome after the publication of the *Life* although she stayed with Emily's sister-in-law Emma Shaen who could not go out very much for health reasons. It was Catherine who received, preserved and shared the prized description of Brontë dated 25 August 1850 (Chapple and Pollard 1966, pp. 123–6) that has been cited in the controversy over Brontë's *Sharpe's Magazine* obituary ('A Few Words about "Jane Eyre"' 1855; Hughes and Lund 1999, pp. 124–30). This letter was circulated by the Winkworths at a time when there was also ongoing competition for Gaskell's attention. Susanna wrote to Catherine from Bonn on 26 August 1850 complaining that the Gaskells had misunderstood the nature of her task for Bunsen (Winkworth 1883, pp. 247–9). Catherine wrote back on 30 August: 'I am going to write to Lily, and shall try to make her comprehend how much more correct your appreciation of your enterprise has been all along than hers' (p. 250). Selina then 'put in a line': 'A letter from Lily telling us about her visit to Lady Kay-Shuttleworth at Windermere to meet Miss Brontë, who seems by all accounts to be a veritable Jane Eyre (in appearance certainly), but alas! without the Mr Rochester' (p. 250). Emily then wrote to Catherine and Selina at Malvern from Crix also on 30 August acknowledging the circulation of the letter: 'Thanks for Mrs Gaskell's. Poor Miss Brontë, I cannot get the look of the grey, square, cold, dead-coloured house out of my head' (p. 246).

This circulation of the original 25 August letter demonstrates that the Winkworth sisters were unsure how to interpret Charlotte Brontë herself and how to cope with Gaskell's enthusiasm. Emily continued on 30 August: 'One feels that her life at least *almost* makes one like her books, though one does not want there to be any more Miss Brontés' (Winkworth 1883, p. 246). When Catherine wrote to Susanna on 12 August 1854, her comment that 'Miss Bronté is very nice' had to be finished with editorial ellipses (p. 447). The Winkworths also played their part in the retelling of misinformation. Catherine wrote to Eliza Paterson on 5 December 1849 that *Shirley* did not have the 'disagreeable parts' of *Jane Eyre* and was not as good as *Mary Barton* and (Harriet Martineau's) *Deerbrook*. With its 'stiffness and dryness', Catherine found *Shirley* 'altogether painful' but linked the novel's effects with Brontë's alleged life: 'the author herself is threatened with consumption at this time, and has lost her two sisters, Ellis and Acton Bell, by it. Their real name is Bronté of the Nelson family' (p. 215). Catherine reported to Emily on 10 November 1851: 'a downcast letter from Miss Bronté, as if her lonely life were weighing on her spirits' (p. 299). Brontë's letter was to Gaskell, and such a reference reinforced the later *Life* accounts of Brontë. These themes, of melancholy and of the life in the fiction, continued when Catherine herself met Brontë and wrote to Emily on 16 March 1853 about the 'terrible sadness' of *Villette*: 'Lily says that the journey to London and Belgium is drawn from her own life, she can recognise numerous little touches in it that she had heard' with characters 'literally drawn from life' (p. 387). On 25 March, Catherine continued: 'her men are so much better than other women's men. But, poor creature, how she must have suffered in that lonely Yorkshire life, and when she was a governess!' (pp. 391–2). Sympathy for Brontë as a woman had grown over these four years, cultivated by Gaskell, and this culminated in two significant letter-written contributions to life writing: Catherine's long letter about their joint visit to Gaskell at Plymouth Grove in 1854 (pp. 437–40) and Brontë's letter to Catherine from her honeymoon two months later (pp. 445–6).

On 8 May 1854, Catherine wrote to Emma Shaen, having held back in order to write about meeting Brontë and the conversations about her impending marriage. Catherine assumes that they will see Brontë less once she is Mrs Nicholls (Winkworth 1883, p. 437). Catherine's words to Brontë reported by Catherine and retained by Susanna were that 'one's home ought to be the one fixed point, the one untroubled region in one's lot; at home one wants peace and settled love and trust not storm and change and excitement' (p. 439). She thus defended quite dramatically the character of Arthur Nicholls whom Brontë herself described as 'a Puseyite and very stiff' (p. 439). To Emma privately and for later family consumption, Catherine rated Nicholls much less highly as a husband than Will Shaen, Emily's husband and Emma's brother, a lawyer who promoted women's education. Arthur Nicholls was, of course, still alive when *Letters and Memorials* appeared but not in the public eye or likely to have been known to the limited audience of the original publication. Catherine concluded, 'I *guess* the true love was Paul Emmanuel after all, and is dead' (p. 440), a startling conclusion for a 'grave' lady. The fiction was thus being intertwined with the life within a circulating letter as a further strand of the misinformation promoted by Gaskell herself.

Brontë's 30 July 1854 letter from her honeymoon (Winkworth 1883, pp. 445–6) was an almost direct response to their conversation in May. The letter was addressed from Cork care of Plymouth Grove and redirected to Alderley so Gaskell would have been aware of the communication as perhaps Brontë wished her to be. The original is now in the Brotherton collection and it appeared in Thomas Wise's Brontëana collection in the 1930s. Catherine was, of course, safely Anglican as far as correspondence with Arthur Nicholls's wife was concerned and the letter duly circulated as part of the trading in friendship. On 1 January 1855, Gaskell exclaimed, 'Miss Brontë's letter *is* very nice; I wish she'd write to me' (p, 480; Chapple and Pollard 1966, p. 327), and it seems likely that the July letter was under discussion since the younger woman would surely have yielded any other available material for the *Life* to her 'affectionate Lily'. Around this time during 1855, the arrangement and acquisition of material for lives also became a factor in correspondence involving Gaskell, the Winkworths and Brontë. The only source for Gaskell's incomplete 1 January letter is the printed copy in *Letters and Memorials* where it continued with a long extract printed by Susanna from a letter by Florence Nightingale detailing nursing in the Crimea (Winkworth 1883, pp. 480–81). Gaskell was already moving on to a new enthusiasm for Nightingale: 'great beauty, and of her holy goodness, who is fit to speak' (p. 480). Gaskell advised Catherine a week later on 7 January 1855 about the arrangement of the hymns in *Lyra Germanica* to match each to a Sunday and its readings (Winkworth 1883, p. 481) since the daily life of the Christian Year was a framework for hymn writing (Macknight 2014, p. 19; Drain 1989, p. 85). The embedding of dated reading was also under discussion in Gaskell's reports on the progress of her novel *North and South* (Chapple and Pollard 1866, pp. 328–9, 330–31; Chapple and Shelston 2000, p. 123) and her dispute with Dickens over its serialisation in *Household Words* to which Brontë referred in July 1854 (Winkworth 1883, p. 446). By the end of August 1855, a footnote in *Letters and Memorials* read: '*Charlotte Brontë Nicholls had ended her brief eight months of bright happy married life on the 31st March, and, shortly after, her husband and father had requested Mrs Gaskell to write her "Life"'(p. 501). In the main body of the text, Susanna wrote to Catherine after the visit to Haworth that Gaskell's 'quest for materials [for Miss Brontë's "Life"*] has been most successful, and I really think that now she will make a capital thing of the "Life" and show people how lives ought to be written' (p. 501). In *Letters and Memorials*, this commendation was also presented in parallel with a request by Julius Hare's widow to Susanna in February 1855 to complete the translation of her husband's *Life of Luther* (pp. 483–4). The ongoing commentary about how dateable lives ought to be written occurred within a life hedged about by life-writing methodologies that Susanna latterly controlled in *Letters and Memorials*.

Susanna did not have enough of her life left to complete her task, and her agenda was partially revised when Margaret Shaen provided an introductory note to the posthumous Volume 2 of *Letters and Memorials*. Susanna had left 1856, 1857 and 1858 'nearly complete' (Winkworth 1886, p. 41) but had authorised the printing of additional material annotated by Shaen that would reinforce Susanna's final adherence to the Anglican Church after her period of Unitarianism (pp. 35, 180, 691). In Volume 2, the handover of the memorial was signalled at the point where 'I' became 'Susanna' in the linking narrative (p. 233). The title of Shaen's much abridged *Memorials of Two Sisters* (1908) suggests that the interwoven lives of all the Winkworth sisters were then repurposed as a conduct and recovery narrative. Shaen explained in her revised text that the grandson of Christian Socialist F.D. Maurice had urged her to produce her edition as a 'picture of family life of sixty years ago' (1908, p. viii), and the title of the work may itself be traced via Maurice through *Letters and Memorials*. It was he as well as his sister who asked Susanna in a letter dated 1 February 1855 to undertake the completion of his brother-in-law Hare's *Life of Luther* (Winkworth 1883, p. 483). Mary Maurice, another of Maurice's sisters, was a teacher who also published on educational matters and had produced her own *Memorials of Two Sisters* (1833) as a devotional guide in letters and journals commemorating two other sisters, Anne (1799–1826) and Emma (1807–32). Given the renewed contact with Maurice's grandson signalled in Shaen's introduction, this seems to have been the source of the revised title and direction of Shaen's abridged edition.

It is fortunate that *Letters and Memorials* was not expected to circulate, despite its published form. Susanna might otherwise have been tempted not to preserve in public some of the less grave behaviour that sheds light on the character of her family. On 1 January 1852, Catherine wrote to Susanna, 'I inform you that Niebuhr is lying on the table looking so grand in his new dress. He looks larger than I expected and highly respectable' (Winkworth 1883, p. 325). *Letters and Memorials*, as a private family record, can be less respectable and so allow Niebuhr to be appropriated as a family member when Catherine, in a family full of aunts, announces, 'I am a sort of *Aunt* to the book' (Winkworth 1883, p. 325). Writing in the late twentieth century, Sidonie Smith describes women as 'doubly estranged' in the 'autobiographical contract' because of their role at the margins and their denial of self writing (1987, p. 49). In the mid-nineteenth century, the women writing women's lives through letters would have found themselves doubly marginalised and tortured by their position in relation to the biographical subject: a woman whose life is told in letters. *Letters and Memorials* was written like a widow's domestic memoir to a family enlarged by the sisters' mode of life and by the adoption of external members through correspondence. The Wink-worths may appear to have been self-silenced because their channel to market was translation. Their existence in *Letters and Memorials* gave them a new voice, however, and it is precisely because Susanna was also a published author of guided letter writing that her choices should be re-examined within the terms of the nineteenth-century model.

Bibliography

'A Few Words about "Jane Eyre."' (1855) *Sharpe's London Magazine*, 6 (June), pp. 339–42.

Austen-Leigh, Richard (ed.) (1942) *Austen Papers, 1704–1856*. Colchester: Spottiswoode Ballantyne.

Austen-Leigh, William and Austen-Leigh, Richard (1913) *Jane Austen: Her Life and Letters: A Family Record*. London: Smith Elder.

Baly, E.C.C. (1943) 'John Norman Collie 1859–1942', *Obituary Notices of Fellows of the Royal Society*, 4 (12), pp. 329–56.

Bennett, William Sterndale and Goldschmitt, Otto (1863) *Chorale Book for England*. London: Longman.

Bunsen, Charles (1856) *Signs of the Times*. Translated by Susanna Winkworth. London: Smith Elder.

Bunsen, Charles (1868–70) *God in History* (3 vols). Translated by Susanna Winkworth. London: Longman.

Chapple, John A.V. and Pollard, Arthur (eds) (1966) *The Letters of Mrs Gaskell*. Reprint, London: Mandolin, 1997.

Chapple, John and Shelston, Alan (eds) (2000) *Further Letters of Mrs Gaskell*. Manchester: Manchester University Press.

Coillard, François (1897) *On the Threshold of Central Africa: Translated from the French and edited by Catherine Winkworth Mackintosh*. London: Hodder and Stoughton.

Cross, John Walter (ed.) (1885b) *George Eliot's Life as Related in Her Letters and Journals. Volume 2*. Edinburgh: Blackwood.

Drain, Susan (1989) *The Anglican Church in Nineteenth-Century Britain: Hymns Ancient and Modern (1860–1875)*. Lampeter: Edwin Mellen Press.

Honan, Park (1987) *Jane Austen: Her Life*. Reprint, London: Phoenix, 1997.

Hughes, Linda K. and Lund, Michael (1999) *Victorian Publishing and Mrs Gaskell's Work*. Charlottesville: University Press of Virginia.

Kœnig, Gustav (1855) *The Life of Luther*. With explanations by Archdeacon Hare. Continued by Susanna Winkworth. London: Longman.

Lee, Elizabeth (1900) 'Catherine Winkworth', in Lee, Sidney (ed.) *Dictionary of National Biography. Volume 62*. London: Smith Elder, pp. 194–6.

Lingard, Christine (2014) 'Primitive, Cheap and Bracing: the Gaskells and the Alps', *Gaskell Society Newsletter*, 58 (Autumn), pp. 2–6.

Lyra Germanica (1855). Translated by Catherine Winkworth. London: Newnes.

Mackenzie, Charlotte (1992) *Psychiatry for the Rich: A History of Ticehurst Private Asylum, 1792–1917*. London: Routledge.

Mackintosh, Catherine Winkworth (1907) *Coillard of the Zambesi*. London: Fisher Unwin, 1907.

Macknight, Lorraine (2014). *Minding the Hymn: Catherine Winkworth and the Transmission of German Hymnody to Australia.* Unpublished PhD thesis. Charles Sturt University, New South Wales.

Martin, Moira (2002) 'Guardians of the Poor', *Regional Historian,* 9 (Summer), pp. 6–11.

Maurice, Mary Atkinson (1833) *Memorials of Two Sisters.* London: Seeley & Sons.

Morgan, Simon (2007) *A Victorian Woman's Place: Public Culture in the Nineteenth Century.* London: Tauris.

Müller, Freidrich Max (1858) *German Love. From the Papers of an Alien.* Translated by Susanna Winkworth. London: Chapman and Hall.

Pfeiffer, Franz (ed.) (1854) *Theologica Germanica.* Translated by Susanna Winkworth. London: Longman.

Poel, Emma (1863) *Life of Amelia Wilhelmina Sieveking.* Translated by Catherine Winkworth. London: Longman.

Prayers from the Collection of Baron Bunsen (1871). Translated by Catherine Winkworth. London: Longman.

Shaen, Margaret J. (ed.) (1908) *Memorials of Two Sisters: Susanna and Catherine Winkworth Edited by Their Niece.* London: Longmans.

Shaen, M.J (1912) *William Shaen: A Brief Sketch.* London: Longman.

Smith, Sidonie (1987) *A Poetics of Women's Autobiography: Marginality and the Fictions of Self-Representation.* Bloomington: University of Indiana Press.

Stark, Susanne (1999) *'Behind Inverted Commas': Translation and Anglo-German Cultural Relations in the Nineteenth Century.* Clevedon: Multilingual Matters Ltd.

The History and Life of the Reverend Doctor John Tauler of Strasbourg (1857) London: Smith Elder.

Uglow, Jenny (1993) *Elizabeth Gaskell: A Habit of Stories.* London: Faber and Faber.

Webster, Rachel (2018) 'Defending Christ's Divinity: The Theological Message of Susanna and Catherine Winkworth's Translations', *Literature and Theology,* 31(2), pp. 17–38. doi:10.1093/litthe/frw041

Winkworth, Catherine (1867), 'Life of Pastor Fliedner of Kaiserworth', in *Kaiserworth Almanack* 1866. Translated by Catherine Winkworth. London: Longman.

Winkworth, Catherine (1869) *Christian Singers of Germany.* London: Macmillan.

Winkworth, Susanna (ed.) (1852) *Life and Letters of Barthold George Niebuhr* (3 vols). London: Chapman and Hall.

Winkworth, Susanna (ed.) (1852a) *Life and Letters of Barthold George Niebuhr. Volume 1.* London: Chapman and Hall.

Winkworth, Susanna (1868) 'Translator's Preface', in Bunsen, Charles (ed.), *God in History. Volume 1.* London: Longman, pp. xi–xvii.

Winkworth, Susanna (1883) *Letters and Memorials of Catherine Winkworth. Volume 1.* Clifton: Austin.

Winkworth, Susanna (1886) *Letters and Memorials of Catherine Winkworth. Volume 2.* Clifton: Austin.

Young Soldier of France and Jesus Christ: Letters of A. E. Casalis (1915). Translated by Catherine Winkworth Mackintosh. Eastbourne: Strange.

6 *Letters of Jane Austen* (1884)

The Family Record

When *Letters of Jane Austen* was published, her great-nephew Lord Brabourne devoted the first 100 pages of Volume 1 to family information about himself, even though he was not born until 12 years after Austen's death. The apparently collected *Letters* was a result of family efforts both to preserve and to reshape the life of the novelist, beginning with the first 'Biographical Notice' by Henry Austen (1818). Brabourne was reacting particularly to his cousin James Edward Austen-Leigh's *A Memoir of Jane Austen* (1870, 1871) and to Sarah Tytler's *Jane Austen and Her Works* (1880), whose biographical sections were based on the *Memoir*. Brabourne used the distribution of Austen's letters preserved and bequeathed by Cassandra Austen as an opportunity to aggrandise his mother, Lady Knatchbull, previously Fanny Knight, who was the Austen sisters' niece. Brabourne also made specific reference to Burney's *Diary and Letters* in the wake of the frequent allusions to Austen and Burney as sister novelists. This chapter assesses the response to Austen's celebrity in the *Letters* and the parallel paths of family letters in the Victorian quest to domesticate the author.

Austen's letters were made public within the family project of making and remaking her image for the nineteenth century and their publication demonstrates how the life and survival pattern of correspondence inflects future life writing. The chapter considers the context for Brabourne's edition that was created from three strands: first from the distribution of papers bequeathed by Cassandra Austen at her death in 1845 and secondly from the appearance of the *Memoir* in 1870. The third contributing factor was the life writing produced by Tytler and by other reviewers of the letters in print such as Margaret Oliphant and H.F. Chorley. As this process unfolded, the influence of Frances Burney's reputation on Austen's brought Brabourne to the pinnacle of critical concern demonstrated by the *Letters*. The answering review of his work by Mary Augusta Ward in *Macmillan's Magazine* was both scathing and constructive of the life as it had emerged by 1885. The chapter finally traces the impact of the letters in their new context where a female circle of correspondents challenged the surrounding corporate public image of the nineteenth-century family record. In this the variants of life writing reveal how a woman writer's words might defy biographical intervention.

Cassandra and Burney

The emergence of Jane Austen's letters into a collected edition was informed by two other assertions about her life made in print during the nineteenth century: first the elision of the letters with the novels and secondly the comparisons between Austen and Frances Burney. After Austen died on 18 July 1817, the first publication to emerge from the family in terms of the Austen life-writing project was a collaboration in which her sister and correspondent Cassandra remained a shadowy figure. Henry Austen, Jane's fourth brother, used the publication of his sister's two previously unpublished complete novels to write his 'Biographical Notice' of 1818 in which he announced: 'Short and easy will be the task of the mere biographer. A life of usefulness, literature and religion, was not by any means a life of event' (Austen 1818, p. v). The uneventfulness of Austen's life was a much repeated 'fact', reinforced later by the contents of the letters and the homeliness of her existence. Henry claimed that Austen's correspondence was written in the same style as her novels in that 'Every thing came finished from her pen' (p. xvii), and in a postscript he brought the first two of those letters into public view (p. xvii). One was the famous 'little bit of ivory' letter to their nephew Edward, later James Edward Austen-Leigh, and the other was a now untraceable non-family letter. In this second letter, Austen acknowledged the attentions of 'my dearest sister, my tender, watchful, indefatigable nurse' as well as the fashion for 'longer petticoats' (p. xviii). Cassandra's *post-mortem* care was demonstrated here by her not yielding any of her surviving letters for print although she was, of course, the owner of the manuscript novels. This would suggest that Austen's public and private writings were being separated by her sister but elided by her brother.

Austen's letters were initially yoked to the novels because of this 'Biographical Notice' that accompanied first publication of *Northanger Abbey* and *Persuasion*. In 1818, the *Edinburgh Magazine and Literary Miscellany* commented that 'the few prefatory pages which contain a sketch of her life, almost come upon us like the melancholy invitation to the funeral of one whom we had long known and loved' ('Review: *Northanger Abbey* and *Persuasion*', 1818, p. 455). This review also claimed that the 'last' letter printed in Henry Austen's postscript was 'more truly descriptive...than any thing the pen of a biographer can produce' (p. 455). Austen was to be an auto/biographer in retrospect. The reviewer in 1818 concluded: 'Such was this admirable person, the character of whose life fully corresponds with that of her writings' (p. 455) so that the letters and the novels were being elided as life writing. The letters were also being made safe within this account as they would be again in the pious writings of her nephew Austen-Leigh where the letters would also be accompanied by new work of Jane Austen. The 'Notice' preceded the posthumous novels in 1818 and Austen-Leigh would include in his second edition of the *Memoir* (1871) the complete, unpublished novella *Lady Susan* together with an unpublished fragment he named *The Watsons* along with the cancelled chapter of *Persuasion*.

The 'Notice' was expanded in 1833 into a 'Memoir' written by Henry Austen for publisher Richard Bentley's 'Standard Novels'. The 'Memoir' quoted extensively from two further articles: one by Maria Jewesbury in the *Athenaeum* in 1831 and another by Richard Whately in the *Quarterly Review* in 1821 (Sutherland 2002, pp. 258–9). It incorporated the same two letters from the 1818 postscript into the main body of the text (Austen 1833, pp. ix–x) and the 'bit of ivory' was also quoted directly from the Jewesbury review itself (p. xi). Writing during the interim between the 'Notice' and the 'Memoir', Jewesbury had bemoaned the 'chasm in our light literature' caused by Austen's early death (1831, p. 553) and her approach demonstrated the hold over the imagination gained by the 1818 'Notice'. Her *Athenaeum* piece on 'Literary Women' absorbed the already circulating ideas of miniature painting and lack of life events, and once again came the comment that 'there seldom appears to have been a more beautiful accordance between an author's life and writings' (p. 553). The article reiterated the lack of action and social commentary in the novels, and its tone suggested a frivolous past world where Austen lived in 'easy and elegant circumstances' (p. 553). The earlier Whately review quoted by Henry took nearly ten pages in its original context to reach 'Austin' herself and then quoted extensively from *Mansfield Park* and *Persuasion* by way of agreeing that Austen had provided instruction with amusement (1821, p. 375). Whately also, however, offered a view on the epistolary novel's 'continual splicing' that would later impact on the presentation of Austen's life in letters: 'to give the letters the appearance of reality...they must contain a very large proportion of matter which has no bearing on the story' (p. 362).

From the use of these articles in the 1833 'Memoir', it is clear that the Austen family was keeping abreast of Jane's press. The remainder of this section argues that one particular association, between Austen and Frances Burney, probably affected the survival and dispersal of Austen's letters inherited by Cassandra. Burney died aged 87 in January 1840. Between February 1842 and early 1843, with Cassandra still living, the first five volumes of Burney's *Diary and Letters* were published. The chosen title re-imposed a sense of domesticity despite the public life that was also presented. The Endpaper to Volume I announced that the 'results' of Burney's resolution to keep a diary 'are now to be given to the world precisely as they left the hand of the writer' if not, in Henry Austen's words, 'finished from her pen'. Charlotte Barrett's 'Introductory Memoir' to Volume I outlined the role of the editor and inheritor of the letters of a sister and author. Barrett was keen to stress that her aunt had 'herself arranged these Journals and Papers with the most scrupulous care' (1842a, xxi) so that the letters were in effect new work from beyond the grave. Having established her ownership and commission as an editor, Barrett described her edition as 'a journalizing memoir' (p. iii) to define the hybrid between journal and letter that would emerge from Burney's retrospective style. Charlotte Barrett and Cassandra Austen were thus custodians of the memorial records of two women who were often linked in the public imagination and also in private. In 1797, Austen's father offered *First Impressions*, subsequently *Pride and Prejudice*, to the publisher Cadell and likened it to *Evelina* (Austen-Leigh 1871, p. 129). Jane Austen was a named subscriber to Burney's *Camilla* (Gilson 1982, p. 432) and she referred to *The Wanderer* and *Evelina* in a letter dated 26 November 1815 (Le Faye 1995, p. 302). *Evelina* is also mentioned along with *Sir Charles Grandison* in *Northanger Abbey* which, although it was only published after Austen's death, was read within the family circle. In one of her letters dated 3 November 1813, Austen jokingly suggested that she might in future 'marry young M^r D'Arblay' (Brabourne 1884a, p. 207) who was Burney's son born in 1794. Austen's godfather the Reverend Samuel Cooke was vicar at Great Bookham in Surrey where the d'Arblays lived from 1793 to 1801 (Le Faye 1995, pp. 508–9). In public, when Thomas Babington Macaulay reviewed Burney's *Diary and Letters* in January 1843 he also compared Austen with Shakespeare (1843, pp. 561–2) and this section of his *Edinburgh Review* article was often quoted. Macaulay concluded his article, however, by saying that he was grateful that two of Madame d'Arblay's successors had surpassed her 'for in truth we owe her not only Evelina, Cecilia, and Camilla, but also Mansfield Park and the Absentee' by Maria Edgeworth (p. 570).

Henry himself promoted Austen's association with Burney in the 'Notice' in which he announced that his sister's novels 'have been placed on the same shelf as the works of a D'Arblay and an Edgeworth' (Austen 1818, p. vii). A further editorial paragraph used by the publisher after his 'Memoir' drew attention to contemporary female novelists at the time of the publication of *Sense and Sensibility*, namely 'Madame D'-Arblay, Miss Edgeworth, Miss Opie, Miss Porter' (Austen 1833, p. xv). In private, Cassandra was aware of her sister's admiration for Burney's *Evelina* (Brabourne 1884a, p. 213) as well as for the novels of Samuel Richardson (Austen 1818, p. xv) which Austen had turned into satire in her earliest work such as 'Love and Freindship', 'Lesley Castle' and *Lady Susan*. These fictional versions of life writing passed into Cassandra's keeping in 1817 along with the factual life-written letters, and the publication of Burney's letters may have influenced Cassandra's indirect editorial decisions about her inheritance during the 1840s. In 1844, she received an extract from another article from her niece Anna Lefroy in which Austen was described by the novelist G.P.R. James as 'the greatest of all female novelists' with 'her power of investing common-place with interest...and the unexpected turns which surprise and disappoint in daily life' (1843, p. 459). James discussed Burney, Edgworth and the Porter sisters on the same page. Cassandra wrote back to Anna on 1 February 1844: 'The Article was quite new to me & could not fail of being highly gratifying to my feelings ... Is it not remarkable that those Books should have risen so much in celebrity after so many years?' (Austen-Leigh, Austen-Leigh and Le Faye, 1989, pp. 242–3). In addition to Henry Austen's use of the Jewesbury and Whately articles in 1833, this would seem to suggest that the family was sensitive to allusions to Austen and it is hardly likely that the publications concerning Burney would have escaped their notice. Barrett, inheritor of the role of Burney's original sister correspondents, announced as editor that the letters had been left to her 'with full permission to publish whatever might be judged desirable' (1842a, xxxi–ii). Cassandra was 70 years old by this time but still living at Chawton with the papers of her sister about her, and possibly even Volume 4 of the *Diary and Letters* in which she could read the courtier Mr Fairly's critique of Burney's letters and her consignment of the papers to the delicate understanding of a sister (Barrett 1842d, p. 208). Cassandra's actions in the 1840s reflected her concern about the impact of letters on the representation of the two authors' lives for posterity.

Burney bequeathed to Barrett 'the whole of my own immense Mass of manuscripts, collected from my fifteenth year...with full and free permission according to her unbiassed taste and judgement to keep or destroy' (Hemlow, Douglas and Hawkins 1984, p. 980). To Cassandra, Jane Austen did 'give and bequeath ... every thing of which I may die possessed' (Le Faye 1995, p. 339), and Cassandra wrote to their niece Fanny Knight on 29 July 1817 to acknowledge 'the precious papers which are now my property' (Brabourne 1884b, p. 341). As discussed in Chapter 2, Burney reviewed and edited her vast hoard of material in the last 20 years of her life, and Cassandra, on the evidence of her niece Caroline, is known to have 'burnt the greater part, (as she told me), 2 or 3 years before her own death' (Sutherland 2002, p. 174). Peter Sabor makes a case for Cassandra as a 'far-sighted archivist', suggesting that it was her own papers that she destroyed (2002, p. 130) but on 9 May 1843, she wrote to her brother Charles:

> As I have leisure, I am looking over & destroying some of my Papers – others I have marked "to be burned", whilst some will still remain' including 'a few manuscripts of our dear Jane, which I have set apart for those parties to whom I think they will be mostly valuable.
>
> (Austen-Leigh, Austen Leigh and Le Faye 1989, p. 243)

Cassandra died on 22 March 1845 leaving a clear indication of her distribution of the 'precious papers'. The letters that were subsequently legacies to brothers and nieces had parts missing. The cancelled *Persuasion* chapters went to Anna and still bear the instruction 'The contents of this drawer for Anna'; and the first volume of what have been termed 'Minor Works' went to her brother Charles for 'I think I recollect that a few of the trifles in this Vol[ume] were written expressly for his amusement' (Gilson 1982, p. 383). Cassandra died suddenly away from home while staying with her brother Frank and so must have prepared this distribution. She was perhaps recollecting Fairly's warning: 'Think but how they will be seized; everybody will try to get some of them; what an outcry there will be!' (Barrett 1842d, p. 208). She had seen the impact of one set of journal letters on the world and chosen to edit her own private and familial distribution.

The fire and the excisions from Austen's letters were reported as having taken place in 1842 or 1843 when Cassandra, in the retirement of private life, sought control over the public memory of her sister in response to Burney-Barrett's narrative of the life of Madame D'Arblay. After the first five volumes of Burney's *Diary and Letters* were published, the Croker (1842) and Macaulay (1843) reviews emerged, and Cassandra's letter of 1844 suggests continued interest and awareness of the literary world. By comparison with Austen's 160 extant letters, Burney handed on to posterity 1,200 documents, 7½ times as many as her fellow author, and it has been estimated that Jane Austen could on the basis of her known output have written 3,000 letters in her lifetime (Southam, 2000, p. 59), dependant, of course, on the absences required to generate that amount of correspondence. If Cassandra received 60% of these potential letters, as is the case with the existing papers, then she destroyed or failed to preserve over 90% of them. This presumed bonfire of the early 1840s could have been a response to the complex negotiation with print demonstrated by Barrett in her publication of the journal letters of Burney.

Austen-Leigh's *Memoir*

The results of Cassandra's distribution impacted on the family's life writing over the rest of the century, specifically the line of inheritance from the Hampshire and Kent Austens through her brothers James and Edward respectively. The death of the last brother Admiral Frank Austen in 1865 was the catalyst for the family papers and recollections to be mustered for a new era. James's son, James Edward Austen-Leigh, took on the task of representing Jane Austen through what he termed, in a postscript to the first edition, 'a family record' (Austen-Leigh 1871, p. 196). This postscript was reprinted for the second edition and the references following are taken from the revised edition of 1871. A modern editor of the *Memoir*, Kathryn Sutherland, sees Austen-Leigh's as a 'project of domestication' that was 'suffused with anxiety' (Sutherland 2002, p. xix; 2005, p. 71). Austen-Leigh misquoted a section from Arthur Helps's *Life of Columbus* claiming he had been 'driven to the enterprise' in default of any other volunteer (Austen-Leigh 1871, p. x). Rather comically, the section quoted from Helps's 1869 work referred to the role of Prince Henry of Portugal in promoting the discovery of America. Austen-Leigh tried to help the cause of domestication by putting himself on the footing of an entrepreneur of the New World.

As members of Victorian society, Jane Austen's family were keen to downplay the surviving records of their sister/aunt's life in their triviality and irrelevance to the novels. Austen-Leigh commented that

> the materials may be thought inferior to the execution, for they treat only of the details of domestic life. There is in them no notice of politics or public events; scarcely any discussions on literature, or other subjects of general interest.
>
> (Austen-Leigh 1871, p. 57)

He was comparing them with the letters of those (men) with a public life that could be justified in print. Continuing his nest-building analogy, his aunt's letters were 'curiously constructed out of the simplest matters...of the twigs and mosses supplied by the tree in which it is placed' (p. 57). Austen-Leigh also, however, displayed his knowledge of the Burney comparison by reflecting the terms of Macaulay's review (1843, p. 565). Following on from a discussion of Richardson's *Sir Charles Grandison*, Austen-Leigh observed: 'It is well that the native good taste of herself and of those with whom she lived, saved her from the snare into which a sister novelist had fallen of imitating the grandiloquent style of Johnson' (Austen-Leigh 1871, p. 84). Austen-Leigh also footnoted Gaskell's *Life of Charlotte Brontë* in his Chapter 7 (p. 110) where he insisted on Austen's 'entire seclusion' from literary recognition (p. 108). Brontë, he claimed, achieved 'personal distinction' as an author despite the 'wild solitude' of her life (pp. 109–10).

The *Memoir* was originally an extended notice of Austen's life. Extracts from the letters available to the Hampshire Austens were interwoven with 11 chapters of narrative (Austen-Leigh 1870). Margaret Oliphant in *Blackwood's Edinburgh Magazine* took the view that Austen-Leigh's style was disarming in its imperfections: 'nothing can be more amusing and attractive than the glimpses...of this girl, through the much trellis-work and leafage of her nephew['s]...biography' (1870, p. 291). Austen-Leigh is not a biographer but the *Memoir* can be deemed a biography partly because of the freshness of the letters that shed 'a passing gleam of light upon the fine vein of feminine cynicism which pervades his aunt's mind' (p. 294). Perversely, it seemed that the added narrative of an amateur writer allowed Jane Austen to speak for herself. In two other reviews of the *Memoir*, Richard Simpson and Henry Chorley were drawn more to the comparison with Burney. Simpson in the *North British Review* was duped by the 'four or five families' (1870, p. 129). He referred to the Macaulay review (p. 136) and to Burney's 'gallery of portraits' from her 'net of literary correspondence and acquaintance' (p. 129). Chorley in the *Quarterly Review* also referred to Austen's 'home simplicity' (1870, p. 197) and drew attention in a footnote to the arguments over Burney's age purveyed by Croker (1833): 'The fable of [*Evelina*] being the work of a girl of seventeen has long been exploded' (Chorley 1870, p. 200). This was an extraordinarily determined onslaught given that the comparison between the authors' ages was inaccurate. Austen may have completed the first draft of *Pride and Prejudice* at the age of 21 but the final revised work was not published until she was 34. Burney was 25 when *Evelina* appeared and her novel, once more tagged by Chorley with the patronage of Dr Johnson, was here described as 'coarse and farcical' by comparison with *Emma* and *Persuasion* (p. 200). Croker's reviews, of course, had appeared in this same *Quarterly Review* (1833, 1842). Chorley also referred to Burney's life writing: 'Madame D'Arblay's diary, which bright and clever as it is, is in too many of its pages little more than a hymn in her own praise sung "at the request of friends"' (1870, p. 217). Brabourne's edition in the following decade (1884a, 1884b) demonstrated that he too had absorbed this information.

In his Preface to the second edition of the *Memoir*, Austen-Leigh played further on his status as an amateur: 'I hope that I may claim some indulgent allowance for the difficulty of recovering little facts and feelings which have been merged half a century deep in oblivion' (1871, p. vi). In the 1870 preface, Austen-Leigh had maintained that the 'family record' was being submitted 'to the public, with all its faults of deficiency and redundancy' and this preface dated 7 September 1869 now became a 'Postscript' as if in correspondence with itself (p. 196). Overall, the second edition of 1871 presented a more complex interaction of letter-writing styles with a revised environment for letters as evidence of a life. The new Preface explaining the new material that would supplement the interwoven letters was dated 17 November 1870 (pp. v–vi) as if the dates of the additional matter were repackaging the letters dated within. The new Chapter 12 was the actual cancelled chapter of *Persuasion*, and Chapter 13 concerned *Sandition*, another fragment that was not, however, published until 1925. The new postscript that had been the preface in 1870 was then followed by the complete *Lady Susan*, a narrative in letters. The expectation of a life being told in letters was therefore built up from a selection of similarly recovered texts.

Within this sequence, the Kent side of the family was implicated for the first time because permission to publish was allegedly given by Austen-Leigh's cousin, Lady Knatchbull (Austen-Leigh 1871, p. 201). This may be one reason why Brabourne had to insulate the letters in his edition from the implication of story-telling or self-narration, and to reinstate his mother outside any concept of the character of Lady Vernon in the novella *Lady Susan*. William May suggests that after *Lady Susan*, Austen's 'subsequent writings resituate the letter as an object co-opted by other readers for nefarious purposes' (2012, p. 116). He sees letters as points of entry 'whose very omissions and evasions permit a dialogue with Austen's work' (p. 117). Mary Favret has also pointed out that Austen's use of letters in the published novels developed beyond that of the epistolary narrative and that 'narrative authority depends on our learning to see and read letters properly' (p. 137). In the second edition of the *Memoir*, Austen-Leigh himself pointed out that *Sense and Sensibility* was originally an epistolary novel which was redrafted, demonstrating that Austen was not satisfied with the form. His preface to *Lady Susan* claimed that, in the publication of this novella, 'the censure must fall upon him who has put it forth, not on her who kept it locked up in her desk' (Austen-Leigh 1871, p. 201) although it was unclear whether this referred to Austen or her inheritors. This new piece of self-deprecation also contradicted the 'Biographical Notice' and its claim of instant accuracy and perfection. The early family publications thus endeavoured to offer more of Austen and found themselves mired in questions of literary value and the reclassification of letter-writing duties. Her letters were about family news and communication and should not be glibly elided with her literary skills in the fictional arena.

Tytler's *Jane Austen*

Austen-Leigh died in 1874, apparently unaware of the Kent family record that had been bequeathed to Lady Knatchbull. There had been contact in 1870 over Lady Knatchbull's alleged permission to publish *Lady Susan* (Austen-Leigh 1871, p. 201), a point that Brabourne later clarified. Lady Knatchbull had inherited the autograph copy from Cassandra, of course, but Austen-Leigh published using another family copy. Brabourne explained in his introduction that his mother had not been capable of agreeing and that permission was granted instead by his youngest sister, who had at the time denied the existence of further papers (1884a, p. x). Brabourne was now keen to countermand accounts of Jane Austen that had used only Austen-Leigh's third of the available material and could now be supplemented by 'his' 79 new letters. Brabourne mentioned early on a little-known work of life writing that was based on the *Memoir* (p. xv): namely *Jane Austen and Her Works*, a young person's guide published by Cassell, Petter and Galpin in 1880. Its author was the evangelical and moral writer Henrietta Keddie, under her penname of Sarah Tytler. Tytler was a self-made, independent woman who had to earn her living by her pen, and her homiletic stance in relation to the life of Austen was explained in her 'Preface': 'My intention in this book is to present in one volume to an over-wrought, and in some respects over-read, generation of young people the most characteristic of Jane Austen's novels, together with her life' (1880, p. vii). Tytler had gleaned from Austen-Leigh that 'the tales and the life are calculated to reflect light on each other', and she claimed to have 'condensed' the novels for her young readers 'with reverent hands' (p. vii). Despite the lack of continuity in the letters, of which there was evidence of only 36 in the *Memoir* at that time, she welcomed 'every trifle' (p. 24). Tytler paid tribute to Austen-Leigh's 'biography' as 'the only authorised memoir of the author' (p. viii) but later reminded her readers that Austen's family biographers were old and not professional writers (p. 2).

In the 'Life' section of Tytler's work, Austen was envisaged 'devouring' *Evelina* or *Cecilia* in the shrubbery (1880, pp. 6–7) and Tytler inevitably described their author Burney's 'transparent literary vanity' (p. 16). The shy Jane Austen rather 'reigned queen' (p. 18) at home, and was also 'queen of her company' (p. 17) and 'a queen of novelists' (p. 25). From her Victorian moral vantage point, Tytler regarded Austen as exclusive, haughty and intolerant (p. 15). She wrote at some length of her concern that Austen could not wholly have concealed that she was mocking her neighbours 'for her mingled instruction and diversion' (p. 19). She was also scathing of Austen's failure to participate in the literary culture of her time. For her own part, Tytler was aware of a need for sociability, networking and gracious behaviour when writing was a livelihood: 'even the most honest and honourable independence has its becoming limits. That of Jane Austen, ultra self-sufficing, fastidious, tinged with haughtiness, is just a trifle repellent out of that small circle in which she was always at home' (p. 32). This was patently unfair since the letters that direct attention to Austen's opinions were private and Tytler also pigeonholed the letters themselves: 'As there is no continuity, either in the letters or the narrative, of which such incidents might supply a part, they fall vaguely and flatly on the reader' (p. 18). The writing of the self is defused and diffused within the text read by Tytler and made safe in the context of the amateur writing of old people that must be re-presented for the impressionable and 'over-wrought' young reader. Tytler indeed read the novels on her readers' behalf so that they might not misinterpret them when presented with, and overexcited by, Austen's actual text.

When the *Letters* appeared, Brabourne also tried to prevent his readers from being alarmed by Jane Austen's actual words and used those of his own mother whose life and actions were significant in the transmission of the texts to be published. Brabourne's introduction and guiding remarks were geared towards her sanctification. 'A son may be pardoned', he explained, 'for saying (when it is simply and literally true) that never was a more exemplary life passed than that of his mother' (1884a, p. 24). The life and writing of Knight, however, was even less well known than Tytler's in this life-writing contest. As Fanny Knight, she was 'her father's right hand and mainstay'; when Lady Knatchbull 'as admirable…in her married life' (p. 25). It was the married life, however, that had threatened the family with scandal three years before the birth of Brabourne. The complex intermarriage of cousins and deceased wife's sisters in the Knatchbull family circle was further compounded in 1826 when Edward Knight, Fanny's brother, eloped to Gretna Green with Mary Dorothea Knatchbull, daughter of Sir Edward Knatchbull by his first wife (Honan 1987, pp. 116–7). This meant that at the age of 33, Fanny became sister-in-law to her own stepdaughter and that when Brabourne was born his half-sister was also his aunt. The couple were remarried at Steventon, however, and received by Cassandra and her niece Anna Lefroy and this was one cause of the rift between the branches of the Austen family put into print by the *Memoir* and *Letters*. Brabourne felt a need to uphold his mother's status in the face of such challenges to respectability but his use of her pocketbooks as verification of Jane Austen's life became a rather desperate exercise. An extract from 1813 announced 'June 6th. – "Aunt Jane and I had a very interesting conversation." June 22nd. – "Aunt Jane and I had a delicious morning together"' (Brabourne 1884b, 120). Brabourne even reproduced an interjection from Fanny herself at the beginning of a letter to Cassandra dated 11 October 1813: 'My dearest At: Cass:— I have just asked At: Jane to let me write a little in her letter but she does not like it so I won't.—Good bye' (1884b, p. 169). In Volume 2 of the *Letters*, this sentence headed the letter but it has become a footnote in the modern edition with the explanation that Austen was keen to express herself privately to the Chawton household on the subject of Fanny's siblings (Le Faye 1995, p. 432, note 20).

Brabourne

It was in the context of both Tytler and Fanny Knight that Edward, Lord Brabourne published his two-volume edition of the letters of his great-aunt in 1884. The *Letters* and the earlier *Memoir* were part of a family confrontation that has come to shape the terms of Austen's biography, making her a sometimes marginal figure within publications claiming to tell the story of her life. Austen-Leigh and his sisters had the advantage of being able to remember Jane Austen in person but Brabourne had possession of the letters inherited by Fanny Knight that constituted the lion's share of the surviving correspondence. His edition of the *Letters* was about his family status, about ownership and provenance, and also about the sanctification of his mother. In spite of some deference to Austen-Leigh, the editor prioritised the Kent Austen connections. He promoted the letters' textual superiority as references to the everyday but at the same time placed Austen's life outside biographical evaluation because of his extensive framing remarks notable, according to one commentator, 'for their diffuse irrelevance' (Rae 1901). Brabourne himself even suggested that his commentary could be omitted but he implied that by doing so the reader would deprive himself of important information (1884a, p. xiv), and anyway that the 'addenda' do not 'detract from the actual value of the genuine letters which I place before him' (p. xv).

The intertwined lines of family succession were highly relevant to Brabourne's project. The letters came into his possession at the death of his mother on Christmas Day 1882. Brabourne indicated that his mother had looked at the letters of her aunt for the last time in August 1856 and that they were thus not seen by Austen-Leigh in the 1860s when the *Memoir* was being planned: 'It is much to be regretted that the "Memoir" should have been published without the additional light which many of these letters throw upon the "Life", though of course no blame attaches to Mr Austen-Leigh in the matter' (Brabourne 1884a, p. xi). Brabourne glossed over the fact that the letters had been unvalued for nearly 30 years but it was not just his second cousin's publication that concerned him. There were also other updated Victorianisations of Jane Austen as a woman including that of Tytler. Margaret Kirkham notes the revisions made to the Austen portrait for the engraving accompanying the *Memoir* and quotes from a letter written by Fanny in 1870 that Austen was 'not so refined as she ought to have been for her talent' (1983, p. 30). The nineteenth century had to adjust and revise the image of Jane Austen and additional material had to be contextualised for the new era. Brabourne even provided an effusive dedication to Queen Victoria by contrast with his great-aunt's reluctance to dedicate *Emma* to the Prince Regent.

As his answer to the *Memoir*, Brabourne claimed in his 100-page introduction to 'attempt 'no "Memoir" that can properly be called so' (1884a, p. i). Austen-Leigh was the eldest son of Jane Austen's eldest brother James and thus represented the Hampshire branch of the family. Brabourne was from the Kent line created when his grandfather Edward Austen, subsequently Edward Knight, inherited from Sir Thomas Knight the estates of Godmersham and Chawton. In Brabourne's edition, there were 96 letters written by Austen, mostly bequeathed by Cassandra to Fanny Knight. In addition to the letters to Cassandra, there were five from Austen to Fanny herself, nine to their other niece Anna Lefroy, one (a comic letter in reverse) to Charles Austen's daughter Cassandra and two from Cassandra to Fanny (Gilson, p. 395). Of these, the five to Fanny have been deposited in the Kent Records Office along with her pocket books but the others have been dispersed in sales as detailed by Deirdre Le Faye in her modern edition. According to her diary, Knight received 47 letters although Brabourne claimed there were 30 of which only those five survive (Brabourne 1884b, p. 118; Le Faye 1995, p. xvii). Fourteen of the originally printed collection of 1884 remain missing and are thus accessible only in the Brabourne version. *Lady Susan* is now in the Pierpoint Morgan Library in New York and the cancelled chapters of *Persuasion* passed from Anna Lefroy to the British Museum in 1925. *Sanditon* was copied for Frank by Cassandra and this copy is in Chawton House Library while the original given to Anna Lefroy is at Kings College Cambridge bequeathed by her descendants in 1930 (Sutherland 2010). Despite describing the documents as 'biographical letters' (Brabourne 1884a, p. 2), Brabourne pointed out that 'they form no continuous narrative and record no stirring events' (p. xiv). 'She does not attract our imagination by sensational descriptions or marvellous plots; but with so little "plot" at all as to offend those who read only for excitement' (p. xiii). At the same time, he was forced to mention that 'the customs and manners which Jane Austen describes have changed and varied so much as to belong to another age' (p. xii) and that 'allusions to things and people…are often made in the purest spirit of playful nonsense, and are by no means to be taken as grave and serious expressions of opinion or statements of fact' (p. xiv). Brabourne seemed to have been unaware that Cassandra destroyed many of the letters or that Austen-Leigh based much of his account on the recollections of his sister Anna Lefroy and their half-sister Caroline. This makes the *Letters* a more valuable resource than perhaps Brabourne intended when he contextualised them within the Knatchbull and Knight families.

Brabourne worked hard to locate himself within the narrative of the opening pages of the *Letters*. Austen-Leigh had been able to open the *Memoir* with the information that he was present at Austen's funeral in 1817. Brabourne began rather testily: 'As circumstances over which I had no control prevented my appearance in the world until twelve years later, I was unfortunately debarred from that personal acquaintance with her and her surroundings' (1884a, p. 1). He could, however, put forward the claims of his mother as 'favourite niece' (p. 1) and also quote from a letter written after Jane's death in which Cassandra told their niece that Jane was 'better known' to Fanny 'than to any human being besides myself' (p. 2). Brabourne later observed in his commentary on the 1805 letters, 'It must be admitted that my beloved great-aunt was a careless speller' (p. 296), and the spelling of 'neice' in that first quotation about his mother, extracted from a letter to Cassandra of 7 October 1808, was immediately footnoted 'Always so spelt in her letters' (p. 2). The spirit of the edition was captured here in miniature. The letters had to be guided into print by his affectionate 'additional information' (and correction) of someone he felt acquainted with because her name was 'a household word in my family from the earliest days of my recollection' (p. 2). In a volume entitled *Letters of Jane Austen*, no other letter then appeared for a further 100 pages. Brabourne felt qualified to 'fill up and complete' (p. 4) the previous *Memoir* with letters ranging from 1798 to 1816. What was 'emphatically a home life' (p. 5) would need his skill at describing the places and family members mentioned in the letters, and he had no scruple about beginning in Kent with his own family line.

The *Letters* were thus accompanied if not engulfed by voluminous accounts of Austen and Knatchbull family connections, not all of them correctly attributed. Brabourne himself was the Liberal MP for Sandwich in Kent from 1857 and held government posts under Lord Russell and Gladstone until 1874. He entered the House of Lords in 1880 and apparently became a Tory sympathiser. His full name at his death was Edward Hugessen Knatchbull-Hugessen, Baron Brabourne of Brabourne. He acquired 'Hugessen' as his given name at birth and changed his surname by royal licence in 1849 at the death of his father, Sir Edward Knatchbull, ninth Baronet of Mersham Hatch in Kent (Rae 1901). Mary Hugessen, Sir Edward's mother, married the eighth baronet in 1780 and died in 1784. Along with her sister Dorothea, the wife of Joseph Banks, Mary was co-heiress to an estate called Provender in Kent that was subsequently inherited by Brabourne (Knatchbull Hugessen 1960, pp. 139, 143). Another family name of Wyndham also came from the female line. It was the maiden name of the fourth Baronet's wife Alice (1676–1723), the given name and revised surname of the fifth and sixth Baronets (p. 97; Pedigree II) and the name of the 12th Baronet, son of Brabourne's half-brother Norton (Pedigree III). Even Brabourne in his notes on the letters confuses the 'Wyndham Knatchbulls' who are Jane Austen's contemporaries (Brabourne 1884b, pp. 218–9). Brabourne inherited Austen's letters when he inherited Provender and claimed them to be the 'confidential outpourings of Jane Austen's soul' (Brabourne 1884a, p. xii).

He could not, however, leave the letters to speak for themselves and provided preliminary guidance notes to each section compiled by year. In his edition, Brabourne also contested other life writing about women. He referred to the work of Charlotte Yonge and expressed his admiration for Charlotte Brontë despite the 'naughty people' in her novels (p. 75). In line with the 'Notice', 'Memoir', *Memoir* and reviewers, he referred at more length to Frances Burney and to the *Diary and Letters* that he had been reading. He described the 'wonderful fidelity' of *Sense and Sensibility* and added that Miss Burney 'approximates both to the vulgar and the horrible, neither of which is to be found in the pages of the immortal Jane' (p. 66). Burney's novels had become doubly significant because Austen-Leigh's *Memoir* had already reproduced George Austen's letter to the publisher Cadell referring to the early version of *Pride and Prejudice* as 'about the length of Miss Burney's "Evelina"' (p. 76; Austen-Leigh 1871, p. 129). In publishing Austen's letters, Brabourne was on guard against the reception received by Burney's letters. He announced that they 'were probably written if not for publication, at least with an idea they might some day be published' (Brabourne 1884a, p. 71). Of Austen, he continued:

> It would have been impossible for her to have written—even for her own private perusal—the flattering words which it delighted Miss Burney to inscribe in her Diary as having been spoken of or to

herself...In fact whilst Madame D'Arblay's "Diary and Letters" tell us all about herself, who and what she was, how she lived, and with whom she passed her time...Jane Austen's letters on the contrary, leave us to find out all these things for ourselves, and to regret that no further or more minute record is in existence.

(pp. 71–2)

The Burney example gave him an opportunity to re-domesticate Austen and to regret with approval the narrative gaps within the letters.

Brabourne seemed largely oblivious to his own extensive intrusions. He was reflecting also the uncomplimentary views of Burney expressed by Lady Llanover in her *Autobiography and Correspondence of Mary Granville, Mrs Delany* (1861–62) that had been similarly framed with family information over six volumes. Brabourne accepted that the letters of Burney 'are the records of a life which was lived much more before the world than the life of Jane' but also raised the prospect – although in double inverted commas – that Burney's letters were '"made up"' (Brabourne 1884, p. 71). He intended to substitute the 'sensitive and delicate nature' of Jane Austen for the 'chronicle [of]...praise and approval' presented by Burney although he dared not approach the memory of George Eliot 'too recently taken from us to allow of the impartial discussion of her work' (p. 73). It was too dangerous to have Eliot's irregular domestic life discussed in 1884 although John Cross would publish her letters as life writing only a year later.

Mary Augusta Ward in *Macmillan's Magazine* criticised Brabourne's 'half edited matter' with its incongruous and boring 'family pedigrees'. Austen-Leigh was for her the 'first biographer' and she commented that '[t]he virtue of literary reticence is fast becoming extinct' (1884, p. 84). She saw the letter as only for 'family use' and criticised the 'ponderous effect of the introductory chapter' (p. 85). Ward also, however, found the records themselves not worthy of printing because of the absence of Austen 'sprightliness' in the later correspondence (p. 85), that is once novel writing was no longer discussed within letter writing. Ward was seeking 'the workshop which precedes the novels' but once Austen has turned 31 the letters are, for her, just the 'ordinary chit-chat of the ordinary gentlewoman' (p. 86). Brabourne was probably horrified to discover that Ward thought he should have merely printed an addendum to the *Memoir*. Elsewhere, however, Thomas Kebbel, in the *Fortnightly Review*, praised the edition: 'Lord Brabourne's criticism is interesting and his judgment carries great weight; but the explanatory prefaces attached to each division of the correspondences are more valuable still' (1885, p. 262). A brief notice in the *Saturday Review* wisely pointed out that Austen had had no need to write an autobiography for her own sister. The reviewer accepted the narrowness of Austen's life as the reason why her letters were 'mere gossip–written conversation of a quality it is pretty safe to say Jane Austen would have been the very last to think worthy of print' ('Letters of Jane Austen' 1884, p. 637). The *Gentleman's Magazine* reviewer, George Barnett Smith, had found the *Memoir* 'very entertaining biography' (1885, p. 27) but thought that the letters added 'very little knowledge of a personal character' and were not 'valuable from a literary point of view' (p. 38). Smith also believed that Austen would have been angry at their publication (p. 38).

In making Jane Austen public, Brabourne caused her to enter into a correspondence with this wider circle that could now sit in judgement. In private, the Lefroy family of Hampshire Austens also produced an immediate commentary that can be read in the so-called 'Bellas' edition. The annotations on this copy of the *Letters* owned by Anna's daughters Fanny Caroline and Louisa have been published online in the twenty-first century and include a cutting from a review in the *Standard* dated 9 January 1885 (Lank 2008). Louisa Bellas also revealed here how Fanny Knight was frustrated in her matrimonial aims when her younger sister married before she became of an age to be their father's housekeeper. For this reason, Fanny had to wait for her next sister in line, Marianne, to take up the reins and so release Fanny for marriage to Brabourne's father, Edward Knatchbull.

More recently, Claudia Johnson has described Brabourne's edition as 'an exercise in local history' (2012, p. 81) and Cheryl Wilson suggests that the letters were being presented 'on the boundaries of history and fiction' (2017, p. 175). In her analysis of the 'recoverable narrative', Kathryn Sutherland points out that Brabourne makes wild claims by contrast with Austen-Leigh who 'worries that the letters may reveal anything at all' (2009, pp. 16–7). The *Letters* were emerging from a context created by the preceding family publications reinforced by reviews and the progression of Victorian life writing. The generic distinction between the *Letters* and the *Memoir* as life writing was being made in scholarly output at the time of original publication. Among biographers with access to the *Letters*, Goldwin Smith, who was later a major benefactor of Cornell University, described Brabourne's 'genial industry' but decided that the letters were disappointing 'in a biographical point of view' (1890, p. 12). John Anderson of the British Museum compiled a bibliography for Smith's book that described the *Memoir* as 'biography' (p. v) and listed the *Letters* among Austen's 'works' (p. i). The work of the family biographers had reinforced the sense of the letters as new work and further trivialised them by causing them to be read as literature along with a designedly plotted fictional letter sequence such as that of *Lady Susan*.

Duty and Rebellion

Despite these concerns about the 'value' of the letters as life writing, acts of female power can be read even from within the extended and choking commentary. Deborah Kaplan discusses the Austen sisters' pride in domestic experiences (1992, p. 76) and Kathryn Sutherland points out the 'formal limits' of letters (2009, p. 21). Examples from the letters Brabourne annotated nonetheless reinstate a sense of the women's ability to situate and narrate their lives through the available vehicle of the letter. This is demonstrable from the letters written to Cassandra within the collection and also from Brabourne's rearrangement of the letters to the 'neices'. Austen's sense of occasion and of the environment of composition emerged, for instance, in a letter dated 15 September 1813: 'Here I am, my dearest Cassandra, seated in the Breakfast, Dining, sitting room, beginning with all my might' (Brabourne 1884b, p. 145). This letter was being written over a number of days to meet a deadline and it was thus being implied that Henry Austen's new home in London was somewhat smaller than Godmersham, country seat of their brother Edward Knight. The modern edition of Austen's *Letters* also notes that the letter was conveyed in a parcel to Alton and thence to Cassandra in Chawton 'by favour of Mr Gray'. In other words, the letter could be longer because it was not subject to the usual charges (Le Faye 1995, p. 420, note 21). The physical appearance and transmission of the letters occupied many of the transactions. To Fanny on 25 March 1817: 'I have had various plans as to this letter, but at last I have determined that Uncle Henry shall forward it from London' (Brabourne 1884b, p. 303) with more outlets for the mail and some impact on the contents. 'Your close-written letter makes me quite ashamed of my wide lines' (p. 29), Austen wrote to Cassandra on 25 October 1808 when she attempted to give value for money. She promised to 'write very close from the first' on 14 October 1813: 'When I have followed up my last with this I shall feel somewhat less unworthy of you than the state of our correspondence now requires' (p. 177). Within the edition, Brabourne noted Austen's 'pretty' hand and the remarkably beautiful writing of *Lady Susan* (p. 205) which had, of course, the effect of reiterating his ownership of the physical manuscripts. In revisiting the letters as texts, however, Jo Modert now points out that Austen's writing became smaller because of the rising cost of postage (1990, p. xx): therefore for reasons of economy rather than aesthetics.

The beginning of Volume 2 of the *Letters* concerning the death of Brabourne's grandmother Elizabeth provided characteristic evidence of the handling of information. The juxtaposition of texts also demonstrates how Austen's letters have come both to defy and to camouflage their contents. On 7 October 1808, Cassandra was away again at Godmersham attending the Knight family on the occasion of their sister-in-law Elizabeth's eleventh confinement when Austen wrote to her from their temporary home in Southampton. A letter had arrived from Cassandra's 'Winchester correspondent' who was unaware of her absence from home. Austen told her sister: 'I took complete possession of the Letter by reading, paying for, & answering it' (Brabourne 1884b, p. 11). Since the recipient paid the postage, this statement encapsulated the whole process of ownership, telling and retelling. This 'Letter' was in fact from their nephew Edward Knight who was at Winchester school and expecting to be sent some biscuits by Aunt Cass. We can trace the survival path of Austen's letter and the short further sequence of letters presented by Brabourne because they were among those bequeathed to Edward's elder sister Fanny by Cassandra. The sequence probably has an ongoing existence because it is marked as a record of Edward and Fanny's mother Elizabeth who was already dead on 10 October by the time Cassandra read Jane's letter posted on 9 October. The ensuing letters discussed rather the arrangements for her sons' mourning dress and for their reception by their aunt in Southampton, albeit with other local gossip to make good value of the communication. At a further remove, the letter has also been magnified in importance because of debates about the gap in Austen's writing during her time in Southampton between her long-term residence at Steventon and her later mature output at Chawton: a house only made over for the use of the Austen women after their brother, also Edward, was widowed 'during' this very letter.

Austen's letters defy their context when they contradict the biography Brabourne had chosen to write. For the rearrangement of the nieces' letters, Brabourne grouped the letters to his mother and Anna Lefroy, daughter of James Austen and sister of Austen-Leigh, after the main sequence in Volume 2. In his commentary, Brabourne initially struggled over the publication of Austen's five letters to his mother because of their content regarding Fanny's rejection of her suitor John Plumptre (1884b, pp. 268–76). Brabourne announced, however, that the overall lack of material was enough justification for putting the letters into print although accompanied by a long introductory explanation. He initially claimed he would not comment further, since the first two letters from November 1814 'speak for themselves and comment would only weaken their effect' (p. 276), but for February 1816 he emphasised that the right man, his own father, arrived three years after Austen's death, and that she 'would have sincerely and heartily rejoiced could she have seen her [Fanny] in the position which she so long and so worthily occupied' (p. 277). These interventions initially seem to reflect the style of the overall edition in reframing a narrative of Fanny Knight. Brabourne, however, failed to differentiate the roles of the correspondents when he included the exactly contemporaneous letters to the nieces dated November 1814. It has also been noted that the letter to Lefroy was slightly garbled by him (Le Faye 1995, p. 440). The separated groups of letters, however, also drew attention to Austen's role-playing and to her corresponding styles as part of family difference since these letters of the same date have survived.

Kathryn Sutherland describes the 'cultural suppleness and multivocality' (2009, p. 20) of Austen's letters, and even where Brabourne has rearranged the text, it becomes clear that Austen was using the letter as a vehicle for female subversion. In the nieces' section of the *Letters*, Austen wrote from Chawton to Fanny on 18 November 1814:

> I read yours through the very even^g I received it – getting away by myself ... Luckily your Aunt C. dined at the other house, therefore I had not to manœuvre away from her; & as to anybody else, I do not care.
>
> (Brabourne 1884b, p. 279)

Conscious of the circulation of letters within the family Austen wrote again from London 12 days later, on 30 November, adding 'write *something* that may do to be read or told' (p. 288). On the same day as she wrote this second letter, Austen also wrote to Anna about Anna's draft novel. The heroine's suitor has been in love with her aunt and Austen described this as 'a very proper compliment to an Aunt!—I rather imagine that Neices are seldom chosen but in compliment to some Aunt or other' (p. 323). She moved from fiction to family in the next sentence with an allusion to Ben Lefroy to whom Anna has been married for less than two weeks: 'I dare say Ben was in love with me once, & w^d never have thought of You if he had not supposed me dead of a Scarlet fever' (p. 323). Despite his explanation of the difference in character between the letters to nieces and those to Cassandra (p. 269), Brabourne seemed impervious to Austen's ability to vary her character as an aunt between nieces. Even in the *Letters*, her distinctive involvement in Anna's novel writing as opposed to Fanny's matchmaking had already set up the terms on which her life writing would be divided between the two families in Hampshire and in Kent.

Brabourne pointed out that the letters for 1813 provided details of Austen's last visits to Godmersham and it was here that he moved on to his mother's pocket books (1884b, pp. 119–20). For the following year, he observed 'I imagine that the sisters were but seldom separated in 1814, since I have but five letters belonging to that year' (p. 217) and thus the letters withdrew their life-writing potential. His mother and Cassandra had destroyed the texts, and the life lived at the time no longer generated the narrative opportunities provided by separation. Deborah Kaplan has suggested that Brabourne was jealous not just of Austen-Leigh's personal relationship with Aunt Jane but also of the Austen sisters themselves, and that their 'women's culture inverted the value structure of the domestic ideology' to value women's private lives over men's public ones (1992, p. 74). Susan Wheeler has also discussed the negative commentaries of H.W. Garrod and E.M. Forster who reviewed the Chapman edition of Austen's *Letters* (1932) in the *Times Literary Supplement* for 10 November 1932. Wheeler highlights Austen's 'private sense of control' in the letters, coupled with 'the constant and contrasting knowledge of subordination' (1993, p. 193). This inversion may be clearer in editions of the letters now unhindered by the Brabourne commentary but even the 1884 edition negotiates from within a position for the letter as a written act of both duty and rebellion.

Despite the fact that specific letters have guided reception, family preservation and the life-writing inheritance, the original correspondents used the letter as a vehicle for writing in spite of their subordination. Absences such as those of Cassandra Austen produced life writing or at least life evidence and this letter evidence was then segmented across the family. When Frances Burney's mock heroic tone in her edited letters and journals dictated the reaction of critics to women's life-writing output, the Austen family was, in turn, made cautious by comparisons with Burney as a novelist. The editors of 1870 and 1884 became wary of the control over Austen's life given by the possession of her letters, and used counter-indications for Austen's alternate character and habits in their framing arguments with evidence from letters preserved by Cassandra in the 1840s. Letter-written lives that were given narrative forms through acts of publication, and archival suppression expanded the ongoing Burney-Austen comparison. Brabourne may have read Burney also in the context of reviews of Llanover's *Autobiography and Correspondence* of Delany, but he responded in print to the *Memoir* and to the *Life* by Tytler, and to his own interpretations of both Burney and Brontë. Brabourne had provenance and greater volume in his favour, and he squandered both these advantages in a Llanover-like approach to family rivalry and ancestry. The diffuse text of the *Letters*' introduction and editorials did not, however, finally engulf the life of the auto/biographical subject. Recovery from Brabourne's framing narrative demonstrates how survival and shortage are features of the Austen archive that paradoxically provide a shape and a 'multivocal' challenge for life writing.

Bibliography

Austen, Henry (1818) 'Biographical Notice of the Author' and 'Postscript', in *"Northanger Abbey" and "Persuasion" by the Author of "Pride and Prejudice", "Mansfield Park" &c. Volume 1*. London: Murray, pp. v–xix.

Austen, Henry (1833) 'Memoir of Miss Austen', in Austen, Jane. *Sense and Sensibility* 'Standard Novels 23'. London: Bentley, pp. v–xv.

Austen-Leigh, James Edward (1870) *A Memoir of Jane Austen, by Her Nephew*. London: Bentley.

Austen-Leigh, James Edward (1871) *A Memoir of Jane Austen, by Her Nephew*. 2nd edn. London: Bentley.

Austen-Leigh, William, Austen-Leigh, Richard Arthur and Le Faye, Deirdre (1989) *Jane Austen: A Family Record*. London: British Library.

Barrett, Charlotte (ed.) (1842a) *The Diary and Letters of Madame D'Arblay. Volume 1: 1778–1780*. London: Henry Colburn.

Barrett, Charlotte (ed.) (1842d) *The Diary and Letters of Madame D'Arblay. Volume 4: 1788–1789*. London: Henry Colburn.

Brabourne, Lord (Edward Knatchbull-Hugesson) (ed.) (1884a) *Letters of Jane Austen. Volume 1*. London: Bentley.

Brabourne, Lord (Edward Knatchbull-Hugesson) (ed.) (1884b) *Letters of Jane Austen. Volume 2*. London: Bentley.

Chapman, Robert W. (ed.) (1932) *Jane Austen's Letters to Her Sister Cassandra and Others*. Oxford: Oxford University Press.

Chorley, Henry (1870). 'A *Memoir of Jane Austen* and *A Life of Mary Russell Mitford*', *Quarterly Review*, 128, pp. 196–218.

Croker, John Wilson (1833) '*Memoirs of Dr Burney*', *Quarterly Review*, 49, pp. 97–125.

Croker, John Wilson (1842) '*Diary and Letters of Madame D'Arblay, Vols I, II, III*', *Quarterly Review*, 70, pp. 243–87.

Favret, Mary A. (1993) *Romantic Correspondence: Women, Politics and the Fiction of Letters*. Cambridge: Cambridge University Press.

Gilson, David (1982) *A Bibliography of Jane Austen*. Oxford: Clarendon Press.

Hemlow, Joyce, Douglas, Althea and Hawkins, Patricia (eds) (1984) *The Journals and Letters of Fanny Burney. Volume 12: 1825–1840*. Oxford: Clarendon Press.

Honan, Park (1987) *Jane Austen: Her Life*. Reprint, London: Phoenix, 1997.

James, G.P.R. (1843) 'American Works of Fiction', *Foreign and Colonial Quarterly Review*, 2 (October), pp. 458–88.

Jewesbury, Maria (1831) 'Literary Women II: Jane Austen', *Athenaeum* 200 (27 August), pp. 553–4.

Johnson, Claudia (2012) *Jane Austen's Cults and Cultures*. London: University of Chicago Press.

Kebbel, Thomas (1885) 'Jane Austen at Home', *Fortnightly Review*, 37 (February), pp. 262–70.

Kirkham, Margaret (1983) 'The Austen Portraits and the Received Biography', in Todd, Janet (ed.) *Jane Austen: New Perspectives*. New York: Holmes and Meier, pp. 29–38.

Knatchbull-Hugessen, Sir Hughe (1960) *Kentish Family*. London: Methuen.

Lank, Edith (2008) 'List of Annotations in the Bellas Copy of Lord Brabourne's *Letters of Jane Austen*', *Persuasions On-Line*, 27(1). Available at: www.jasna.org/persuasions/on-line/vol29no1/lank.html (accessed: 22 May 2019)

Le Faye, Deirdre (ed.) (1995) *Jane Austen's Letters*. Oxford: Oxford University Press.

'Letters of Jane Austen' (1884) *Saturday Review*, 58 (15 November), pp. 637–8.

Llanover, Lady (Augusta Hall) (1861–62) *The Autobiography and Correspondence of Mary Granville, Mrs Delany* (6 vols). London: Bentley.

Macaulay, Thomas Babington (1843) 'Diary and Letters of Madame D'Arblay', *The Edinburgh Review*, 76, pp. 523–70.

May, William (2012) 'Letters to Jane: Austen, the Letter and Twentieth-Century Women's Writing', in Dow, Gillian and Hanson, Claire (eds) *Uses of Austen: Jane's Afterlives*. Basingstoke: Palgrave Macmillan, pp. 115–31. doi:10.1057/9781137271747

Modert, Jo (ed.) (1990) *Jane Austen's Letters in Facsimile*. Carbondale: Southern Illinois University Press.

Oliphant, Margaret (1870) 'Miss Austen and Miss Mitford', *Blackwoods Edinburgh Magazine*, 107, pp. 290–313.

Rae, William Fraser (1901) 'Edward Hugessen Knatchbull-Hugessen', in Lee, Sidney (ed.) *Dictionary of National Biography: Supplement. Volume 3.* London: Smith Elder, p. 69.

'Review: *Northanger Abbey* and *Persuasion*.' (1818) *Edinburgh Magazine and Literary Miscellany*, 2, pp. 453–5.

Sabor, Peter (2002) 'Jane Austen', in Jones, Derek (ed.) *Censorship: A World Encyclopedia*. London: Routledge, pp. 129–30.

Simpson, Richard (1870) 'Jane Austen', *North British Review*, 52, pp. 129–52.

Smith, George Barnett (1885) 'More Views of Jane Austen', *Gentleman's Magazine*, 258 (January), pp. 26–45.

Smith, Goldwin (1890) *Life of Jane Austen*. London: Scott.

Southam, Brian (2000) *Jane Austen and the Navy*. Reprint, London: National Maritime Museum, 2005.

Sutherland, Kathryn (ed.) (2002) *A Memoir of Jane Austen and Other Family Recollections*. Oxford: Oxford University Press.

Sutherland, Kathryn (2005) *Jane Austen's Textual Lives*. Oxford: Oxford University Press.

Sutherland, Kathryn (2009) 'Jane Austen's Life and Letters', in Johnson, Claudia L. and Tuite, Clara (eds) *A Companion to Jane Austen*. Oxford: Wiley Blackwell, pp. 13–30.

Sutherland, Kathryn (ed.) (2010) *Jane Austen's Fiction Manuscripts: A Digital Edition*. Available at: www.janeausten.ac.uk. ISBN: 978-0-9565793-1-7

Tytler, Sarah (1880) *Jane Austen and Her Works*. London: Cassell, Petter & Galpin.

Ward, Mary Augusta (December 1884) 'Style and Miss Austen.' *Macmillan's Magazine* 51, pp. 84–91.

Whately, Richard (1821) 'Modern Novels: A Review of "Northanger Abbey" and "Persuasion"', *Quarterly Review*, 24 (January), pp. 352–76.

Wheeler, Susan C. (1993) 'Prose and Power in Two Letters by Jane Austen', in Mackenzie, Alan T. (ed.) *Sent as a Gift: Eight Correspondences from the Eighteenth Century*. London: University of Georgia Press, pp. 173–200.

Wilson, Cheryl A. (2017) *Jane Austen and the Victorian Heroine*. London: Palgrave Macmillan. doi:10.1007/978-3-319-62965-0

7 *George Eliot's Life* (1885)

Letters as Life Writing and the Response to Biography

When the novelist George Eliot died suddenly in December 1880 executive power over her letters passed into the hands of her 'stepson', Charles Lee Lewes. Moral power, however, came to be invested in her new husband and former 'nephew' John Walter Cross, a banker with family links to a powerful Scottish merchant house. Cross had been the Leweses' financial advisor and tennis coach, and his subsequent approach to writing Eliot's *Life* betrayed both his accounting style and his procrastination over the market for biography. *George Eliot's Life as Related in Her Letters and Journals* was published in 1885 under a cloud of suspicion about Cross's motives, and he was accused of suppressing the character of Eliot.

Cross's *Life* appeared two years after the 'Eminent Women' biography *George Eliot* by Mathilde Blind (1883). This work built on other articles of 1881–82, including those by Edith Simcox, Frederick Myers and Charles Kegan Paul, that had claimed intimate knowledge of Eliot. Cross, however, 'judged it best to let George Eliot be her own interpreter' (1885a, p. viii), confining himself to 'the work of selection and arrangement' (p. vii) in which he was carefully reductive in his use of material. He exploited and pruned the evidence of the original documents and produced chapter summaries and an index that were highly selective. The design of Cross's *Life* allowed him to claim the use of Eliot's own words but his treatment of the letters and journals emerged from a requirement to respond to a market he understood very little. The chapter first explores what can be recovered of George Eliot's views on life writing and considers how Blind and Cross replaced her life within periodical culture using Eliot's own commentaries to justify their auto/biographical approaches.

In the context of the Barrett-Gaskell model and its recovery narrative, Cross's *Life* is then discussed as a riposte to other claimants on Eliot's biography. The chapter reviews Cross's use of Eliot's own words and the production of a generic hybrid auto/biography in letters. This includes the representation of Eliot's domestic role in parallel with Gaskell's recuperation of Brontë, and these 'hearthside affections' are traced using references to members of the Cross family who were retrospectively cultivated into Eliot's life and *Life*.

George Eliot and Life Writing

Eliot wrote to Frances Eleanor Trollope in 1879 that '[t]he best history of a writer is contained in his writings' (Haight 1955, p. 230) although this becomes highly ambiguous for all the biographers attempting to recover the life of Eliot from her novels. Eliot's published writing on the subject of life writing appeared in early, although anonymous, articles in *The Westminster Review* (1852a, 1852b) that were particularly noted by Blind (1883, pp. 79–80). To Trollope, Eliot described biography as 'a disease of English Literature' but autobiography as 'a precious contribution to knowledge' (Haight 1955, p. 230). Her widower was therefore keen to insist that his methods allowed Eliot to write her autobiography posthumously.

In January 1852, Eliot had reviewed Thomas Carlyle's *Life of Sterling* observing that 'the conditions required for the perfection of life writing' are 'personal intimacy, a loving poetic nature,…and the artistic power which seizes characteristic points and renders them with life-like effect' (1852a, p. 133). The review recommended qualities that would later be apportioned across Eliot's two biographers: Cross representing intimacy and loving, and Blind poetic and artistic power. Eliot concluded that

> the facts noted, the letters selected, are all such as serve to give the liveliest conception of what Sterling was, and what he did; and though this book speaks much of other persons, this collateral matter is all a kind of scene-painting and is accessory to the main purpose.
>
> (p. 133)

The concepts of 'scene-painting' and a foregrounded character resembled the task Cross would set himself in the years after Eliot's death. Blind, however, quoted a different section of this article in which Eliot commended biography 'instead of the three- or five-volume compilations of letter, and diary and detail, little to the purpose' (Eliot 1852a, p. 133; Blind 1883, p. 79). Eliot provided a definition for Blind's task of producing 'a real "life" setting forth briefly and vividly the man's inward and outward struggles, aims and achievements, so as to make clear the meaning which his experience has for his fellows' (Eliot 1852a, p. 133; Blind 1883, p. 79). It was Blind who would claim to be able to divine the 'meaning' and purpose in her biography leaving Cross to tackle the 'compilation'.

Blind also detected Eliot as the author of a review in the *Westminster* of the *Memoirs of Margaret Fuller Ossoli* (1852b) and so a 'correspondence' between them about life writing could appear in Blind's biography. Blind quoted Eliot's suggestion that Fuller was 'so self-conscious that her life seemed to be a studied act' (1885b, p. 353; Blind 1883, p. 80).

Eliot had also concluded that 'admiration and sympathy' for the life of Fuller was changed by the drowning that shaped the 'closing scenes' of the rather disorganised *Memoirs* (1852b, p. 353). Blind, in turn, aligned Eliot's life with Fuller's as a 'studied act' shaped by its closure when she described the essay writing of the novelist as a visit 'behind the scenes of her mind' (1883, p. 82). 'Marian Evans had not yet hidden herself behind the mask of George Eliot', Blind claimed, nor yet enacted her 'dramatic impersonation' of a novelist (p. 82). Further correspondences emerged. Eliot returned to Fuller and linked her with Mary Wollstonecraft in a later essay for the *Leader* (1855) while Blind too wrote a biographical essay about Wollstonecraft in the *New Quarterly Magazine* in July 1878. James Diedrick suggests that Blind read Eliot on Fuller at the same time (2016, p. 177). This circle of writers was also linked to the Brontës and to Gaskell by collected biographical output. Fuller was the subject of a biography by Julia Ward Howe in the second 'Eminent Women' series in which Blind produced her second title, *Madame Roland* in 1886. *George Eliot* (1883) appeared in the same (first) series as *Emily Brontë* by Agnes Mary Frances Robinson (1883). When these two lives published in 1883 were reviewed together in *The Times* on 9 January 1884, Blind was criticised for her cosmopolitan style (Diedrick 2016, p. 185) by comparison with Robinson's poetic and rhetorical approach to the scarce information on Emily Brontë. Robinson's biography was, however, basically rewritten from Gaskell's *Life* of 1857 (Peterson 2006) and by extension from Charlotte's letters and the 'Biographical Notice' of her sisters. The two lives by Blind and Gaskell were thus circulating in close textual proximity in the 1880s.

Unlike Gaskell, however, Blind had never actually met her biographical subject and so lacked the 'personal intimacy' recommended by Eliot in 1852. This meant that Blind had to work harder to insert herself into her version of Eliot's life. Blind did this by opening a debate about French women writers (1883, pp. 1–2) whom Eliot had surveyed in another essay for the *Westminster Review* (1854). In addition, Blind introduced women authors, seen to be counterparts of Eliot, whose lives and letters were also in the marketplace, notably Burney and Austen as well as Brontë (1883, pp. 6, 7–8). Blind later quoted Charlotte Brontë's letter on Lewes's novel *Ranthorpe* (p. 109) together with a reference to Jane Eyre who should, according to Blind, have been able to marry Rochester in the context of Eliot's 'union' with Lewes. Blind adjudged that Eliot 'was called upon to make her private judgment a law unto herself' (p. 114) just as her letters would be made to stand in for a public narrative.

Having inserted Brontë's fiction into Eliot's life, Blind then appeared to promote and justify her factual sources through letter evidence. In her preface, she thanked Eliot's Coventry friends the Brays and Sara Hennell as sources and gave them roles as narrators through their letters within the biography, at the same time fictionalising her contributors as 'more like some delightful characters in a first-rate novel' (1883, p. 34). Letters much later from March 1873 were inserted into the biography early on as illustrations of real-life 'friendly relations subsisting to the end' (p. 37), an image that had to be announced and sustained to promote the Coventry family's veracity as observers. The Hennell-Brays belonged to an early period of life that had to be established in the biography in advance of Blind's overall interpretation of Eliot's 'real' life. In Coventry, Cara Bray lived 'a life of saintly purity and self-devotion' (p. 35) and Sara Hennell was 'as a sister... importing all the ardour of feeling into a life of austere thought' (p. 37). Many of the characters of Eliot's life came to be equated with those of her novels precisely because the information available during her lifetime was closed down. Blind had linked Eliot's father with the eponymous Adam Bede and with Caleb Garth in *Middlemarch* (p. 13), her brother with Tom Tulliver in *The Mill on the Floss* (p. 19) and now the Brays with the Meyricks from *Daniel Deronda* (p. 36). Lewes himself was Deronda (p. 109). Blind later suggested that 'The child-life of Tom and Maggie Tulliver was in many respects an autobiography; and no biographer can ever hope to describe the early history of George Eliot as she herself has done in "The Mill on the Floss"' (p. 164). The absence of letters from a period pre-dating her celebrity had to be filled with an account unauthorised as life writing. It was also thus suggested that Eliot had already written her autobiography long before Cross reached the market.

Like Gaskell in *The Life of Charlotte Brontë*, Blind was forced to interpret and manage gaps and frequently adapted her letter evidence to this purpose. The Victorian reader would have recognised the significance of Eliot's religious and matrimonial crisis points where letter communication was actually absent or had broken down. The early religious divisions within the family and with her friend Maria Lewis became a 'new religious synthesis' (Blind 1883, p. 45). Blind surmised 'a new birth' from 'a letter written at this period' (p. 50) and commented that 'there exists a letter' (p. 60) written to a man who would be the prototype for Casaubon in *Middlemarch*. A letter to Cara Bray 'many years later' about 'an evil generation who would not read "Clarissa"' (p. 65) appeared anachronistically around this time in the biography, and an 1876 letter occurred during the 1850s *Westminster Review* chapter (p. 75). Other correspondents were marshalled in Blind's cause. One of the already published letters claiming to be Eliot's 'Last Words' (Phelps 1882) used Positivism to gloss over her relationship with Herbert Spencer, the philosopher who repelled Eliot's advances (Blind 1883, p. 104). Blind indicated that correspondence with Anne Gilchrist 'has been kindly placed at my disposal' (p. 247) but theirs was only a brief contact over Eliot's rental of her cottage during the composition of *Middlemarch*. Gilchrist was the author of *Mary Lamb* in the 'Eminent Women' series and Cross would quote from a letter about her 'methodical thoughtfulness' in preparing for the Leweses' stay (1885c, p. 130). Most significantly, Eliot's two 'elopements' and their surrounding communication would be anachronistically relocated through letters from the future inserted at key moments. In real time letters went unposted or at least unreceived while Eliot underwent her transformations into Mrs Lewes and later Mrs Cross (Hughes 1998, p. 338).

Blind, however, unlike Cross, could also be more liberated in her assessment of her characters. Lewes had 'a general shagginess of beard and eyebrow not unsuggestive of a Skye terrier' (1883, p. 280) and his 'tenderness' was described as 'doglike fidelity' (p. 113). Cross later included repeated references both to his own 'tenderness' and to that of his family in the *Life* (Cross 1885c, pp. 311, 312, 279) and, in turn, his loyalty to Eliot was privately described as 'canine' by the poet and critic Edmund Gosse on 16 June 1883 (Mathiesen and Mulligan 1965, p. 114). This canine relationship with Lewes and Cross remained mysteriously unresolved in an illustration that appeared at the end of the *Life* (Cross 1885c, opposite p. 440) in which there is a dog on the pavement outside the house where Eliot died at 4 Cheyne Walk in addition to the small figure of a man at the railings looking in. More controversially, Blind observed that Lewes 'helped to reveal George Eliot to herself, and after that there was little left for him to do' (1883, p. 123). In her biography, as in the press after Eliot's death, the later works were relegated along with Lewes. *Middlemarch* was 'a story without a plot' (p. 240) and in *Felix Holt* there is 'too conscious a seeking for effect' (p. 236). This was the received wisdom on Eliot in the 1880s: that she did her best work in the early novels. After the publication of *Romola* in 1863, Blind commented: 'Few are the external events to be now recorded of George Eliot's life' (p. 213). Publishing landmarks and domestic routine were summarised in a phrase reminiscent of the claimed uneventfulness of the lives of Austen and Brontë (Austen 1818, p. v; Peterson 2006, pp. 78, 300, 358). Blind might have been attempting a critical detachment reminiscent of Eliot's own but she also set up some of the criteria against which Cross's *Life* would be judged. She created an anticipation of unpublished correspondence and an interwoven discussion about Eliot's appearance (1883, pp. 54, 274–5) There was also an understanding that the plots of the novels would be part of any biographical revelations so that the novels as well as the letters were expected to stand in for autobiography.

In the aftermath of Blind's biography, Cross used his 'autobiography' to reproduce Eliot's opinions on life writing that had been formed by her reading of lives such as those of Charlotte Brontë, Lord Byron and particularly Harriet Martineau. A letter to Sara Hennell of 16 April 1857 demonstrated Eliot's response to Gaskell's *Life*: 'Deeply affecting throughout; in the early part romantic, poetic, as one of her own novels; in the later years tragic, especially to those who know what sickness is' (Cross 1885a, p. 441). Whether this referred to Gaskell's or Brontë's novels remained ambiguous in its suggestion of an auto/biographical distinction. Eliot continued: 'Mrs Gaskell has done her work admirably, both in the industry and care with which she has gathered and selected her material, and in the feeling with which she has presented it' (p. 441). On 22 May, Eliot wrote again to Hennell about 'the life of Currer Bell': 'Some people think its revelations in bad taste – making money out of the dead, wounding the feelings of the living etc.... We thought it admirable, cried over it, and felt better for it' (p. 449). Cross was here seeking vindication for his 'industry and care' despite Eliot's other reactions to auto/biography unearthed by Blind.

One particular life provided supporting material for Cross's approach in his *Life*. With the death of Harriet Martineau in 1876, Eliot wrote in a birthday letter to Hennell: 'All biography diminishes in interest when the subject has won celebrity... But autobiography at least saves a man or woman that the world is curious about from the publication of a string of mistakes called "Memoirs"' (Cross 1885c, p. 214). Eliot was demonstrated as showing concerns about shaping and about the balance of material. When Martineau's *Autobiography* came out the following year, having been first written in 1855, Eliot wrote to Cara Bray on 20 March 1877: 'as in all books of the kind, the charm departs as the life advances, and the writer has to tell of her own triumphs' (p. 305). Cross too had a problem caused by a lack of early autobiographical detail. He provided in Eliot's own words the suggestion that the narrative of growth was important but that it was difficult to provide a personal assessment. Eliot wrote that she regretted Martineau's commentary on 'her intercourse with many more or less distinguished persons' and 'her gratuitous rudeness' towards people who would have been living if the autobiography had appeared as planned (p. 305), and this discretion was definitely part of Cross's received brief. Margaret Oliphant would write in the *Edinburgh Review* that it is 'the fault of her biographer that she seems to take the great crisis of her life so calmly' (1885, p. 552). Although Cross's method appeared to allow Eliot to compose her autobiography and to make the letters stand in for any commentary, Cross also pruned and smoothed over her opinions.

Eliot was even more stringent in her comments about Maria Chapman's *Memorials of Harriet Martineau* appended to the *Autobiography* and this produced a statement significant within Cross's project for which he supplied a specific entry in the index: 'Autobiography, repugnance to' (1885c, p. 446). Eliot wrote to Sarah Hennell on 15 May 1877, indicating that she would not be reading Chapman: 'the more it deepens my repugnance – or rather creates a new repugnance in me – to autobiography, unless it can be so written as to involve neither self-glorification nor the impeachment of others' (pp. 306–7). This was Cross's plan. Eliot continued that 'a future life in the minds of a coming generation' cannot be used to 'perpetuate personal animosities, which can never be rightly judged by those immediately engaged in them' (p. 307). Eliot and Hennell had previously corresponded on 21 September 1869 on the subject of Byron's 'loss of moral wealth' and 'desecration of family ties' (Cross 1885c, p. 100). Using the May 1877 letter, Cross then sought to exonerate Eliot from any charges of having thought of the publication of her letters when she continued in the letter to Hennell:

> No, I did not agree with you about the Byron case... To write a letter in a rage is very pardonable... But I have no pity to spare for the rancour that corrects its proofs and revises, and lays it by chuckling with the sense of its future publicity.
>
> (pp. 307–8)

Cross therefore favoured the 'three-volume compilation' and termed this an 'autobiography' (1885a, p. viii), a form that was for him clearly sanctioned by Eliot evidence. Cross claimed somewhat ambiguously that 'the whole book is a long record of debts due to other friends for letters' (p. viii). The letters were written in real time to redress the balance of correspondence as dictated by letter manuals. The letters also provided evidence that he had been able to obtain the correspondence through his own credit as a husband and family advisor. The first 27 pages that he had to write himself were an account of Eliot's early life through references to her fiction; this he had to reclaim from Blind at the same time as he reclaimed Eliot as his wife.

Riposte and Recovery

Blind's 'Prefatory Note' had explained that 'the dearth of published materials' had directed her efforts to 'private sources' (1883, p. v). Like Gaskell visiting Haworth, Blind was active in research and had the 'privilege' of meeting Isaac Evans, Eliot's estranged brother 'gleaning many a characteristic trait from old people in the neighbourhood' (p. v). It seemed convenient to ignore the fact that the Evans family had not officially communicated with Eliot from the time of her elopement with Lewes until her marriage to Cross 23 years later, although Cross too would be keen to promote the Evans family given his reliance on Isaac for his opening chapter (1885a, p. viii). Blind and Cross would have other sources in common for the narrative of growth, '[f]or valuable help in forming an idea of the growth of GEORGE ELIOT's mind' (Blind 1883, p. v). Where Blind thanked 'her oldest friends' the Hennell-Brays, Cross's compilation would cumulatively suggest that Eliot corresponded with them only sporadically in later years, most often around Christmas and their November birthdays, Eliot's on 22nd and Sara's on 23rd. Blind added that 'Miss Jenkins, the novelist's schoolfellow, and Mrs John Cash, also generously afforded me every assistance in their power' (pp. v–vi).

Jenkins was not in Eliot's life after they both excelled in French at school and Cash was Mary Sibree whom Cross also interviewed and extracted in the *Life* (Cross 1885a, pp. 155–63). Blind's role was to research and to stand in for Eliot and to act as a new correspondent within the lives of these lapsed 'friends'.

Others who had become adherents latterly had already joined battle for ownership over her biography, appearance and reputation. Although Blind's explanation that '[a] great part of the correspondence in the present volume has not hitherto appeared in print' (1883, p. vi) reflected the hunger for information about Eliot, she also summarised as her sources the printed material that Cross would have to contest. Blind used letters that appeared in *Harper's Magazine* (Phelps 1882) and referenced articles by Charles Kegan Paul (1881) and Frederick Myers (1881) as well as an anonymous tribute in *Blackwood's Edinburgh Magazine* ('George Eliot' 1881). She drew attention also to an article in *Century Magazine* that claimed the character of Dinah Morris was based on that of Eliot's aunt, Elizabeth Evans (Bulkley 1882, pp. 550–52). In addition, Blind mentioned Edith Simcox writing in the *Contemporary Review*, assuming that 'One Who Knew Her' must be Simcox whereas the article entitled 'The Moral Influence of George Eliot' was actually written by Julia Wedgwood (1881) who would go on to publish *The Moral Ideal* (1888). She was the same 'Snow' Wedgwood who had helped with the compilation of Gaskell's *Life of Charlotte Brontë* nearly 25 years before (Chapple 1979, p. 288) and who had been claimed privately by Gaskell's daughter Meta as a 'Mother-Confessor' in a letter dated 8 November 1856 (Wiltshire 2012, p. 51). Simcox was the named author of another article in *The Nineteenth Century* in May 1881, where she had in fact protested about the 'One Who Knew Her' article and another by Leslie Stephen in *Cornhilll Magazine* (1881). In her *Autobiography of a Shirtmaker*, Simcox noted on 20 March 1881 that she planned such a riposte and that she had gained support for it from Cross and from another Eliot worshipper, Elma Stuart (Fulmer and Barfield 1998, pp. 153–4). Cross was also personally aware of the *Cornhill* and *Nineteenth Century* articles through the correspondence of Simcox and Stuart. Blind, however, broadly encapsulated the terms on which battle had been drawn up.

Some of these articles required Cross to provide his own riposte and others gave him guidance once he had finally settled on the form of letters for his commemoration of the woman he had originally called 'Aunt'. Eliot's publisher Blackwood had recorded a prompt tribute in their magazine in February 1881 while pointing out 'we have in her works, and in our private correspondence relating to them, all that is requisite for constructing a brief history of her genius' ('George Eliot' 1881, p. 267). This pinpointed the location of the texts themselves but also gave out a vague threat about their publication. The article also reiterated the suggestion of life writing in the works that recurred often in the obituary notices and in Blind's biography. In *Cornhill Magazine*, where *Romola* had actually appeared as a serial (July 1862–August 1863) followed by 'Brother Jacob' (July 1864), Leslie Stephen promoted the idea that the novels were Eliot's life and presented her as a late developer compared with Brontë and Fielding, allying her work pattern rather with that of Scott. It was from the novels that he felt able to conclude: 'The so-called masculine quality in George Eliot – her wide and calm intelligence – was certainly combined with a thoroughly feminine nature' (1881, p. 160). Stephen did not stray into the life but described Eliot 'teaching' with 'a power and delicacy unsurpassed in her own sphere' (p. 168). The life was being aligned with the career in a balance between preparation and fulfilment through fiction. This was an obvious approach in a magazine dedicated to fiction although the *Cornhill*'s publisher Smith Elder had not benefited in kind from the serialisation of *Romola* by comparison with the successes recorded for Eliot's fiction at Blackwood (Glynn 1986, pp. 137–41). Writing in *Harper's New Monthly Magazine*, Charles Kegan Paul, editor of *Mary Wollstonecraft's Letters to Gilbert Imlay* (1879), also laid down guidelines for Cross:

> Whenever the life of George Eliot is written, it is plain that the interest will be found to lie chiefly in the records of her mind, as shown by what of her conversation can be preserved and by her correspondence.
>
> (1881, p. 912)

He added a caution: 'of outward events her life had few. She shunned rather than courted publicity, and there will be nothing to satisfy any of those who look for exciting narratives in biography' (p. 912).

The immediate obituaries were suggesting that the life evidence claimed by publishers and correspondents was distributed between the letters and the works. A more sinister development in *Harper's Monthly* for March 1882 came in the form of 'Last Words from George Eliot' by Elizabeth Stuart Phelps, an American writer who was briefly in correspondence with Eliot about a course on 'Representative Modern Fiction'. Phelps wrote: 'I make no apology for sharing with the readers of this Magazine my little portion of our now precious memories of her, almost without comment of my own' (1882, p. 568). This seemed to be suggesting that Eliot could speak for herself using Phelps as a medium. Phelps had approached the subject already in a tribute poem that had appeared in the same issue as Kegan Paul's article in May 1881; the two pieces were separated by a four-page article on English Parliamentary procedure that made Phelps's short displaced poem appear to be a filler item. Phelps was named, as she was for the article, in the index to the volume edition of the magazine and her poem was listed in the index as 'Eliot, George: Her Jury' so as to follow the Kegan Paul article despite their separation in the issue of the magazine ('Contents of Volume LXII' 1881, p. v). In sentimental style, the poem claimed that Eliot was 'A lily rooted in a sacred soil' (Phelps 1881, p. 927). According to the poem, Eliot was to be judged by the pleading of her own fictional women, Dinah and Dorothea, whose existence replaced the Christian beliefs questioned by Eliot. At the same time, Eliot acquired a Christ-like significance in the poem because of Phelps's capitalisation of the personal pronoun: Dinah 'Shall plead for Her' and the characters are 'Of Her great hand, the moulded, breathing clay' (p. 927). Phelps asked a final rhetorical question: 'Shall they...possess the life eternal and not She?' (p. 927).

In 'Last Words', Phelps later explained that their correspondence arose as a result of her seeking a biography of Eliot at 'the beginning of an occasional, and by no means confidential, but to me most valuable correspondence, interrupted only by the death of Mrs Cross' (1882, p. 568). She claimed that theirs was an 'unfinished friendship' and that George Eliot 'must live despite herself' (p. 571). Phelps offered her own 'little invertebral membrane in the shape of an explanatory word or two' (p. 568) and also claimed to be keeping some pages to herself, quoting only 'shattered crystals' (p. 570). It may be that this technique recommended itself to Cross as a counter-weight to the more free-flowing account supplied by Blind. Cross was, however, once more threatened by the manuscript holdings of people prepared to go into print. Despite her claims of simplicity and non-intervention, Phelps made extravagant claims for her material 'like fossil ferns': 'Continually upon these few well-worn sheets the fine outline falls' (p. 569). In addition, at the very beginning of the article, came the threat that would highlight Cross's own concerns and failings in the context of all the tributes: 'It is to be hoped that he of all now living most fitted for such a task will give to the world the memorial volume for which we now wait' (p. 568).

The waiting, however, went on. Over a year later, on 16 June 1883, Edmund Gosse wrote to Robert Underwood, editor of *Century Magazine*, suggesting that the 'world' did not think Cross 'fitted' and that the *Life* 'will not see the light of day for many years unless pressure is put on Cross by threatened publication' (Mathieson and Mulligan 1965, p. 114). '[T]hreatened publication' had already included the Phelps 'Last Words' and the revelations of Blind's biography in which Blind had unearthed rumours of an early engagement to a picture restorer (1883, p. 33) in addition to drawing parallels between Eliot's own life and the events of *The Mill on the Floss* (p. 164). Despite his role in the image-making discussed below, Gosse added, 'To save his wife's character he may be forced to publish, as he has been forced to write his book, against his will' (Mathieson and Mulligan 1965, p. 114). The campaign for Cross's publication was also conducted in public. Gosse had seen a brief entry by 'an admirer of George Eliot' in the 'personal' column of

Harper's Weekly that seemed to challenge the hesitant auto/biographer. The writer of this entry claimed that 'Had it not been for the busy and bustling GEORGE HENRY LEWES...the world would most likely have been without such precious possessions as *Adam Bede*, *Romola* and *The Mill on the Floss*' ('Personal' 1883, p. 339). It was Lewes, in capital letters, who had promoted Eliot in the past and oiled the wheels of publication. This view was then complicated by the suggestion that Eliot lacked energy because of her 'mere industry and application' with its 'wealth of unused potentialities' (p. 339). The magazine itself provided the potentially threatening postscript that '[t]he forthcoming *Life of George Eliot*, by her second husband, Mr. CROSS, is nearly finished' (p. 339), to be read as both a call for a riposte and a riposte in itself.

The *Harper's Weekly* campaign continued three months later, when the Norwegian author Hjalmar Boyesen once again described Lewes both as a philosopher and as the 'husband of George Eliot' (1883, p. 615). Eliot was a 'gifted wife' who did not like anyone to speak of her works. The Russian novelist Turgenev was reported to have described her style as 'unfortunate' because 'she expressed herself in an overelaborate and cumbrous manner' (p. 615). Harper's would be the American publishers of the *Life*, but it was a further 15 months before Cross's publication appeared, and this criticism would surely have hit home. Cross's younger brother Richard and his family were influential in New York society at this time, even though Cross himself was now based in London. His nephews John Walter and Eliot Buchanan Cross would be responsible as architects for many of New York's landmark buildings (Pennoyer and Walker 2014). John Walter Cross I was described as a 'second husband' (Boyesen 1883, p. 615) in conjunction with Lewes. Cross too was by implication lacking in energy since, unlike Lewes, he had not yet promoted the figure and works of George Eliot in the world. Gosse commented of Cross in June 1883, 'He is extremely rich, without literary ambition, disdainful of popularity, activated by no feeling but a sort of unreasoning canine loyalty to his wife's memory...he only wants to be let alone' (Mathieson and Mulligan 1965, p. 114).

The three volumes Cross finally produced were given narrative shape by their subtitles: 'Unknown', 'Famous' and 'Sunset'. This life trajectory re-evaluated Eliot's later work as part of an uneventful period as was proposed by Blind. Cross the insider was supposed, however, to reveal George Eliot to a world awaiting revelations: revelations in which they were disappointed. In response, *Blackwood's Edinburgh Magazine* was inevitably supportive since the *Life* was a Blackwood publication ('The Life and Letters' 1885) and John Morley in *Macmillan's Magazine* pronounced the book 'a striking success' that 'leaves her life to write itself' (1885, p. 242). Morley was himself the general editor of Macmillan's 'English Men of Letters' and future biographer of Gladstone, and he referred in his review to the letters of Scott, Macaulay, Voltaire and Byron

(p. 242). A life of Macaulay had appeared in the first 'English Men of Letters' series. Gaskell, Eliot and Burney would feature in the second so this was a review designed to develop his own market for biography. Margaret Oliphant, who had written a biography of Sheridan for Morley, was unimpressed with the 'absence of all personal comment and gossip' and the 'reticence' of the *Life* (1885, p. 553). She devalued letter evidence when she observed that 'George Eliot needs no expositor' other than her characters Maggie Tulliver and Dorothea Brooke (p. 553). In the same 'Book of Appreciation' where Eliza Lynn Linton would savage Eliot's 'private life and character' (1897, p. 63), Oliphant would later comment on 'the ruthless art of Biography' in an account of the Brontës (1897, p. 56). This article commended Emily for being 'no correspondent' (p. 56) and observed that Gaskell herself had wisely fended off similar treatment by leaving children to 'protect her memory' (p. 58). With no remaining children of her own, Oliphant refused to allow her own life to be written and left her editor Annie Coghill with the problem of providing a thread of storyline between her letters and prose accounts of her life (1899), a process that has been described as 'simultaneously auto/biographical and epistolary' (Regis 2019, p. 68). In 1885, Oliphant was already wresting with such methodology when she relegated both Cross himself and Eliot's other correspondents to being 'smaller voices' that 'die away' 'even when, by some mystery of nature, they are joined and echoed by her own' (Oliphant 1885, p. 553).

Richard Hutton in the *Contemporary Review* called Cross's *Life* a 'sombre book' (1885, p. 372) and suggested that Eliot's correspondence proved that 'the richest part of her was almost a secret from herself' (p. 373). This seemed to indicate that Eliot was not even capable of being her own autobiographer and that the letters could not write a real life because she was barely in correspondence with herself. Henry James, who knew Cross personally, was more circumspect in *Atlantic Monthly* when he commented on Eliot's lack of 'animal spirits' (1885, p. 678) and on 'her rich and complicated mind' (p. 668). James pointed out that the public may have been expecting revelations from behind the scenes and had learned only of Eliot's depression and poor health but he concluded that '[t]here is little that is absent that it would have been in Mr Cross's power to give us' (p. 668). This might mean that there was no other evidence but also hinted that Cross was not capable or worthy to access that evidence in the first place. Such underwhelming commentary reflected the task faced by Cross in producing his recovery narrative in the wake of Blind's biography. Cross took on the role of judging the immediacy in the letters while also excising their spontaneity, and this prompted Oliphant to describe the *Life* as 'a gigantic silhouette... Background and figure are alike dull' (1885, p. 517). Cross had had to reclaim both Eliot and her circle of correspondents from the 'Eminent Women' text that had preceded him.

'Her Own Interpreter'

The emergence of the *Life* can be traced through the preferred image presented by Cross and by his response to key events within Eliot's life as well as his planned importation of the Cross family. Cross was forced to write a recovery narrative by revelations emerging in magazines and in Blind's biography, and his work to control the circulation of Eliot's image led to a compromise in November 1881. When Gosse commented in 1883 that '[p]ublic feeling... has obliged him to write this book' (Mathieson and Mulligan 1965, p. 114), he would have been aware of his own role in goading Cross into publication. Gosse was the author of a brief article (1881) accompanying a picture of Eliot, reproduced in agreement with the widower, that appeared as a frontispiece to *Century Magazine*. Eliot's appearance had become a battleground for her worshippers and her detractors. Blind randomly remarked that 'her personal appearance improved with time' but that Eliot never had 'any real youthfulness' with her 'general heaviness of structure, the complexion being pale but not fair' (1883, p. 54). Kegan Paul had written: 'To the casual observer there was but little of what is generally understood to be beauty of form' (1881, p. 920). The Gosse article reiterated Cross's ownership of the published image of Eliot engraved from a chalk drawing made in 1866–67 by Frederick Burton. Gosse explained that the only other two images were in private hands. One, from 1849, had been drawn and was owned by François d'Albert Durade in Geneva where Eliot lived for about a year after her father's death, while a Samuel Laurence image from 1861 was owned by the publisher Blackwood. Gosse explained that there might also be a silhouette of her aged 16, a photograph from 1850 and a pencil drawing by Mrs Alma Tadema from March 1877 but that Mr Cross was 'determined to record in a monumental way what he felt to be the best existing likeness' (1881, p. 47). When he published the *Life* in 1885, Cross subsequently presented the letters as standing in for Eliot's appearance: 'I have endeavoured to combine a narrative of day-to-day life with the play of light and shade, which only letters, written in various moods, can give, and without which no portrait can be a good likeness' (1885a, pp. vi–vii). The Burton etching evolved into the frontispiece to Volume 1 of the *Life* and Durade's 'George Eliot at 30', by this time in Cross's possession (p. xi), appeared in Volume 2. Cross himself was represented in Volume 3 by the illustration of the house in Cheyne Walk where Eliot died and by another illustration, opposite page 298, of Witley Heights. This was a house that he himself obtained for the Leweses in 1876, and the illustration was included on the page preceding a letter dated 18 January 1877 in which Eliot commended to John Blackwood the services of Helen Allingham, the illustrator used here in the *Life* (Cross 1885c, p. 302).

Images were thus being positioned within the *Life* but Cross encountered greater difficulty in answering written commentary. Frederick Myers's account of 'a deeply venerated friend whom death has newly taken' (1881, p. 57) appeared in the same issue of *Century* as the engraving. Myers insisted that the story of Eliot's life was 'simple and unsuggestive' (p. 60) but his article promoted many of the accounts of Eliot circulating despite the attempts of other writers such as Simcox (1881) and the writer of the Blackwood tribute ('George Eliot' 1881) to maintain her privacy. From being 'an obscure sub-editor of an unfashionable review, she rose at a bound to the first place among the imaginative prose writers of her time' (Myers 1881, p. 58); her success was the result of work over 20 years during which 'her mind was fed by strenuous and constant study' (p. 58) and the learning of the gloomy sage was reflected in her 'strenuous seriousness' (p. 59). Myers called her 'Mrs Lewes' and painted the picture of a humourless reclusive woman without 'any buoyancy or contagious quality' at her 'Sunday afternoon receptions' (p. 59). Myers promoted the idea of the studious author then added his personal story of their meeting. The description of 'her grave majestic countenance turned towards me like a sibyl's in the gloom' (p. 62) was reinforced by the appearance of this countenance as frontispiece to the actual magazine. The sage and sibyl characterisations of Eliot attributed by many commentators to Cross were being promulgated here four years before the 1885 *Life*. Despite having no personal contact with Eliot, Blind would describe 'a certain weird sibylline air' (1883, p. 214) and Richard Hutton would later quote Myers's article at length in his review of Cross's *Life* in the *Contemporary Review*, claiming that '[t]his sombre book reads like one long illumination of a passage contained in Mr Myers' essay' (1885, p. 372).

It was clear that even Eliot's friends wrestled with the image-making and gossip-mongering that followed Eliot's death. Her life and career were variously engineered in public by writers with much more influence than Cross in the periodical and life-writing markets. Her letters as finally presented to the reading public offered a reiteration of her working life managed by Lewes and John Blackwood but a long catalogue of ailments and upheavals also emerged. In order to allow Eliot to speak for herself, Cross removed the visual trappings of the letter but used the outer margins (left on the verso and right on the recto) to indicate the name of the correspondent and the date of the letter. He explained his technique at the beginning of Volume 1 of the *Life*:

> With the materials in my hands, I have endeavoured to form an *autobiography* (if the term may be permitted) of George Eliot...[b]y arranging all the letters and journals so as to form one connected whole, keeping the order of their dates, and with the least possible interruption of comment.
>
> (1885a, p. v)

This was what Rosemarie Bodenheimer has termed 'Cross's patchwork manufacture of a continuous narrative' (1994, p. 3), a method intended to give the reader an uninterrupted flow as if from the pen of Eliot herself. Cross claimed 'I have confined myself to the work of selection and arrangement' but he also confessed that '[e]ach letter has been pruned of everything that seemed to me irrelevant to my purpose' (1885a, p. vii). After the introductory chapter that followed this preface, he reiterated his scheme for the *Life* by alluding to Boswell's *Life of Johnson* and the letters of Hannah More although not to Burney (Barrett 1842–46) whose letters had also been treated as 'continuous narrative'. He explained that he would not give any single letter in full and that:

[t]he slight thread of narrative or explanation which I have written to elucidate the letters, where necessary, will hereafter occupy an inside margin, so that the reader will see at a glance what is narrative and what is correspondence, and will be troubled as little as possible with marks of quotation or changes of type.

(1885a, pp. 38–9)

Despite naming his traditional forebears in life writing, Cross the banker was returning the letter in appearance to its function as a balance sheet.

The divisions created by Cross's layout exacerbated a further discrepancy between the letter-writing moment and the life-writing moment. The technique kept track of dates but also removed the sense of letters' having a correspondent, as if the reader should assume that Eliot was speaking directly without postal intervention. The life was presented through a medium adapted too far from its original context and created the curious effect of nullifying Eliot's voice because it no longer had either a context or a justification within the life being lived and narrated. Cross was praised for his originality ('The Life and Letters of George Eliot' 1885, p. 175; Morley 1885, p. 242) but the method of minimal interjection followed on from that adopted by Barrett (1842–46) and Lady Llanover (1861–62) in arranging for the subject to speak for herself. In Cross's *Life*, however, the excisions that allowed for the flow of material suggested omission and censorship rather than shaping, and the outer marginal dating on the one hand presented factual evidence but on the other highlighted the gaps that would be taken for reticence.

It thus became clear that the year 1850, when Eliot changed her name to 'Marian', was missed out altogether. Inevitably Cross also had to tread warily around the subject of Lewes, to reveal 'the deeper side of his character' (1885a, p. 261). On 28 March 1853, Eliot remarked to Hennell: 'Lewes, as always, genial and amusing. He has quite won my liking, in spite of myself' (p. 307). Her friends were in reality, however, kept in ignorance of her plans and Cross had to manoeuvre his material into an acceptable form to maintain the support of his letter evidence.

In this, he used a letter to the Brays dated 20 July 1854 that adopted a different tone and format from other letters to this family when it concluded: 'Dear friends – all three – I have only time to say good-bye, and God bless you... Ever your loving and grateful Marian' (p. 325). Cross was careful here not to prune the greeting and adieu, and he also imported a further letter '(out of its place as to date)' from September 1855 since '[h]ere as elsewhere, it seems to be of the first importance that she should speak for herself' (p. 326). He aimed to present 'the point of view from which she regarded her own action' and then claimed that 'No words that any one else can write, no arguments any one else can use, will I think, be so impressive as the life itself' (p. 326). This letter ended the chapter with 'I am your affectionate and earnest friend' (p. 329) but also included the words 'I should never like to write about myself again' (p. 326). Cross was struggling here and decided to justify the 'union' with Lewes at the expense of undermining his sources. In a letter to Clementia Taylor dated 5 May 1856, Cross has already had Eliot bemoan the 'uncertain process of letter-writing' and the 'weaving and unweaving of false impressions' (p. 294) created by letters. Eliot has experienced 'misunderstanding created by letters, even to old friends' (p. 293). The Brays, however, must appear to have known about the elopement with Lewes to allow a justification to be put in the right place for Cross's argument. Many more letters would follow and Eliot would also be made to write about the resulting 'new birth' (p. 413) herself for a further two volumes, with the term reiterated early in Volume 2 in a quotation from Lewes's Journal dated 28 January 1859 (1885b, p. 55). When Eliot became engaged to Cross more than 20 years later, she would describe 'the wonderful renewal of my life' in a letter of 13 April 1880 to Cross's sister Eleanor (1885c, p. 387), and this was one of the areas where the Cross family were employed to renovate Eliot's life retrospectively.

Cross combined his use of Eliot's words with the restoration of her domestic character or 'hearthside affections'. He echoed Gaskell's objective in writing *The Life of Charlotte Brontë* to make 'the world...honour the woman as much as they admired the writer' (Chapple and Pollard 1966, p. 345) which had been announced in a letter to George Smith dated 31 May 1855. On 4 June 1855, Gaskell reiterated to Smith 'the more she was known the more people would honour her as a woman, separate from her character as an authoress' (p. 347). Cross announced in his prospectus that '[i]n dealing with the correspondence I have been influenced by the desire to make known the woman, as well as the author, through the presentation of her daily life' (1885a, p. v). He insisted that '[t]he letters now published throw light on another side of her nature – not less important, but hitherto unknown to the public, – the side of the affections' (p. vi). This would be his unique contribution to the life of Eliot. He explained that Eliot shrank from 'the position of a public character' while cherishing 'the reward of the artist' but that 'the joys of the

hearthside, the delight in the love of her friends, were the supreme pleasure of her life' (p. vi). In July 1842, at a time when domestication within
the Cross family was not yet available, 'intellectual sympathy' had been
provided by Sara Hennell (p. 114) but Cross also reconstituted Eliot's
estranged half-sister Fanny Houghton in 1848 as having 'more intellectual sympathy' than the rest of the Evans family (p. 228). The death of
Robert Evans at this time was presented through halting letters different
in style from those around them (pp. 186–205). Eliot wrote to Hennell
at the end of 1848, 'I am living unspeakable moments, and can write no
more' (p. 194) and in April 1849, 'My letters would be a sort of hermit's
diary' (p. 201). The Houghton correspondence, however, was designed
to reinforce Eliot's domestic fireside character although few letters had
been preserved and seemed mostly to demonstrate the conventions of
letter writing. On 6 September 1849, Eliot wrote: 'I begin to feel the full
value of a letter...I shall always reckon it among the first duties to sit
down without delay, giving no ear to the suggestions of my idleness and
aversion to letter-writing' (p. 220); and then on 4 October 'The blessed
compensation there is in all things made your letter doubly precious for
having been waited for' (p. 228). In the context of Cross's *Life*, such
letters were perhaps designed to distract from the unusual step of Eliot's
being alone as a single woman alone in Europe, and the half-sisters were
estranged afterwards by Eliot's co-habitation with Lewes.

The estrangement from correspondents and the constitution of domesticity within a culturally suspect 'hearthside' had to be managed for
public consumption. The 'union' with Lewes was named on the contents page to Volume 1 (Cross 1885a, p. xiv) and in its place in July 1854
(p. 326). Letters to Hennell here compensated by becoming more dutiful
in content, and on 19 February 1859, despite her declaration to Taylor,
Eliot wrote: 'You have the art of writing just the sort of letters I care
for – sincere letters like your own talk' (Cross 1885b, p. 60). The Leweses were reading out loud the *Life of Scott*: 'Our home is very comfortable, with far more of vulgar indulgences in it than I ever expected to
have again' (p. 60). The new hearthside was represented by the domestic
duties of letter writing and collaborative learning. For Hennell, Eliot
called Lewes '[a] model husband!' (p. 99) on 15 April 1859 restoring a
sense of domesticity where Blind had more bluntly commented that 'she
became his wife in every sense but the legal one' (1883, p. 116). Cross
also preserved a type of anti-domestic discourse to signal a growing
distance in the relationship with her Coventry correspondents. Hennell
had been offended by a critique of her work according to a letter of 27
August 1860 in which Eliot had decided that letters are not suitable
for writing 'on large questions' (Cross 1885b, p. 270). The next letter
in the sequence appeared to be a birthday letter on 13 November and
Eliot then maintained a distance on 20 December when complaining
to Hennell, after the awkward patch in their relationship, 'Such is life,

seen from a furnishing point of view' (p. 282). When she moved to the
Priory in 1863, Eliot told Cara Bray on 14 November, again around her
birthday:

> Such fringing away of precious life in thinking of carpets and tables,
> is an affliction to me, and seems like a nightmare from which I shall
> find it bliss to awake into my old world of care for things, quite apart
> from upholstery.
>
> (p. 367)

With Eliot's final illness approaching, Cross restored domestic cares in
a further digression on the subject during his survey of Eliot's character in his own words (1885c, pp. 416–31): 'Nothing offended her more
than the idea that because a woman had exceptional intellectual powers
therefore it was right that she should absolve herself, or be absolved,
from her ordinary household duties' (p. 428).

The rest of Cross's *Life*, however, had to negotiate the absence of a
public life too. When Eliot resumed her correspondence with Clementia
Taylor on 1 and 6 April 1861, she explained that it had been no 'trial'
to be 'cut off from what is called the world' (1885b, p. 294) since without the 'usual reciprocity of visits' (p. 297) she could dedicate herself to
work without causing offence (p. 296). She also told Taylor that she had
ceased to be '"Miss Evans"... – having held myself under all the responsibilities of a married woman, I wish this to be distinctly understood'
(p. 294). Eliot described this new family being completed by Lewes's
sons who called her mother and Charles Lewes was 'our oldest boy' in
her Journal for 1 July 1860 (p. 255). She told Taylor, 'the point is not one
of mere egoism or personal dignity, when I request that any one who has
a regard for me will cease to speak of me by my maiden name' (p. 295).

Conversely, the 'hearthside' became an important factor in the cultivation of the Cross family, essential to Cross's own position in the *Life*. The
Crosses occupied a whole column in the index (Cross 1885c, p. 450), and
their role was to take the place of both Eliot's actual family and the Coventry family as well as of their fictional embodiments. Lewes had met
Cross's mother Anna on a walking tour in 1867, and the acquaintance
was consolidated during a visit to Rome in 1869 when Cross first met
the Leweses while on a trip to Europe from America where he was then
in business. Cross anticipated his future marriage by including a letter to
Barbara Bodichon dated 2 July 1877 about the marriage of Anne Thackeray to a much younger man: 'nearly twenty years difference between
them was bridged hopefully by his solidity and gravity...young men with
even brilliant advantages will often choose as their life's companion
a woman whose attractions are chiefly of the spiritual order' (1885c,
p. 313). Cross too was also more than 20 years Eliot's junior and he was
careful to include any early references to himself where they occurred in

Eliot's own words. Eliot's letter to his sister Florence Nightingale Cross on 11 May 1874 included a reference to 'J' and closed 'Best love to all, the mother being chief among them all' (1885c, pp. 230–31). A letter to Anna Cross in September 1872 included 'Particular regards to J' (pp. 168–9). Cross understandably omitted references to himself as 'Nephew' but unsqueamishly included a letter to Florence in which Eliot claimed, 'You are our children, you know' (p. 398). Florence was born in 1857 so Cross (born 1840) was old enough to be her father. His other sisters were, however, Anne (born 1841), Mary (born 1843), Eleanor (born 1847) and Emily (born 1849). A letter from their brother, the wealthy Richard James Cross in America, sealed Eliot's welcome into the Cross family according to another letter to Florence dated 25 May 1880 (p. 397) but at this point there was also a long extract from Eliot's letter to her own brother Isaac who wrote his congratulations after their 23-year estrangement. Eliot told him on 26 May, 'our long silence has never broken the affection for you' although for Cross's purposes she also conveniently acknowledged in the same letter that she had known the Cross family for 11 years (p. 398).

Cross's choices are, of course, now made visible by the Eliot collected letters (Haight 1954–55, 1978). In a letter to Cara Bray dated 28 November 1880 about the 'desecrating fate' of the preserved letter, Eliot wrote that '[b]urning is the most reverential destination one can give to relics which will not interest any one after we are gone' (Haight 1955, pp. 340). She contrasted the resulting 'lumber' of the material and 'hard curiosity' of future readers with the 'eyes full of living memory' of the original recipients and inheritors (p. 341). It is perhaps unsurprising that Cross omitted this passage and extracted instead from the same letter an account of their plans to move into 4 Cheyne Walk and his 'tenderest watching and nursing' during Eliot's recent illness (1885c, p. 434). Cross had, however, already preserved a similar passage that suggested his more proper approach to the use of letters. On 20 February 1874, Eliot had written to John Blackwood about 'the reform of our habits in the matter of literary biography' (p. 226) with reference to Forster's *Life of Dickens*: 'Is it not odious that as soon as a man is dead his desk is raked, and every insignificant memorandum which he never meant for the public is printed for the gossip and amusement of people too idle to read his books?' (p. 226). This was surely provided as a commentary on Cross's own project that acted as a counter-weight to the search for biographical titillation. At the same time however, the *Life* drew attention to the existence of this and many other letters retained by Blackwood that were part of Eliot's writing life and had been used as bargaining in the publisher's memorial tribute article ('George Eliot', 1881).

Eliot herself thwarted the correspondence seekers by destroying letters to herself and having Lewes's letters buried with her. On 29 November 1879, she recorded in her Journal 'I read his letters, and packed them together, to be buried with me. Perhaps that will happen before next November' (Harris and Johnston, p. 187). This entry was excluded from the *Life* in which Cross quoted at this point from the convenient annual birthday letter to Sara Hennell: 'I am exceptionally blessed in many ways; but more blessed are the dead who rest from their labours, and have not to dread a barren, useless survival' (1885c, p. 385). Eliot wrote to Clementia Taylor on 6 December, a week after the journal entry that bemoaned the absence of Lewes as secretary: 'I have now to write a great many letters, such as used to be written for me' (p. 385). Cross noted that she was seeing 'old friends again', including him '[b]ut her life was nevertheless a life of heart-loneliness. Accustomed as she had been for so many years to solitude *à deux*' (p. 387). The sensationalism of the loss of letters that could have provided key information was replaced with these more sentimental reflections.

It was not just the authorised illustration in *Century Magazine* that recorded Eliot 'in a monumental way'. Cross's decision to make Eliot speak for herself was based on his interpretation of her preference for autobiography. He then had to embrace all the elements of the Barrett-Gaskell model that contorted Eliot's letters as life writing. It had to be demonstrated that the letters had not been written for publication, despite their authorship, and Eliot herself had to be shown to be wary of self-narration and performance. Her own words were preferred, but Cross's pruning methods suggested withholding as well as a sense of duty letter writing, which might itself be a kind of fiction. Cross thought he would be able to mould a life to re-present and protect Eliot, but the letter-writing form was a false friend in this enterprise. When he fell back on the domestic narrative, this clashed with the gloomy sage and sibyl model purveyed by the more experienced writers who had pre-empted him.

Bibliography

Austen, Henry (1818) 'Biographical Notice of the Author' and 'Postscript', in Austen, Jane. *"Northanger Abbey" and "Persuasion" by the Author of "Pride and Prejudice", "Mansfield Park" &c. Volume 1*. London: Murray, pp. v–xix.

Barrett, Charlotte (ed.) (1842–46) *The Diary and Letters of Madame D'Arblay* (7 vols). London: Henry Colburn.

Blind, Mathilde (1883) *George Eliot*. London: W. H. Allen.

Bodenheimer, Rosemarie (1994) *The Real Life of Mary Ann Evans: George Eliot, Her Letters and Fiction*. Ithaca, NY: Cornell University Press.

Boyesen, Hjalmar H. (1883) 'Reminiscences of Tourgénoff', *Harper's Weekly*, 24 (29 September), p. 615.

Bulkley, Louisa (1882) 'Dinah Morris and Mrs Elizabeth Evans', *Century Magazine*, 24 (August), pp. 550–52.

Chapple, John A.V. (1979) 'An Author's Life: Elizabeth Gaskell and the Wedgwood Family', *Bronte Society Transactions*, 17, pp. 287–92.

Chapple, John A.V. and Pollard, Arthur (eds) (1966) *The Letters of Mrs Gaskell*. Reprint, London: Mandolin, 1997.

Coghill, Mrs Harry [Annie Louise] (1899) *Autobiography and Letters of Mrs M.O.W. Oliphant*. London: Blackwood.

'Contents of Volume LXII' (1881). *Harper's New Monthly Magazine*, 62, pp. iii–viii.

Cross, John Walter (ed.) (1885a) *George Eliot's Life as Related in Her Letters and Journals. Volume 1*. Edinburgh: Blackwood.

Cross, John Walter (ed.) (1885b) *George Eliot's Life as Related in her Letters and Journals. Volume 2*. Edinburgh: Blackwood.

Cross, John Walter (ed.) (1885c) *George Eliot's Life as Related in her Letters and Journals. Volume 3*. Edinburgh: Blackwood.

Diedrick, James (2016) *Mathilde Blind: Late-Victorian Culture and the Woman of Letters*. Charlottesville: University of Virginia Press.

Eliot, George (1852a) 'Carlyle's Life of Sterling', *Westminster Review*, 57, pp. 132–4.

Eliot, George (1852b) 'Contemporary Literature of America', *Westminster Review*, 57, pp. 351–9.

Eliot, George (1854) 'Women in France: Madame de Sablé', *Westminster Review*, 62 (October), pp. 448–73.

Eliot, George (1855) 'Margaret Fuller and Mary Wollstonecraft', *The Leader*, 6 (13 October), pp. 988–9.

Fulmer, Constance M. and Barfield, Margaret E. (eds) (1998) *A Monument to the Memory of George Eliot: Edith J. Simcox's 'Autobiography of a Shirt-maker'*. New York: Garland.

'George Eliot' (1881) *Blackwood's Edinburgh Magazine*, 129 (February), pp. 255–68.

Glynn, Jenifer (1986) *Prince of Publishers: A Biography of George Smith*. London: Allison and Busby.

Gosse, Edmund (1881) 'The Portrait of George Eliot', *Century Magazine*, 23 (November), pp. 47–8.

Harris, Margaret and Johnston, Judith (eds) (1998) *The Journals of George Eliot* Cambridge: Cambridge University Press.

Haight, Gordon (ed.) (1954–55) *The George Eliot Letters* (7 vols). New Haven: Yale University Press.

Haight, Gordon (ed.) (1955) *The George Eliot Letters. Volume 7*. New Haven: Yale University Press.

Haight, Gordon (ed.) (1978) *The George Eliot Letters* (2 vols). New Haven: Yale University Press.

Hughes, Kathryn (1998) *George Eliot: The Last Victorian*. Reprint, New York: Cooper Square, 2001.

Hutton, Reginald Holt (1885) 'George Eliot', *Contemporary Review*, 47, pp. 372–91.

James, Henry (1885) 'George Eliot's Life', *Atlantic Monthly*, 55 (May), pp. 668–78.

Linton, Eliza Lynn (1897) 'George Eliot', in *Women Novelists of Queen Victoria's Reign: A Book of Appreciations*. London: Hurst and Blackett, pp. 61–105.

Llanover, Lady (Augusta Hall) (1861–62) *The Autobiography and Correspondence of Mary Granville, Mrs Delany* (6 vols). London: Bentley.

Mathiesen, Paul F. and Mulligan, Michael (eds) (1965) *Transatlantic Dialogue: Selected American Correspondence of Edmund Gosse*. Austin: University of Texas.

Morley, John (1885) 'The Life of George Eliot', *Macmillan's Magazine*, 51, pp. 241–56.

Myers, Frederick W. H. (1881) 'George Eliot', *Century Magazine*, 23 (November), pp. 57–64.

Oliphant, Margaret (1885) *'George Eliot's Life as related in Her Letters and Journals'*, *Edinburgh Review*, 161 (April), pp. 514–53.

Oliphant, Margaret (1897) 'The Sisters Brontë', in *Women Novelists of Queen Victoria's Reign: A Book of Appreciations*. London: Hurst and Blackett, pp. 1–59.

Regis, Amber K. (2019) 'Un/making the Victorian Literary Biography', in Bradford, Richard (ed.) *A Companion to Literary Biography*. Chichester: Wiley-Blackwell, pp. 63–86.

Paul, Charles Kegan (1881) 'George Eliot', *Harper's New Monthly Magazine*, 62 (May), pp. 912–23.

Pennoyer, Peter and Walker, Anne (2014) *New York Transformed: The Architecture of Cross & Cross*. New York: Monacelli Press.

'Personal' (1883). *Harper's Weekly*, 27 (2 June), p. 339.

Peterson, Linda H. (ed.) (2006) *The Life of Charlotte Brontë*. Volume 8 of Shattock, Joanne (ed.) *The Works of Elizabeth Gaskell*. London: Pickering and Chatto. doi:10.4324/9781351220149

Phelps, Elizabeth Stuart (1881) 'George Eliot: Her Jury', *Harper's New Monthly Magazine*, 62 (May), p. 927.

Phelps, Elizabeth Stuart (1882) 'Last Words from George Eliot', *Harper's New Monthly Magazine*, 64 (March), pp. 568–71.

Robinson, A[gnes] Mary F[rances] (1883) *Emily Brontë*. London: W. H. Allen.

Simcox, Edith (1881) 'George Eliot', *The Nineteenth Century*, 9 (May), pp. 778–801.

Stephen, Leslie (1881) 'George Eliot', *Cornhill Magazine*, 43 (February), pp. 152–68.

'The Life and Letters of George Eliot' (1885) *Blackwood's Edinburgh Magazine*, 137 (February), pp. 156–76.

Uglow, Jennifer (1987) *George Eliot*. London: Virago.

Wedgwood, Julia 'One Who Knew Her' (1881) 'The Moral Influence of George Eliot', *Contemporary Review*, 39, pp. 173–85.

Wedgwood, Julia (1888) *The Moral Ideal: A Historic Study*. London: Trubner and Co.

Wiltshire, Irene (ed.) (2012) *Letters of Mrs Gaskell's Daughters*. Penrith: Humanities E-Books.

8   Women's Letters as Life Writing
Hidden Lives and Afterlives

The letters of women authors have many postscripts, and this chapter takes three approaches to reading these postscripts within the model established for the period 1840–85. The chapter first explores the immediate afterlife of women's letters as life writing using the 'Lives' of Christina Rossetti, published between 1895 and 1908. Rossetti was an author famously private within both her own poetic output and the public spectacle of Pre-Raphaelitism. Returning to the core texts, the chapter then uses information laid out in an Appendix to follow revised and modern collection projects within the continuum established by the earlier chapters. This continuum extends from Burney/Barrett's *Diary and Letters* (Barrett 1842, 1843, 1846) and Brontë/Gaskell's *Life* (1857) to Austen/Brabourne's *Letters* (1884) and Eliot/Cross's *Life* (1885). The chapter finally introduces some of the hidden or tangential lives emerging from the letter-writing evidence of new collections.

The Case of Christina Rossetti

Christina Rossetti's writing has been described as designedly resisting auto/biography (Easley 2004, p. 153) and as 'a mythological construction...deprived of history' through which Rossetti becomes 'an unknowable biographical subject' (Chapman 2000, pp. 49, 63, 171). At the same time, however, the storylines of her poems and her time-based devotional works offered the possibility of correspondence with current and future public readers. Christina's *Time Flies: A Reading Diary* (1885) was also used for the *post-mortem* reinterpretation of biographical events by her biographers where the process of revisiting a timed collection or diary of Rossetti's thoughts re-presented the entries as letters reaching out to a new public.

William Michael Rossetti made heavy-handed factual interventions into the actual letter collection of Christina Rossetti published in 1908 as *The Family Letters of Christina Georgina Rossetti with Some Supplementary Letters and Appendices*. He had made similar rearrangements of her published poems in *New Poetry* (1896) and *Poetical Works* (1904), insisting on a thematic presentation of his sister's work as opposed to a collection-based order for the poetry that had been composed and published in his sister's lifetime. *Family Letters* was effectively a companion volume to the two volumes of *Dante Gabriel Rossetti: His Family Letters with a Memoir* (1895). William was both archivist to the Pre-Raphaelites and a chronicler of the Rossetti family. In an allusion to his employment as a tax collector with the Inland Revenue, he was damned as a 'fact-collector' by the *Saturday Review* (Gosse 1898, p. 177). William was careful to associate himself with two early lives of Christina by Ellen Proctor (1895) and Mackenzie Bell (1898), and, in 1908, found himself being held almost to ransom over letters that he (William) had sold to Bell (1908, p. vii). Document-based evidence became a battleground for the persona of Christina when practical and logistical personal letters apparently undermined her cultivated mythical and sibylline status.

Rossetti (1830–94) lived during the period of the published letter writing discussed in this book. Her image was thus formed and cultivated within the context supplied by the life-writing events of 1840–85. She was familiar with Burney's *Diary* and involved briefly in the 'Eminent Women' series that produced lives of women writers including *George Eliot* by Mathilde Blind (1883). Control over her life and over life writing about her was exerted specifically by William whose role as Pre-Raphaelite archivist caused him to react to traceable life-writing emergencies in the 20 years after her death including the Proctor and Bell texts, and reviews by those claiming knowledge of his sister such as Edmund Gosse (1898) and William Sharp (1895). The use of letters to present a recovery narrative within these publications supports the model of letters as life writing. The documentary evidence suggests also that Christina herself was conscious that her life might be subject to the attentions of what Dinah Craik had called 'literary ghouls' (1858, p. 113). Despite the saintly image conjured by biographers and the corrections issued by William, Christina herself appears to have cultivated a sense of two lives being lived. In her 'family letters' we can read the domestic responsibility for elderly relatives separated from any suggestion of biographical links within the poetry itself. This section looks at links with the other lives in letters being written in the nineteenth century and then at the deployment of letters or 'letters' within the life-writing context supervised by William.

In January 1850, Christina Rossetti's Aunt Charlotte Polidori took her niece on a visit to Longleat around the time when her seven poems appeared in the short-lived Pre-Raphaelite journal *The Germ* (January–April 1850). These were published at first anonymously and then under her pseudonym of Ellen Alleyne. On 31 January 1850, Christina wrote to William in his capacity as editor: 'Should all other articles fail, boldly publish my letters; they would doubtless produce an immense sensation...by substituting initials and asterisks for all names, and adding a few titles, my correspondence might have quite a success' (Marsh 1994, p. 108). Jan Marsh claims that the stay at Longleat with its court connections drew Christina to this suggestion (1994, p. 108) but it is not unrealistic to suggest that the *Diary and Letters of Madame D'Arblay* (Barrett 1842–46) was available in the library and being referenced in Christina's letter. Rossetti and her mother certainly later owned the four-volume Bickers and Son edition of the *Diary and Letters* that was published in 1875. References to this edition appear in the letters published by William. Gabriel commends ownership of the volumes on 3 November 1875 (Rossetti 1895, p. 320) and Christina writes in her letter of 18 July 1876: 'I hope you like Mme D'Arblay in moderation: we both do' (Rossetti 1908, p. 57). It may be that 'moderation' referred to the reduced volume of material provided by the abridged edition as well as to a moderate 'liking' of the reading experience. There was a further ambiguous reference in August when Gabriel requested the loan of the same volumes to help him through sleepless nights without chloral (Rossetti 1895, p. 336).

Other experiments with letters were also taking place during Christina's early career. The fragment of an epistolary novel by Christina, *Corrispondenza Famigliare*, appeared in 1852 in a privately printed magazine entitled *The Bouquet from Marylebone Gardens* (Easley 2004, pp. 166–7). In 1895 and 1908, the Italian title of the fragment is translated into *Family Letters* in the more prosaic hands of William. In 1852, however, the *Bouquet* was dedicated or 'inscribed' by the editor 'Thistle' to Lady Mary Knatchbull who has two claims to notice in the history of women's letters. First, she was the wife of Norton Knatchbull, tenth Baronet of Mersham Hatch and half-brother to Lord Brabourne who was Jane Austen's 1884 editor. Lady Mary was also the daughter of Mary and Jesse Watts-Russell whose family had acquired Ilam Hall in 1809 from the Port family at the death of John Port who was husband to Mary Delany's niece, Mary Port, and grandfather to Lady Llanover. Fictional letters by Rossetti were thus embedded in the reading output of families intent on the use of letters as life writing and on the reiteration of identities dependant on 'family considerations'.

The placement of Rossetti's life within the life writing of the period extended to its fictionalisation in the familiar context of Gaskell's *Life of Charlotte Brontë* (1857). The poet and biographer Arthur Benson drew a cryptic parallel in *The National Review* by claiming that 'the same autobiographical sorrow haunts all her work as haunted the eager dramas of Charlotte Brontë' (Benson 1895, p. 756). This 'sorrow' had been cultivated by the appearance of the earlier published life of Brontë and of the letters quoted by Gaskell as life evidence. In his biography, Bell used the concept of family talents to align the Rossetti siblings with the Brontës, mentioning Charlotte herself and the 'limited genius' of Emily (Bell 1898, p. 3). Mary Robinson's biography of Emily for the Eminent

Women series, substantially based on Gaskell's *Life* of Charlotte, also represents a link in life writing since *Emily Brontë* (Robinson 1883) was published during Christina's negotiations about her own involvement with the series. Bell quoted from a letter to editor John Ingram dated 8 May 1883 that Christina could not write a life of Elizabeth Barrett Browning without Robert Browning's 'co-operation'. Rossetti observed that she strongly sympathised with Browning's 'reticence' (Bell 1898, p. 91), and this remark could be viewed as a riposte to Gaskell's *Life* and the publicity surrounding its original publication. In 1883, Rossetti seemed seriously to be considering Ingram's proposal that she write a life of Anne Radcliffe, and even Bell presented her professional approach to the project when he quoted discussions on word count and research in the British Museum. He included in his biography a letter dated 24 April 1883 in which Christina asked Ingram: 'Are any hopes to be indulged of private letters, journals, what not becoming accessible to us?' (Bell 1898, p. 91). Bell's use of Rossetti's own letters was helpfully validated through Rossetti's demonstrable awareness of the biographical support-ing framework of a life. Her practical approach to the task was then con-veniently dispelled in favour of the saintly unworldly image of the invalid poet, and in the end it was Lucy Madox Rossetti, wife of William who contributed to the Eminent Women series when *Mrs Shelley* appeared in 1890. William had already written his memoir of Percy Shelley in 1870 and supplemented it in 1878 and again in 1886.

The desperation to produce letters as evidence was readily apparent in Bell's biography of Christina and caused the *Saturday Review* to pro-nounce the work 'dull' (Gosse 1898, p. 177). Bell observed in his Pref-ace that some letters 'may be deemed...too slight for publication' but of course 'personal or other interest' and 'felicity of phrase' justified their inclusion and, he added, 'Her punctuation has been carefully preserved' (Bell 1898, p. lx). Bell explained that his subject was 'not unpractical and her methodical and carefully arranged account books of household expenditure were models of neatness' and he linked this virtue with a *Time Flies* entry for 31 May about the dishonesty of using time for 'non-duties' (Bell 1898, p. 159). William too in his memoir preceding *Poetical Works* of 1904 described how the poems appear in 'impeccably neat manuscript...in one of her little notebooks' that are also dated at least until 11 June 1866 (Rossetti 1904, p. lxix; p. 462).

This need to track down, elucidate and rearrange Rossetti's life in her own words was a factor in the printed information supplied by both William and others. Despite the pursuit of biographical fact, however, there was traceable evidence of Christina's manipulation of the medium within the letters utilised by Bell. Sometime before June 1865, Christina wrote to her future sister-in-law then Lucy Madox Brown, 'I am in fact only Maria's [her sister's] pen', concluding, 'I won't send kind regards, because Maria's message is somewhat in the nature of a "private"' (Bell

1898, p. 41). She was enquiring about the suitability of a gift for Lucy's younger half-brother Oliver. Bell then perversely included a letter to Lucy from Frances Rossetti, Christina's mother, enclosing a 'knobbed bodkin' from herself as a birthday gift with 'Christina's love' (1898, p. 42). The letters thus seemed to substitute for the religious differences and personality clashes that caused Christina, her mother and aunts to live separately from Lucy and William from October 1876 onwards. On 18 July 1876, Christina wrote to Gabriel: 'I am evidently unpleasing to Lucy, and, could we exchange personalities, I have no doubt I should then feel with her feelings' (Rossetti 1895, p. 57). In his biography, Bell even left in 'Ah perdona' as a footnote referring to a blot occurring in a strategic place in another letter to Lucy dated 21 January 1889. The letter concerned the death of Lucy's brother-in-law Francis Hueffer but concluded: 'I am the more impressed by your achievements of economy because I had understood Biarritz to be particularly dear' (Bell 1898, p. 118). The blot occurred after 'understood', the very physical appearance of the letters seeming to represent the religious division that defined their relationship.

At the same time the division of the letters between printed resources set up a new correspondence between the later biographers. In the 'Memoir' that introduced the 1904 *Poems*, William presented the 'hushed life-drama' (p. liii) of his sister through accounts of her suitors and in particular Charles Cayley. Henry Austen before him had claimed for his sister Jane that '[a] life of usefulness, literature and religion, was not by any means a life of event' (1818, p. v). William represented Christina's life as having 'hardly any incident' (p. liv) beyond religion and affection and the two marriage proposals by Cayley and James Collinson. William repeated this mantra for 'a life marked by so few external incidents' (p. lvi) and 'a life which did not consist of incidents' (p. lviii) in an apparently planned repulsion of biography hunters. He was answering Bell's claim that despite the 'outwardly uneventful life', '[v]ery rarely has a life so lacking in incident as hers been passed amid such noteworthy surroundings and in such constant touch with eminent persons' (Bell 1898, p. 2). For William, Christina's life was 'replete with the spirit of self-postponement' (Rossetti 1904, p. lxvii). He described the production of 'poems which the world has not as yet been willing to let die' but nonetheless felt the need to outline her income on the same page (p. li). William described his biographical task as an act of 'rummaging' (1895, p. xiii) in which it appeared that letters were studiously defused by their failure to shed any further light on Christina's life.

Rossetti's was an image that must be cultivated from lack of evidence. Letters in their dailiness could both complete and compete with the idea of her secluded life. At the same time, however, letters allowed other correspondents to prove their alternative claims on the Rossetti image. Bell and William had themselves been pre-empted by other writers deploying letters including Ellen A. Proctor whose *A Brief Memoir of Christina G.*

Rossetti (1895) was published by the Society for the Propagation of Christian Knowledge (SPCK). *Time Flies* (1885), *Verses* (1893) and Christina's devotional prose works were sponsored by SPCK, and Proctor made use of this coincidence. Pronouncing her subject 'a cloistered nun' (1895, p. 83), Proctor's sequencing extended the quoted texts in a series leading from Rossetti herself so that these letters might be seen both as insights into the life and as new work. Ownership of the letters also validated the role of the correspondent, in this case with the collusion of William who wrote a 'Prefatory Note' to confirm Proctor's role and provide forensic evidence of her presence in Christina's life. William also felt the need to mention that he had acted as an intermediary in reading Proctor's letters to Christina when his sister was beyond this capability (p. 8). The battle continued when William's encroachment was countered by Proctor with her account of kissing Christina's cold forehead on her last visit to her (p. 76) albeit five days before Rossetti's actual death.

In June 1895, the writer and biographer William Sharp deployed letters in 'Some Reminiscences of Christina Rossetti' in *Atlantic Monthly*. The control of imagery that had beset John Cross in his representation of George Eliot was also brought into play since the problematising of Rossetti's appearance outside the Pre-Raphaelite/nun-like model was raised by Sharp as it would be in both the Bell and William Michael biographies. Sharp described Christina as 'cloistral' and saintly, 'a born apostle' (Sharp 1895, pp. 736, 738) and also used the sense of personal acquaintance exploited by Proctor and later by Bell. Like Bell, Sharp referenced *Time Flies* and his article evinced the sense of withholding that is part of the life-writing model since 'most of her letters are too personal for publicity' (p. 744). It was Sharp who coined the term 'artless art' in which 'if not in intellectual impulse [she] is greatly Mrs Browning's superior' (p. 741). He also hinted at the contrast in appearance between the Pre-Raphaelite model and the mature woman who had suffered from Graves disease. This 'disembodied soul of song' had, in Sharp's words, a 'placid, rather stout face' (pp. 742, 749). He likened her indeed to the famed author of *John Halifax Gentleman* Dinah Craik, an opponent of biographical writing. Alexis Easley suggests that 'Christina Rossetti' was a fictional construct (2004, p. 172) as the forgoing discussion has described. As a corollary, the use of letters as a form of fiction within actual life has intriguing relevance to Sharp himself. From 1893, Sharp was writing simultaneously as himself and as the Celtic Revival author 'Fiona Macleod' to the extent that he created letters and a life for his 'twin self' (Sharp 1910, p. 411). His wife explained in her biography of him that he 'lived a new sequent life' (p. 423) although he had to forward 'Fiona's' letters for his sister to copy and send in order to maintain the separateness within this twinning. Such a scenario offers a coincidental commentary on the hidden lives within letters and on the documentary evidence of sequestered image-making supplied by textual readings of Christina.

Edna Charles points out that despite William's claim of a 'secluded life' on his sister's behalf, 40% of her reviewers look to events in her life as the inspiration for her poetry (1985, p. 47). William made the claim that few people were allowed 'behind the scenes of Christina Rossetti's life' (1904, p. 462) but his notes to her 'Monna Innominata' suggested that these sonnets were a 'personal utterance' published with a prose introduction to act 'as a blind to draw off attention from the writer in her proper person' (1904, p. 462). Charles identifies 'a fierce inner struggle against assuming the role of a middle class Victorian woman' (1985, p. 11). In adopting the role of sibyl or seer, however, there is evidence of a construction that nods to the life-writing models evolving during the years of her activity as poet and writer. Christina is avoiding a life that can be scrutinised through documentary evidence while others are trying to fix an image consonant with the cloistered religious poet. Letters and even controlled diary entries evade and escape this constituency, and create an image that can be manipulated and re-read through the acts of correspondents and editors. Letters are the opposite of that confinement in 'a visual moment' (Garlick 2002, p. 170) that was the Pre-Raphaelite image.

In William's hands, letters were being used not to dramatise but to close down the life, and to offer the last word because only the brother correspondent could know the poet. In this process texts that had already gone out came to be reshaped for the life. Christina had produced *Annus Domini* 'a prayer for each day of the year' (1874) and *Called to be Saints* 'the minor festivals devotionally studied' (1881) before *Time Flies* (1885). Her poetical and devotional imposition on the progress of time was thus apparently available as a counterbalance to the domestic family-based form of her letter writing. For Bell, *Time Flies* 'contains many personal allusions, though there are rarely any definite indications as to place or as to time' (1898, p. 9). He nonetheless used the dating of the 'diary' to supplement the biographical chapters of his study (pp. 10–93). The use of a diary framework with dates has drawn one critic to describe *Time Flies* as 'autobiography undisguised' (Mason 1980, p. 233), and another defines the diary as cognitive therapy performed through a 'largely autobiographical text' (Williams 2014, pp. 321, 328). There is now a modern four-volume edition of Christina's letters (Harrison 1997–2004) but suggestions of autobiographical detail in *Time Flies* reoriented the entries towards a self-narration unrecoverable from letters available to the early biographers. *Time Flies* was, however, a 'reading diary'. It was applicable to any year, structured by saints' days and church festivals, and much reprinted. Despite its impersonal detachment from actual life, *Time Flies* was nonetheless presumed to stand in for the poet's own words in opposition to the letters that might appear too prosaic and at odds with the image of the sequestered sibyl.

Time Flies itself remains an illusion in terms of life writing. The sermonising technique of the daily entries and their sense of being read over time presented an evolution and contradiction of ideas not dissimilar to a letter collection. The call to duty and to recovery from fame as a woman of letters had to be made through further biographical intervention, and in this the biographers undermined their own texts by promoting the idea that only those who had met Rossetti could truly know her (Chapman 2000, p. 171, n. 63). The biographers were looking for a life within the fiction of the poet's own identity but no identity could be fixed despite the dating and personal voice. The persona who reaches out from *Time Flies* must be severe and seer-like at the same time as being known to her circle of acquaintance. This makes her life unknowable to the reader of the life writing and precipitates explanatory intrusions by the biographer that efface the biographee still further from the traces of her own life-written text. This suggests that in her documentary life Rossetti was able to reproduce the state of her poetry by obscuring biographical fact and evading the life sought by the 'ghouls'.

Afterlives

Letter (re)discoveries (re)shape lives, and the debate on their function and functionality is wide and varied. English Showalter, for example, has questioned the trend for 'maximal inclusiveness and annotation with a single chronological arrangement and extensive indexing' (1986, p. 126). There are, however, as demonstrated in the Appendix below, new collaborations and dialogues in the re-collection of letters such as the long-running Burney project, the integration of the Austen collections, the new edition of Brontë's letters and the Haight edition of Eliot's letters. Lyndall Gordon who herself wrote a biography of Charlotte Brontë was unhappy with the Smith edition of Brontë's letters when it began to appear in 1995. She objected to the use of a biographical introduction that interposed itself between the reader and the letters 'instead of trusting the letters to speak for themselves' (Gordon 1995). Gordon insisted that the letters were works of art and not 'a set of useful commentaries'. In an essay in the *Guardian*, Ruth Scurr points out, however, that inclusiveness is an illusion since letters have been burned to thwart the 'life hunters' during the 'biographical chase' (2015, p. 18).

The afterlives of the letters of four of the letter-writing women discussed in this book were extended by the work of Reginald Brimley Johnson, an amateur scholar who published the early work of G.K. Chesterton. The Appendix shows his assiduous use of the letter material of all the authors except for the Winkworths whose text was abridged by their niece Margaret Shaen (1908). In 1918, Johnson published a work of commentary and biography called *The Women Novelists* in which he claimed of Austen that 'her letters do not suggest the uneasiness attached to the possession of a soul' (p. 271). He linked the so-called 'manners comedy' of Burney and Austen to the 'moral campaign' of Brontë in the person of Eliot whose task was 'to weld the message of woman into modernity' (p. 280). He had by this time added Brabourne's *Letters* (in 1912) to his ten-volume edition of the novels of Austen, and would go on to publish Austen's selected letters (1925b) and *Mrs Delany at Court* (1925a), abridging Llanover's edition. He also selected the letters of George Eliot (Johnson 1926b), two years after Cross's death, and brought forward new Burney material in *Frances Burney and the Burneys* (1926a). The actual letters of Charlotte Brontë were out of Johnson's hands. Having been poorly managed by Ellen Nussey, they were variously wrested from the possession of Margaret Wooler, Arthur Nicholls and relatives of the publishers Smith Elder by Wemyss Reid (1877), Clement Shorter (1896, 1908 and 1914) and, of course, Wise and Symington (1932). These afterlives are outlined in the Appendix.

Although this study is largely confined to discussion of English editions, it is significant that in the USA Sarah Chauncey Woolsey (1835–1905), the novelist Susan Coolidge, edited the letters of Mary Delany (1879), Frances Burney (1880) and Jane Austen (1892) for American audiences. This continuity of editorship, like that of Johnson and Shorter later, suggests a continuity across the lives and letters of the authors. The situation over copyrights for transatlantic publication introduced the further complication of material circulating outside official family control. After the publication of the first five volumes of Burney's *Diary and Letters* in 1842, for instance, a two-volume edition was published in New York, expecting an indulgent reception (Berkeley 1844, Vol. 1, p. v) in an echo of Charlotte Barrett's own preface (1842a, p. vi). The editor of *Memoirs of Madame D'Arblay* was the novelist Helen Berkeley, later actress Anna Cora Mowatt (1819–70), and she described the *Diary and Letters* as 'unwieldy and voluminous in form, made tedious by so many details that are foreign and uninteresting' (Berkeley 1844, Vol. 1, p. v). She complained that 'the expensive character of the publication has rendered it a sealed book to the great majority of American readers', and her task was thus to 'separate the gold from the dross' (p. v). Notwithstanding the fact that the official publication had only reached the year 1792 some 47 years before Burney's death, Berkeley concluded Burney's life for her by quoting wholesale from travel-writer Anne Katherine Elwood's *Memoirs of the Literary Ladies of England from the Commencement of the Last Century* (1843, Vol. 2, pp. 33–65). This process summarises the issues arising from letters as a source of biographical information. If true they need to be accurate and if accurate they become 'voluminous'. They are unreadable because indigestible and also because they are too expensive to be acquired by the general reader.

Elwood (1796–1873) referred only briefly to Burney's recently published 'Diary'. She also included in her publication Delany 'with few letters extant' (1843, Vol. 1, p. 81), and the Austen entry drew on the 'Memoir' (Austen 1833) including the letter about her last illness and petticoats (Vol. 2, p. 182). Letters in their published form had an impact on later collective biographies, however, signalling a further transition into life writing. This is a wide field (Booth 2004) but two examples serve to emphasise that letter migration became common practice for life writing in the later nineteenth century. *The Book of Noble Englishwomen: Lives Made Illustrious by Heroism, Goodness and Great Attainments* edited by children's author Charles Bruce appeared in 1875. The collection included chapters on Delany, Burney, Austen and Brontë. 'The Life and Letters of Mrs Delany' (Bruce 1875, p. 212) was an abridged version of a chapter from Bessie Rayner Parkes's *Vignettes: Twelve Bibliographical Studies* of 1866. Parkes described the piece as a 'biographical review cast into the shape of a short story' (1866, p. vi) because it was itself reprinted from her review in the *English Woman's Journal* (March 1862) of the Llanover edition of Delany's letters (1861–62). Parkes quoted extensively from letters and categorised them within the context of Delany's life and relationships. The Frances Burney section of the Bruce collection was taken from Julia Kavanagh's *English Women of Letters* (1862) but the chapter closed with direct extracts from the *Diary and Letters*. Although Kavanagh had also discussed Jane Austen (pp. 247–51), Bruce's Austen chapter favoured Austen-Leigh's *Memoir* (1871) which had appeared since Kavanagh's work. Bruce's Charlotte Brontë chapter drew heavily on Gaskell's *Life* but ended rather differently with extensive quotations from Brontë's novels leading into his following chapter about Grace Darling. Having deployed letters as life writing, the last line quoted incongruously from *Villette*, 'Let them picture union and a happy succeeding life' (Bruce 1875, p. 427), once more suggesting both the fictionalisation of letters and direct communication with the reader through correspondence.

The Book of Noble Englishwomen was itself abridged into *Inspiring Stories: Biographies for Girls* in 1895, tapping into a market for school and Sunday school prizes. In 1887, Helen Gray Cone and Jeanette Gilder published their *Pen Portraits of Literary Women by Themselves and Others*, aimed at a more academic section of the market and published by the educational publisher, Cassell. Gilder (1849–1916) was a journalist and Cone (1859–1934) a poet and professor at Hunter College, New York. Burney, Austen and Brontë featured in this two-volume collection as well as Eliot whom the authors scrupulously named 'Marian Evans (Lewes) Cross (George Eliot)'. They claimed that the *Diary and Letters* had embalmed Burney's memory with its 'somewhat unmerciful bulk' (Cone and Gilder 1887, Vol. 1, p. 47) relieved by the American editor Woolsey. They also quoted extensively from Macaulay's review (1843) of the *Diary and Letters*. Macaulay then also featured in the Austen section together with Austen-Leigh, Cassell's author Sarah Tytler (1880) and two references to Brabourne's edition. Life writing in letters itself had a further life, and the authors of the letters were seen to be part of an ongoing correspondence about women as writers.

Hidden Lives

Within the published letter collections forming the core texts of this study, there are unformed and silenced lives that have been recorded or withheld by the knowledge and experience of letter-written life writing. These 'silences' include the lives of Burney's nieces and great-nieces, of Emily and Anne Brontë, Cassandra Austen, the daughters of Gaskell, and of the other Winkworth sisters, Emily, Selina and Alice. Burney appears within the letters of Delany, and *vice versa*. Gaskell writes herself into the life of Brontë and becomes an apologist for women's writing in her own apparently marginalised person. Susanna Winkworth appears in her *Letters and Memorials* of her sister and, through death, hands the editorial role over to her niece Margaret Shaen so that 'I' in the text becomes 'She' (Winkworth 1886, p. 233). The lives of these hidden women can be read in other correspondences such as those with George Smith, Robert Southey and Arthur Young. Cassandra Austen can be recovered as a reverse image from the letters of Jane where she allows herself to be preserved. It seems almost fitting that there is doubt over an 1802 watercolour of Jane painted from behind by Cassandra and that the only confirmed image of Cassandra herself is a silhouette (Honan 1987, illus 4, 29). The nieces of the Winkworth sisters emerge into family letters in addition to the correspondent siblings. Susan Collie (1861–1932) daughter of Selina (Winkworth 1886, p. 328) was an early woman graduate of London University and Head of Bedford High School for Girls (1899–1919). Mabel (1862–1941) daughter of Stephen Winkworth (Winkworth 1886, pp. 369, 379) will attend Newnham College, Cambridge of which her parents were early benefactors (Gardner 1921, pp. 48, 80, 90) and go on to become the mother of archaeologist Winifred Lamb (1894–1963) who was Keeper of Greek Antiquities at the Fitzwilliam Museum from 1920 to 1958 (Gill 2018).

Modern projects have produced the letters of Frances Burney's sister Susan (Olleson 2012) and of her half-sister Sarah Harriet (Clark 1997), and abstracted the letters exchanged by Mary Delany and Lord North (Kerhervé 2009). The inheritors of the lives in letters have themselves produced life writing. Cousin Catherine Winkworth Mackintosh translated the writings of her uncle, François Coillard, and wrote his biography (Mackintosh 1897, 1907). During an interim year in the publication of Burney's *Diary and Letters*, *Letters from Madras* by Julia Maitland, Charlotte Barrett's daughter, was published (Maitland 1843). Other correspondents were discouraged by the existence of letter collections in print. When Frances Anne Burney's *A Great-Niece's Journals* was published by her granddaughter Margaret Rolt, the editor described Frances-Anne (1812–60), the daughter of Frances Burney's nephew, Charles Parr Burney, as 'not a very fervent admirer of her aunt's work' (Rolt 1926, p. xxviii). Rolt suggested that 'Fanny no.1' had snatched away the ambition of 'Fanny no.2' (pp. xxviii–ix) quoting from her grandmother: '[Who] having waded through Aunt Fanny's interminable and tedious pages...would have the courage to embark on another series of journals by another member of the family?' (p. xxx).

The number of other lives to be recovered within the letters is vast and work has been done through letter editions on the Austen, Brontë and Burney families and their correspondents. Descendants of Delany have reviewed their own material (Hayden 2000) and Alain Kerhervé has added extensive research on the available archives and 'le corpus delanyen' (2004, p. 55). The Haight edition of George Eliot's letters, the *Journals* published in 1998 and subsequent biographies have helped to uncover the correspondents of Marian Evans Lewes, and the Cross family has been discussed in Chapter 7. This hidden lives section therefore focuses on two contributors to women's letters becoming life writing who were themselves hidden in the works they put into print: namely Charlotte Barrett and Elizabeth Gaskell. Their roles in the publication of letters have brought down criticism and opprobrium as discussed in Chapters 2 and 3. The roles assumed by Barrett and Gaskell, however, also provide a compact overview of the letter-written life-writing continuum.

Before handing the task to her niece Charlotte Barrett, Frances Burney acted as her own editor when she described the preface 'to Nobody' that introduced Volume 1 of her *Diary and Letters* as a 'strange medley of thoughts and facts ...written at the age of 15 for my genuine and most private amusements' (Barrett 1842a, p. 32). The history of this entry provides a background to the ongoing life of Burney's letters and also some clues to the actions of her editor-niece. The remark was preserved by Barrett to be inscribed on a facsimile of the re-transcribed 'Nobody' letter for the published edition. The combined preface, expressly chosen by Burney, led an endangered life in the subsequent 'new editions' and reworkings of Burney-Barrett's seven-volume original that took place between 1875 and 1892 as demonstrated in the Appendix. In Annie Raine Ellis's edition of Burney's previously unpublished early diaries, an extensive editorial preface was supplied by Ellis and the 'Nobody' entry restored to its proper place on 27 March 1868 albeit headed up 'Juvenile Journal' (Ellis 1889a, p. 5). This 1889 publication of new material that Barrett had withheld in 1842 and bought back from Colburn's estate in 1857 also restored the conclusion to this first entry that the teenage Burney had preserved from 1768 but not published in 1842 – a conclusion that perhaps dangerously observed: 'why, permit me to ask, must a *female* be made Nobody?' (Ellis 1889a, p. 6).

It was in the wake of this increased interest in the diary that Austin Dobson contributed his volume on Burney to the 'Men of Letters' series in 1903. Burney was the second woman to feature in the series after George Eliot, and this, in turn, prompted Dobson to reproduce the original version of the diary, now in six volumes, in 1904–5. In his version, Dobson included some trenchant if polite remarks about Barrett's editing, and the life-writing community was further expanded to include a dedication to Burney's great-nephew, Charles, brother of Frances Anne, together with an epigram from Macaulay's review (Dobson 1904, p. viii). The printed 'Nobody' Preface and its facsimile remained in their places as before with Barrett's intervention highlighted and Ellis's expanded version mentioned in a footnote (Dobson 1904, pp. 19–20). Finally, in the twentieth and twenty-first centuries, the McGill University Burney Centre has restored the whole to its place, written 'to the moment' in the five-volume *Early Journals* with all its appropriate editorial apparatus (1988, p. 2). In fact, the recovery of Burney's original texts has occupied the Burney Centre for nearly 60 years. The overall edition, comprising 25 volumes including six devoted to the Court Journals, represents a kind of life writing in reverse, recreating a text that was itself a collaborative project between the 15-year-old and 75-year-old Burneys.

Much of the discussion in this long-running edition arises from a painstaking re-reading of the jigsaw puzzle left by Frances Burney and then by her niece who is regarded as an enemy of the recovery process. Charlotte Barrett herself, despite some recent attention (Delafield 2012), continues to be a strange absence from the history of women's authorship. Barrett kept a journal of a tour to Europe in 1819 but she confided in the agriculturalist Arthur Young: 'my book will never disgrace me, for it will never be printed. I have it here to curl my hair with' (1819, p. 115). It is not certain, however, how far she intended to erase herself from the retelling of those lives she moved in. She was a guardian of the literary remains of the Burneys and her life brought her into contact with the memoir – or memorial – of a vast family in which she remains a somewhat shadowy figure. She has been characterised as an over-scrupulous and destructive editor (Hemlow, Cecil and Douglas 1972, pp. xliv–lii; Troide 1988, pp. ix–xxix) whose 'disfiguring editorial work' has had to be 'undone' (Cooke 2015, p. xxv). It was otherwise at the time of original publication, however, when critics felt that it had been Barrett's responsibility to curb Burney's self-publicising instincts (Croker 1842, p. 259; Rolt 1926, p. 337). Lady Llanover inevitably suggested that Barrett had preserved 'pert and vulgar dialogue' to further family interests (Llanover, 1862c, p. 127).

The fictional editor of Burney's novel *Evelina* describes the editor of letters being 'happily wrapped up in a mantle of impenetrable obscurity' and the lives of Barrett and Cassandra Austen were themselves obscured by their various actions as editors. This book has suggested that the ways they handled their inherited texts in the 1840s were not wholly unconnected. Barrett's own life included the early deaths, over the course of only four years, of her brother Clement (1792–1829) and her sister Marianne (1790–32), and of her children Henrietta (1811–33) and Henry (1814–29). Barrett's life can be glimpsed both in the letters that survive in the modern edition of *Journals and Letters* and in the recovered text she originally sacrificed for 'family considerations' and on the advice of the publisher Henry Colburn. Barrett herself is effectively an invisible woman although Reginald Brimley Johnson reproduced a family sketch of her by Edward Burney in *Frances Burney and the Burneys* (1926a, p. 384). Edward was Frances Burney's cousin and artist of the portrait of Burney reproduced as the frontispiece to Volume 1 of the *Diary and Letters*, and this stylistic link through portraiture goes a little way towards restoring Barrett's heritage. This seems like progress for an effaced and 'obscure' editor in the context of the dubious silhouette of Cassandra Austen but Barrett's place in life writing was to write herself out of it, and to write her aunt Burney into the conventions of a *post-mortem* period of history.

Barrett's own life could be recreated as a developing photographic negative image of the life she helped to write, and she briefly appeared in Annie Raine Ellis's text of the *Early Journals* as 'a very little old lady' who could read Hebrew and make jelly (Ellis 1889b, p. 273). By this time, Barrett's fellow biographer Elizabeth Gaskell had died, having actively refused to offer biographical information about herself (Shattock 2005, pp. xii–xiii). Although Gaskell's second daughter Meta eventually authorised a biography by Clement Shorter, the work was never completed (Shattock 2005, p. xiii). Gaskell's correspondence, however, provides in microcosm a sense of women's letters as life writing since modern scholarship has more completely recovered her original texts. Chapple and Pollard's edition (1966) gives a vivid sense of letters sent, forwarded, shared, burnt (or not burnt), lost and preserved. The re-reader of the letters is presented with 'angles' because of the letters preserved. Greater prominence is given, for instance, to her eldest daughter Marianne during Gaskell's lifetime because over a quarter of the surviving letters were addressed to Marianne. Other perspectives emerge from alternative accounts of events sent to Gaskell's American friend Charles Eliot Norton. These were not written in the moment but accumulated in the manner of weekly correspondence similar to that written by Burney and Austen before the advent of the penny post. Letter survival was subsequently controlled by second daughter Meta who inherited both the actual ongoing correspondence with Norton and the physical copies of her mother's letters including those to her father William Gaskell.

Most of the surviving Gaskell letters were published for the centenary of Gaskell's death and the texts brought into focus her own written attempts to organise daughters, husband and editors as well as Arthur Nicholls and Patrick Brontë. Gaskell coded her letters for their planned destruction despite the forwarding and re-sending that was part of her own life as a correspondent. Her twentieth-century editors have, in turn, numbered, coded and cross-referenced the letters by correspondent which has the effect of allowing the reader to follow her regular contacts and her characterisation of herself according to these sequences. The editors wanted to minimise their intervention and so presented 'the letters themselves as spontaneous literature' (Chapple and Pollard 1966, p. xxvii). We are still left, however, with curious gaps such as those around the deaths of Aunt Lumb and the child Willie. Gaskell needed time to process the experience of these significant losses and the letters are missing in the case of her aunt and re-contextualised in the case of her son. Willie died on 10 August 1845 aged nine months according to his gravestone in Sankey Street, Warrington. Within surviving letters, Gaskell wrote about him to Annie Shaen, Emily Winkworth Shaen's sister-in-law, on 24 April 1848 (Chapple and Pollard 1966, p. 57) and to her friend Eliza Fox on 26 April 1850 (p. 111). Further Gaskell letters were added to a new edition in 1997 followed by an actual *Further Letters* (Chapple and Shelston 2000) in which letters surface that were written within days if not hours of each other. This creates a sense of the revisions possible with later discoveries. *Further Letters* also has a fuller back-up commentary and notes simply because it is a shorter piece of work that has benefited from the research into these new letters and also from the intervening work of biographer Jenny Uglow (1993). The letter discoveries discussed by the editors have uncovered factors that remained hidden such as the loss of another son, which emerges in a letter to her early friend Harriet Carr (Chapple and Shelston 2000, p. 156), and the identification of the 'Daddy' of the 1966 *Letters* as nanny Barbara Fergusson to whom six of the *Further Letters* are addressed (p. xii).

The categorisation of letters and the injunction against publication suggest the extent to which Gaskell operated as her own editor. The parallel research of Clement Shorter into Gaskell and Bronte's letters also suggests a need to assess the role of her daughters in the final transmission process. Meta Gaskell is believed to have burned family papers in the last months of her life (Chapple and Pollard 1966, p. xiii; Shattock 2005, p. xiii) and she corresponded with Shorter in the early 1900s (Wiltshire 2015, pp. 242, 249). Meta also featured in Winkworth correspondence. She was an amusing letter writer according to the Winkworths' sister-in-law Emma, 'Mrs Winkworth the mountaineer' and future mother of Mabel Lamb (Winkworth 1886, pp. 303, 401). Meta was expected in Clifton by Catherine Winkworth on 22 November 1867 (p. 464) and helped with the care of Emily Shaen in 1874 (p. 629). In 1895, Meta also appeared with her younger sister Julia in the *Journal of Beatrix*

Potter where the two women were described by the future creator of Mrs Tiggywinkle as 'exceedingly stout' (Linder 1966, p. 396). This journal was written in a code not broken until 1958 (p. xxiv), and was sometimes addressed, Burney-like, to 'My dear Esther' (pp. 203, 365, 431). Esther (1749–1832) was Burney's eldest sister, and in May 1890, Potter described her entry as 'a stroke in humble imitation of my heroine Fanny Burney' (p. 203). The Gaskell sisters have more recently been discussed by Irene Wiltshire in her edition of their letters (2012) and in an article entitled 'What the Gaskells Did Next' (2013). The life-writing circle then widens back in time to letter editor Sarah Chauncey Woolsey who wrote, under her penname of Susan Coolidge, a number of sequels to *What Katy Did* (1872) including *What Katy Did Next* (1886). There are thus lost and alternative lives within collections of letters. These lives appear in relief, not always written in letters but inscribed by the act of collection. In public, Charles Burney's life sheltered the life of Madame d'Arblay and Lord Brabourne wrote himself into the life of Jane Austen. In private, Emily Shaen emerged from within Susanna Winkworth's memorial to Catherine, and the Cross family were reconstituted in the letters of George Eliot.

Acts of family memory, collection and academic recovery have affected the lives recorded in letters. Manuscript letters were controlled within families and then subsequently controlled by being in printed form. The printed form ostensibly freed those letters to help compose a life or multiple lives. The letters then engaged in a dance between provenance, presence and readability. 'Rummaging' like that of William Rossetti uncovered new material for publication and new inclusions within biographical record. The Austens produced intergenerational writing albeit in a competition between the Hampshire and Kent branches of the family. Lady Llanover and Susanna Winkworth wrote family histories for future generations but for the Brontë sisters, with no apparent heirs, resistance followed by loss of family ownership left their lives prey to 'letter hunters'.

The control exerted over letter collections has come to shape life writing. Letters advertise reciprocity, exchange and collaboration: and ownership. When texts become objects, they provide not just new material but generate the requisite intimacy with authors now lacking because author and audience are divided by death. In the case of women writers, these were lives lived at a boundary between the public and the private, between fiction and fact. Acts of trading and withholding, self-narration and fictionalisation emerge from the publication of collected letters. Lives can be told in the writer's own words and then reoriented to present duty and recovery from the clutches of fame. In the mid- to late-nineteenth century, women's letters created a complex and contingent series of frames through which lives were narrated and fixed but also questioned and concealed.

Appendix: The Afterlife

Jane Austen (1775–1817)

Henry Austen (1818, 1833) included the extracts from the 'bit of ivory' and near death letters. Austen-Leigh (1870, 1871) presented the Hampshire family account. His two editions utilised 23 and 36 letters respectively (Modert 1990, p. xxvii). Brabourne (1884) was the Kent family account using 96 letters 'edited with an introduction and critical remarks by Edward, Lord Brabourne'. Hubback and Hubback (1906) added five further letters provided by the family of Frank Austen (Modert 1990, p. xxviii). Austen-Leigh and Austen-Leigh (1913) was a riposte from the Hampshire family adding nine more letters (Modert, 1990, p. xxviii).

Johnson (1912) added Brabourne (1884) (without its long introductory passage) to the original ten-volume edition of the novels first published with illustrations by Dent in 1892. The *Letters* formed the second half of volume 11 and the whole of Volume 12. Johnson retained Brabourne's dedication to Queen Victoria and the appendices of linen inventories from the 1884 edition. Volume 11 opens with *Lady Susan* and *The Watsons*, continuing the trend of presenting the letters as new work although Johnson subtitles the Letters 'A Memoir' (volume 11, p. 198). Johnson (1925) was 'selected with an introduction by Reginald Brimley Johnson' and described by Le Faye (2011, p. xi) as the first selected letters. There were 44 letters from those available at the time.

Chapman (1932) was the first consolidated collection stimulated in part by Johnson (1925). The second edition (1952) added five more letters. Chapman had previously edited Austen-Leigh (1871) for Clarendon Press in 1926. Modert (1990) traced the sales of the letters and discussed the actions of Chapman (pp. xxviii–ix). Le Faye (1995) built on Chapman (1932, 1952) providing full accounts of provenance and a concordance of her rearrangements. Le Faye (2011) provided a full history of the letters' preservation and reappearance (pp. ix–xii).

Charlotte Brontë (1816–55)

Note: Margaret Smith gives a full account of Ellen Nussey's 'precarious' (1995, p. 42) control of her manuscript letters in Volume 1 of the modern edition (pp. 27–71). The British Library still has a record of the unpublished book managed by antiquarian Joseph Horsfall Turner in 1885–89.

Gaskell (1857) makes use of some 270 letters, 152 of them written to Nussey. The first edition appeared in March and the second in April. The revised third edition was published in November and there were many reprints. Modern editors such as Alan Shelston (Penguin 1975), Angus Easson (Oxford 1996), Elisabeth Jay (Penguin 1997) and Linda Peterson

(Pickering and Chatto 2006) have debated whether to base their editions on the first (because of its original intent) or the third (because it was the version last edited by Gaskell). While favouring the text of the first edition, Peterson provides an accessible version of the text of the third in her textual notes (2006, pp. 477–515).

The Life and Works of Charlotte Brontë and Her Sisters (1873) was an illustrated edition, prefaced with Brontë's unfortunate dedication (as Currer Bell) of the second edition of *Jane Eyre* to Thackeray. Thackeray's wife spent much of her life in asylums. The edition included *The Life of Charlotte Brontë* as Volume 7. Reid (1877) thanked Nussey and also Margaret Wooler for the sight of their letters (p. ix). 'These letters lie before me as I write' (p. 4) and from them he makes 'a tribute-wreath woven of flowers culled from her own letters' (p. 6).

Shorter (1896) acknowledged Arthur Nicholls and Ellen Nussey along with the daughter of W.S. Williams at Smith Elder. There was a sense of Nicholls being hounded since he had been persuaded to allow publication because the letters he had yielded were already privately printed and had been read by 'not less than eight to ten people' (Preface). This 1896 work was extended by Shorter (1908).

The Life and Works of Charlotte Brontë and Her Sisters (1900) was a reprint of the 1873 edition with Mrs Humphry [Mary Augusta] Ward providing introductions to the novels. The *Life* (Volume 7), however, was introduced by Clement Shorter who wrote:

> Whatever may have been the sorrows of her life, Charlotte Brontë was so far fortunate in death that her biography was written by the one woman among her contemporaries who had most fitness for the task...her fame has been made thrice secure through the ever popular biography of her from the pen of Mrs Gaskell.
>
> (p. xix)

This introduction remained in John Murray reprints of the *Life and Works* and formed the introduction to the Oxford University Press edition as late as 1978 (replaced by the Easson edition in 1996).

Shorter (1908) was subtitled 'being an attempt to present a full and final record of the lives of the three sisters Charlotte, Emily and Anne Brontë from the biographies of Mrs. Gaskell and others, and from numerous hitherto unpublished MSS. and letters'. Shorter noted the expiry of Gaskell's copyright on the *Life* and the new material he had gathered (p. iv). Correspondence was loaned to Shorter by Thomas Wise, whose work has since been discredited over forgery and the illegal dispersal of material. Shorter also had letters by Gaskell on Brontë and letters to George Smith privately printed in 1915 and 1919. He used the Brontë-Heger letters in a further publication: *The Brontës and Their Circle* (1914). Shorter (1906–19) included the *Life* as Volume 11 (1919). Because of its inclusion in *The Life and Works* (1900), the *Life* had not formed part of the Knutsford Works edited by Adolphus William Ward for Smith Elder in 1899–1900 and was also omitted from the first seven-volume collected Gaskell edition of 1873.

Wise and Symington (1932) was the main source of letters until the publication of the three-volume modern edition. Wise had also had letters 'recounting the deaths of Emily, Anne and Branwell Brontë' privately printed in 1913 as well as 'The Love Letters of Charlotte Brontë to Constantin Heger' in 1914. These latter had been published with translations by the art critic Marion H. Spielmann in *The Times* on 29 July 1913. Smith (1995, 2000, 2004) is the modern edition. Barker (1997) revisited the original manuscripts prior to the Smith edition, and was an abridged version in letters of Barker (1994).

Frances Burney (1752–1840)

Barrett (1842, 1843) comprised the first five volumes of *Diary and Letters*, edited so as to open with the publication of *Evelina* and close with Burney's release from court duties in 1792. Berkeley (1844) was described as being 'compiled from her voluminous diaries and letters, and from other sources'. Barrett (1846) compressed the remainder of Burney's life into two volumes and the whole was reprinted as a 'new edition' without the family's knowledge (Barrett 1854).

The Diary and Letters (1875) was abridged to four volumes and 're-vised with portraits', retaining Barrett's introduction. Ellis (1889) used the material prior to Barrett's edition 'with a selection from [Burney's] correspondence and from the journals of her sisters Susan and Charlotte Burney'. The edition was 'reprinted and corrected' (1907, 1913). Ward (1890–91) claimed to be the unaltered popular edition by 'The Cream of the Diarists and Memoir Writers' despite comprising only three volumes. Ward's Preface acknowledged that the entries had been reselected from 'Mrs. Barrett's' edition. Barrett had died in 1870 and Ward described her as the 'former editor' (p. x). Bell (1891), Frederick (1892) and Swan Sonnenschein (1892) retained Barrett's introduction and framing devices. Ward, however, removed Barrett's introduction, used Macaulay's review in its stead and ignored the 'Nobody' preface repositioned by Burney herself for the 1842 edition.

Dobson (1904–5) was compiled after his biography in the English Men of Letters series (Dobson 1903). Johnson (1926) acknowledged new family material including Frances Burney's journal letters written in France (pp. 19–107) that he edited back into the sequence with reference to the 'standard' edition (Dobson 1904–5).

Hemlow, Douglas, Bloom, Bloom, Derry, Warren *et al.* (1972–84) began the publication of a fully edited collection following on from an early biography (Hemlow 1958), textual recovery work (Hemlow 1968) and a comprehensive catalogue (Hemlow, Burgess and Douglas 1971). The Introduction to Volume 1 of *Journals and Letters* sets out the rationale for recovery of the texts (pp. xxi–lix). Troide, Rizzo and Cooke (1988–2012) have continued with *The Early Journals*. Sabor, Cooke, Clark, Sill and Johnson (2011–19) have produced *The Court Journals* and retrospective discoveries have been provided by Cooke and Sabor (2015–18).

Mary Delany (1700–88)

Two letters to Jonathan Swift appeared in Hawkesworth (1766). Delany (1778) listed her 'Paper Mosaicks' which themselves included personal messages and records of their creation.

The Correspondence of Samuel Richardson (1804) included letters from Delany to Samuel Richardson 'author of Pamela, Clarissa and Sir Charles Grandison'. The letters were described as being 'selected from the original manuscripts, bequeathed by him to his family. To which are prefixed a biographical account of that author, and observations about his writings, by Anna Lætitia Barbauld'.

Letters from Mrs Delany (1820) was produced after the death of Frances Hamilton in 1819 but was released in the wake of the death of George III. It provided a biographical sketch of Delany (pp. ix–xxiv) and 21 letters dated from 1779 to 1788. In the last letter, Georgiana Port, later Waddington and mother of Lady Llanover, wrote with news of Delany's death (p. 106). The book was focused partly on the creation of the mosaics but mostly on the Court 'comprising many interesting and unpublished anecdotes of their late Majesties and the Royal Family, etc.'. Kerhervé (2015) points out that no manuscripts of these letters survive (p. xv).

Llanover (1861–62) echoed *Letters* (1820) in being advertised 'with Interesting Reminiscences of King George the Third and Queen Charlotte'. It was also a riposte to Barrett (1842) which had included accounts of Delany in Volumes 2–4. The Llanover edition included 1,084 letters written by Delany (Kerhervé 2004, p. 40).

Geary (1898) combined 'friendships' of Queen Anne and the Duchess of Marlborough, and Queen Charlotte and Mrs Delany 'as derived from histories, diaries, biographies, letters etc.'.

Paston (1900) was abridged from Llanover's edition. The pseudonym (for Emily Morse Symonds) was used for other publications but added to the sense of letter heritage by alluding to the Paston Letters in print since 1787 with further editions appearing in 1872, 1896 and 1904. Johnson (1925) was described as 'a record of a lady of genius in the art of living edited from her [Llanover 1861–62] "Autobiography and Correspondence"', and Vuliamy (1925) accessed the persona of 'Aspasia' adopted by Delany herself. Dewes (1940) appeared to offer a family account with an apparent link to Llanover whose great-grandfather was John Dewes, brother-in-law to Delany but in fact the Dewes pseudonym came from within the author St Clair's own family.

Day (1991) added fragments of letters to those selected from Llanover (1861–62) dating from Delany's time in Ireland, 1731–68. Kerhervé (2009) gives the sense of a single correspondent through the answering letters of Lord North but also locates these letters as part of the rhetoric of letter authorship. Kerhervé (2015) provides an account of the Delany archive and uses 112 letters, 101 of which are from Llanover (1861–62) but not all of which are verifiable. Kerhervé provides a chronological list of the letters dating from 1720 to 1788 (2004, pp. 463–86).

George Eliot (1819–80)

Cross (1885) was 'arranged and edited by her husband' with co-operation from Eliot's early and recent friends, and the enthusiasm of her brother from whom she was so long estranged.

Johnson (1926) was 'selected with an introduction by Reginald Brimley Johnson' after the death of John Cross in 1924. Paterson (1928) included letters of Thornton Lewes and Charles Lee Lewes. It used the opportunity to reclaim Eliot for the Lewes as opposed to the Cross family following Cross's death.

Haight (1978) supplemented Haight (1954–55) and predated the publication of Eliot's *Journal* (Harris and Johnston 1998). Haight's influence on Eliot biography and his use of the letters are unpacked in Henry (2012).

Catherine Winkworth (1827–78)

Winkworth (1883) and Winkworth (1886) were privately printed. Winkworth (1886) was re-edited by Margaret Shaen, who inserted letters as evidence of Susanna Winkworth's Church of England convictions and added several notes by Emily Shaen (Margaret's mother) and Alice Winkworth (her aunt). The connecting passages of Volume 2 start to describe Susanna in the third person from page 233 onwards.

Shaen (1908) abridged Winkworth (1883, 1886) for publication.

Bibliography

Austen, Henry (1818) 'Biographical Notice of the Author' and 'Postscript', in *"Northanger Abbey" and "Persuasion" by the Author of "Pride and Prejudice", "Mansfield Park" &c. Volume 1*. London: Murray, pp. v–xix.

Austen, Henry (1833) 'Memoir of Miss Austen', in Austen, Jane. *Sense and Sensibility* 'Standard Novels 23'. London: Bentley, pp. v–xv.

Austen-Leigh, James Edward (1870, 1871) *A Memoir of Jane Austen, by Her Nephew*. London: Bentley.

Austen-Leigh, William, and Austen-Leigh, Richard Arthur (1913) *Jane Austen, Her Life and Letters: A Family Record*. London: Smith Elder.

Barker, Juliet (1994) *The Brontës*. Reprint: London: Phoenix, 1995.

Barker, Juliet (1997) *The Brontës: A Life in Letters*. London: Viking.

Barrett, Charlotte (1819) 'Letter to Arthur Young', 23 August. Barrett Collection 3703A, British Library.

Barrett, Charlotte (ed.) (1842a) *The Diary and Letters of Madame D'Arblay. Volume 1: 1778–1780*. London: Henry Colburn.

Barrett, Charlotte (ed.) (1842) *The Diary and Letters of Madame D'Arblay* (4 vols). London: Henry Colburn.

Barrett, Charlotte (ed.) (1843) *The Diary and Letters of Madame D'Arblay. Volume 5*. London: Henry Colburn.

Barrett, Charlotte (ed.) (1846) *The Diary and Letters of Madame D'Arblay* (2 vols). London: Henry Colburn.

Bell, Mackenzie (1898) *Christina Rossetti: A Biographical and Critical Study*. London: Burleigh.

Benson, A. C. (1895) 'Christina Rossetti', *The National Review*, 24, pp. 753–63.

Berkeley, Helen [Anna Cora Ogden Mowatt]. (1844) *Memoirs of Madame D'Arblay* (2 vols), New York: Mowatt.

Blind, Mathilde (1883) *George Eliot*. London: W. H. Allen.

Booth, Alison. (2004) *How to Make It as a Woman: Collective Biographical History from Victoria to Present*. Chicago: Chicago University Press.

Brabourne, Lord (Edward Knatchbull-Hugesson) (ed.) (1884) *Letters of Jane Austen* (2 vols). London: Bentley.

Bruce, Charles (ed.) (1875) *The Book of Noble Englishwomen*. London: Nimmo.

Chapman, Alison (2000) *The Afterlife of Christina Rossetti*. Basingstoke: Macmillan. doi:10.1057/9780230286009

Chapman, Robert W. (ed.) (1932, 1952) *Jane Austen's Letters to Her Sister Cassandra and Others*. Oxford: Oxford University Press.

Chapple, John A.V. and Pollard, Arthur (eds) (1966) *The Letters of Mrs Gaskell*. Reprint, London: Mandolin, 1997.

Chapple, John and Shelston, Alan (eds) (2000) *Further Letters of Mrs Gaskell*. Manchester: Manchester University Press.

Charles, Edna Kotin (1985) *Christina Rossetti: Critical Perspectives 1862–1982*. London: Associated University Presses.

Clark, Lorna J. (ed.) (1997) *The Letters of Sarah Harriet Burney*. Athens: University of Georgia Press.

Cooke, Stewart (ed.) (2015) *The Additional Journals and Letters of Fanny Burney. Volume 1: 1784–86*. Oxford: Oxford University Press.

Cooke, Stewart and Sabor, Peter (eds) (2015–18) *The Additional Journals and Letters of Fanny Burney* (2 vols). Oxford: Oxford University Press.

Craik, Dinah Mulock (1858) 'Literary Ghouls: A Protest from the Other World', *Chambers's Edinburgh Journal*, 242 (21 August 1858), pp. 113–7.

Croker, John Wilson (1842) '*Diary and Letters of Madame D'Arblay, Vols I, II, III*', *The Quarterly Review*, 70, pp. 243–87.

Cross, John Walter (ed.) (1885) *George Eliot's Life as Related in her Letters and Journals* (3 vols). Edinburgh: Blackwood.

Day, Angelique (ed.) (1991) *Letters from Georgian Ireland: The Correspondence of Mary Delany 1731–68*. Belfast: Friar's Bull Press.

Delafield, Catherine (2012) 'Barrett Writing Burney: A Life among the Foot-notes', in Cook, Daniel and Culley, Amy (eds) *Women's Life Writing 1700–1850: Gender, Genre and Authorship*. Basingstoke: Palgrave Macmillan, pp. 26–38. doi:10.1057/9781137030771

Delany, Mary (1778) *Catalogue of Plants Copyed from Nature in Paper Mosaick Finished in the Year 1778 and Disposed in Alphabetical Order, According to the Generic and Specific Names of Linnaeus*. London: British Library.

Dewes, Simon [Muriel, John St Clair] (1940) *Mrs Delany*. London: Rich and Cowan.

Dobson, Austin (1903) *Fanny Burney (Madame d'Arblay)*. London: Macmillan.

Dobson, Austin (ed.) (1904) *The Diary and Letters of Madame d'Arblay. Volume 1: 1778–June 1781*. London: Macmillan.

Dobson, Austin (ed.) (1904–5) *The Diary and Letters of Madame d'Arblay* (6 vols). London: Macmillan.

Easley, Alexis (2004) *First-Person Anonymous: Women Writers and Victorian Print Media, 1830–70*. Aldershot: Ashgate. doi:10.4324/9781315255224

Easson, Angus (ed.) (1996) *The Life of Charlotte Brontë*. Oxford: Oxford World's Classics.

Ellis, Annie Raine (ed.) (1889a) *The Early Diary of Frances Burney (1768–1778). Volume 1*. London: Bell.

Ellis, Annie Raine (ed.) (1889b) *The Early Diary of Frances Burney (1768–1778). Volume 2*. London: Bell.

Elwood, Anne Katherine (1843) *Memoirs of the Literary Ladies of England from the Commencement of the Last Century* (2 vols). London: Colburn.

Gardner, Alice (1921) *A Short History of Newnham College Cambridge*. Cambridge: Bowes and Bowes.

Garlick, Barbara (2002) 'Defacing the Self: Christina Rossetti's *The Face of the Deep* as Absolution', in Garlick, Barbara (ed.) *Tradition and the Poetics of Self in Nineteenth-Century Women's Poetry*. Rodopi: Amsterdam, pp. 155–75

Gaskell, Elizabeth (1857) *The Life of Charlotte Brontë*. London, Smith Elder.

Geary, Caroline (1898) *Royal Friendships: The Story of Two Royal Friendships*. London: Digby Long.

Gill, David W. J. (2018) *Winifred Lamb: Aegean Prehistorian and Museum Curator*. Oxford: Archaeopress.

Gordon, Lyndall. (1995) 'Yours Insincerely, Charlotte Brontë', 22 July. *The Independent* [Online] Available at: www.independent.co.uk (accessed 17 April 2019).

Gosse, Edmund (1898) 'Christina Rossetti', *Saturday Review*, 5 February, pp. 177–8.

Haight, Gordon (ed.) (1954–55) *The George Eliot Letters* (7 vols). New Haven: Yale University Press.

Haight, Gordon (ed.) (1978) *The George Eliot Letters* (2 vols). New Haven: Yale University Press.

Hayden, Ruth (2000) *Mrs Delany: Her Life and Her Flowers*. 1980. London: British Museum Press.

Harris, Margaret and Johnston, Judith (eds) (1998) *The Journals of George Eliot*. Cambridge: Cambridge University Press.

Harrison, Antony H. (ed.) (1997–2004) *The Letters of Christina Rossetti* (4 vols). Charlottseville: University of Virginia Press.

Hawkesworth, John (1766) *Letters written by the late Jonathan Swift. Volume 2*. London: T Davies.

Hemlow, Joyce (1958) *The History of Fanny Burney*. Oxford: Oxford University Press, 1958.

Hemlow, Joyce (1968) 'Letters and Journals of Fanny Burney: Establishing the Text', in Smith, D. I B. (ed.) *Editing Eighteenth-Century Texts: Papers Given at the Editorial Conference University of Toronto October 1967*. Toronto: University of Toronto Press, pp. 25–43.

Hemlow, Joyce, Burgess Jeanne M and Douglas, Althea (eds.) (1971) *A Catalogue of the Burney Family Correspondence, 1749–1878*. New York: New York Public Library.

Hemlow, Joyce, Cecil, Curtis D. and Douglas, Althea (eds) (1972) *The Journals and Letters of Fanny Burney. Volume 1: 1791–92*. Oxford: Clarendon Press.

Hemlow, Joyce, Douglas, Althea, Bloom, Edward A., Derry, Warren et al. (eds) (1972–84) *The Journals and Letters of Fanny Burney* (12 vols). Oxford: Clarendon Press.

Henry, Nancy (2012) *The Life of George Eliot: A Critical Biography*. Chichester: Wiley-Blackwell.

Honan, Park (1987) *Jane Austen: Her Life*. Reprint, London: Phoenix, 1997, pp. 210–11, illus.

Hubback, John H. and Hubback, Edith C. (1906) *Jane Austen's Sailor Brothers*. London: Lane.

Jay, Elisabeth (ed.) (1997) *The Life of Charlotte Brontë*. London: Penguin.

Johnson, Reginald Brimley (ed.) (1912) *The Letters and Novels of Jane Austen* (12 vols). Edinburgh: John Grant.

Johnson, Reginald Brimley (1918) *The Women Novelists*. London: Collins.

Johnson, Reginald Brimley (ed.) (1925a) *Mrs Delany at Court and Among the Wits*. London: Stanley and Paul.

Johnson, Reginald Brimley (ed.) (1925b) *The Letters of Jane Austen*. London: Lane.

Johnson, Reginald Brimley (1926a) *Frances Burney and the Burneys*. London: Stanley and Paul.

Johnson, Reginald Brimley (ed.) (1926b) *The Letters of George Eliot*. London: Lane Bodley Head.

Kavanagh, Julia (1862) *English Women of Letters: Biographical Sketches*. Leipzig: Tauchnitz. Reprint (2 vols). London: Hurst and Blackett for Henry Colburn, 1863.

Kerhervé, Alain (2004) *Mary Delany (1700–1788) Une Épisolière Anglaise du XVIIIè Siècle*. Paris: L'Harmattan.

Kerhervé, Alain (ed.) (2009) *Polite Letters: The Correspondence of Mary Delany (1700–1788) and Francis North, Lord Guilford (1704–1790)*. Newcastle: Cambridge Scholars.

Kerhervé, Alain (ed.) (2015) *Memoirs of the Court of George III. Volume 2: Mary Delany (1700–1788) and the Court of King George III*. London: Pickering & Chatto.

Le Faye, Deirdre (ed.) (1995, 2011) *Jane Austen's Letters*. Oxford: Oxford University Press.

Letters from Mrs Delany (Widow of Doctor Patrick Delany) to Mrs Frances Hamilton from the Year 1779 to 1788 (1820). London: Longman.

Linder, Leslie (ed.) (1966) *The Journal of Beatrix Potter from 1881 to 1897*. London: Warne.

Llanover, Lady (Augusta Hall) (1861–62) *The Autobiography and Correspondence of Mary Granville, Mrs Delany: With Interesting Reminiscences of King George the Third and Queen Charlotte* (6 vols). London: Bentley.

Llanover, Lady (Augusta Hall) (ed.) (1862c) *The Autobiography and Correspondence of Mary Granville, Mrs Delany. Volume 6*. London: Bentley.

Macaulay, Thomas Babington (1843) 'Diary and Letters of Madame D'Arblay', *The Edinburgh Review*, 76, pp. 523–70.

Mackintosh, Catherine Winkworth (1897) *On the Threshold of Central Africa: A Record of Twenty Years Pioneering among the Barotsi of the Upper Zambesi*. London: Hodder and Stoughton.

Mackintosh, Catherine Winkworth (1907) *Coillard of the Zambesi: The Lives of François and Christina Coillard of the Paris Missionary Society (1858–1904)*. London: Unwin.

Maitland, Julia (1843) *Letters from Madras during the Years 1836–1839*. London: Murray.

Marsh, Jan (1994) *Christina Rossetti: A Literary Biography*. London: Pimlico.

Mason, Mary G. (1980) 'The Other Voice: Autobiographies of Women Writers', in Olney, James (ed.) *Autobiography: Essays Theoretical and Critical*. Princeton: Princeton University Press, pp. 207–35

Modert, Jo (ed.) (1990) *Jane Austen's Letters in Facsimile*. Carbondale: Southern Illinois University Press.

Olleson, Philip (ed.) (2012) *The Journals and Letters of Susan Burney*. Farnham: Ashgate. doi:10.4324/9781315556444

Parkes, Bessie Rayner (1886) *Vignettes: Twelve Bibliograhical Studies*. London: Strahan.

Paston, George [Emily Morse Symonds] (1900) *Mrs Delany (Mary Granville): A Memoir 1700–1788*. London: Richards.

Paterson, Arthur (1928) *George Eliot's Family Life and Letters*. London: Selwyn and Blount.

Peterson, Linda H. (ed.) (2006) *The Life of Charlotte Brontë. Volume 8* of Shattock, Joanne (ed.) *The Works of Elizabeth Gaskell*. London: Pickering and Chatto. doi:10.4324/9781351220149

Proctor, Ellen E. (1895) *A Brief Memoir of Christina Georgina Rossetti*. London: SPCK.

Reid, Thomas Wemyss (1877) *Charlotte Brontë: A Monograph*. London: Macmillan.

Robinson, Agnes Mary Frances (1883) *Emily Brontë*. London: W. H. Allen.

Rolt, Margaret S. (ed.) (1926) *A Great-Niece's Journals Being Extracts from the Journals of Fanny Anne Burney (Mrs Wood) from 1830 to 1842*. London: Constable.

Rossetti, Christina (1885) *Time Flies: A Reading Diary*. London: SPCK.

Rossetti, Christina (1893) *Verses*. London: SPCK.

Rossetti, Lucy Madox (1890) *Mrs Shelley*. London: W. H. Allen.

Rossetti, William Michael (1870) 'Memoir of Shelley', in Rossetti, William Michael (ed.) *The Poetical Works of Percy Bysshe Shelley: Including Various Additional Pieces from MS, and Other Sources. Vol. 1.* London: Moxon, pp. xxix–clxxix.

Rossetti, William Michael (1878) 'Memoir of Shelley', in Rossetti, William Michael (ed.) *The Complete Poetical Works of Percy Bysshe Shelley: The Text Carefully Revised with Notes and a Memoir: Vol 1.* London: Moxon, pp. 1–154.

Rossetti, William Michael (1886) *A Memoir of Shelley (with a Fresh Preface).* London: Clay.

Rossetti, William Michael (ed.) (1895) *Dante Gabriel Rossetti: His Family-Letters with a Memoir. Volume 2.* London: Ellis and Elvey.

Rossetti, William Michael (ed.) (1904) *The Poetical Works of Christina Georgina Rossetti with Memoir and Notes &c.* London: Macmillan.

Rossetti, William Michael (ed.) (1908) *The Family Letters of Christina Georgina Rossetti with Some Supplementary Letters and Appendices.* London: Brown Langham.

Sabor, Peter, Cooke, Stewart, Clark, Lorna J., Sill, Geoffrey and Johnson, Nancy (eds) (2011–19) *The Court Journals and Letters of Frances Burney* (6 vols). Oxford: Oxford University Press.

Scurr, Ruth (2015) 'Lives, Some Briefer than Others', *The Guardian*, 28 February, Review, pp. 18–19.

Shaen, Margaret J. (ed.) (1908) *Memorials of Two Sisters: Susanna and Catherine Winkworth Edited by Their Niece.* London: Longmans.

Sharp, Elizabeth A. (1910) *William Sharp (Fiona Macleod): A Memoir.* London: Heinemann.

Sharp, William (1895) 'Some Reminiscences of Christina Rossetti', *Atlantic Monthly*, 75, pp. 736–49.

Shattock, Joanne (ed.) (2005) *Journalism, Early Fiction and Personal Writings. Volume 1* of Shattock, Joanne (ed.) *The Works of Elizabeth Gaskell.* London: Pickering and Chatto. London: Pickering and Chatto. doi:10.4324/9781351220422

Shelston. Alan (ed.) (1975) *The Life of Charlotte Brontë.* London: Penguin.

Shorter, Clement K. (1896) *Charlotte Brontë and her Circle.* London: Hodder and Stoughton.

Shorter, Clement K. (ed.) (1906–19) *The Novels and Tales of Mrs Gaskell* (11 vols). London: Oxford University Press.

Shorter, Clement K. (1908) *The Brontes: Life and Letters* (2 vols). London: Hodder and Stoughton.

Showalter Jr., English (1986) 'Authorial Self-Consciousness in the Familiar Letter: The Case of Madame de Graffigny', *Yale French Studies*, 71, pp. 113–30.

Smith, Margaret (ed.) (1995, 2000, 2004) *The Letters of Charlotte Brontë* (3 vols). Oxford: Oxford University Press.

The Correspondence of Samuel Richardson. Volume 4 (1804) London: Philips.

The Diary and Letters of Madame d'Arblay (1854) (7 vols). London: Hurst and Blackett for Henry Colburn.

The Diary and Letters of Madame d'Arblay (1875) (4 vols). London: Bickers and Son.

The Diary and Letters of Madame d'Arblay (1891) (4 vols). London: Bell.

The Diary and Letters of Madame d'Arblay (1892) (3 vols). London: Frederick.

The Diary and Letters of Madame D'Arblay (1892) (3 vols). London: Swan Sonnenschein.

The Life and Works of Charlotte Brontë and her Sisters (1873) (7 vols). London: Smith Elder.

The Life and Works of Charlotte Brontë and her Sisters (1900) (7 vols). London: Smith Elder.

Troide, Lars E. (ed.) (1988) *The Early Journals and Letters of Fanny Burney. Volume 1: 1768–1773*. Oxford: Clarendon Press.

Troide, Lars E., Rizzo, Betty and Cooke Stewart J (eds) (1988–2012) *The Early Journals and Letters of Fanny Burney* (5 vols). Oxford: Clarendon Press.

Uglow, Jenny (1993) *Elizabeth Gaskell: A Habit of Stories*. London: Faber and Faber.

Vuliamy, Colwyn Edward (1925) *Aspasia: The Life and Letters of Mary Granville, Mrs Delaney*. Geoffrey Bles: London.

Ward, William C. (ed.) (1890–91) *The Diary and Letters of Madame d'Arblay* (3 vols). London: Virtue/Vizetelly & Co.

Williams, Todd O. (2014) 'The Autobiographical Self and Embodied Knowledge of God in Christian Rossetti's *Time Flies*', *Literature and Theology* 28(3), pp. 321–33. doi:10.1093/litthe/fru024

Wiltshire, Irene (ed.) (2012) *Letters of Mrs Gaskell's Daughters*. Penrith: Humanities E-Books.

Wiltshire, Irene (2013) 'What the Gaskells Did Next: Life after Mother', *Gaskell Journal*, 27, pp. 49–67.

Winkworth, Susanna (1883) *Letters and Memorials of Catherine Winkworth. Volume 1*. Clifton: Austin.

Winkworth, Susanna (1886) *Letters and Memorials of Catherine Winkworth. Volume 2*. Clifton: Austin.

Wise, Thomas J. and Symington, John Alexander (1932) *The Lives, Friendships and Correspondence of the Brontë Family* (4 vols). Oxford: Blackwell.

Index

For Product Safety Concerns and Information please contact our EU
representative GPSR@taylorandfrancis.com
Taylor & Francis Verlag GmbH, Kaufingerstraße 24, 80331 München, Germany

www.ingramcontent.com/pod-product-compliance
Lightning Source LLC
Chambersburg PA
CBHW071410100726
47908CB00004B/1127

9 781032 239071